Otto Neurath and the History of Economics

AF835167

Although Otto Neurath left his mark across an array of fields in the first half of the twentieth century, he was trained as an economist and wrote extensively about economics. He questioned the philosophical foundations of economic concepts, the fuzziness of economic terminology, the unwarranted reduction of economic theorizing to matters of price, and the misplaced reliance upon certain quantitative approaches.

This book intends to find a place for Otto Neurath in the history of economic thought by examining and analyzing his economic ideas, both on their own terms, albeit with a critical perspective, and in the broader context of their impact. Neurath may be seen as a pioneer in posing ideas and approaches now considered heterodox.

This book will be of interest to students and researchers of the history of economic thought, and especially those interested in the evolution of heterodox economics in the twentieth century.

Michael Turk is professor emeritus in economics at Fitchburg State University, USA.

Routledge Studies in the History of Economics

201 Lionel Robbins on the Principles of Economic Analysis
The 1930s Lectures
Authored by Lionel Robbins
Edited by Susan Howson

202 The Foundations of Political Economy and Social Reform
Economy and Society in Eighteenth-Century France
Ryuzo Kuroki and Yusuke Ando

203 Asia and the History of the International Economy
Essays in Memory of Peter Mathias
Edited by A.J.H. Latham and Heita Kawakatsu

204 The Economic Thought of Henry Calvert Simons
Crown Prince of the Chicago School
G.R. Steele

205 The Economic Thought of William Petty
Exploring the Colonialist Roots of Economics
Hugh Goodacre

206 Greed in the History of Political Economy
The Role of Self-Interest in Shaping Modern Economics
Rudi Verburg

207 Aristotle's Critique of Political Economy
A Contemporary Application
Robert L. Gallagher

208 Otto Neurath and the History of Economics
Michael Turk

For more information about this series, please visit www.routledge.com/series/SE0341

Otto Neurath and the History of Economics

Michael Turk

Routledge
Taylor & Francis Group
LONDON AND NEW YORK

First published 2018
by Routledge

2 Park Square, Milton Park, Abingdon, Oxfordshire OX14 4RN
52 Vanderbilt Avenue, New York, NY 10017

Routledge is an imprint of the Taylor & Francis Group, an informa business

First issued in paperback 2020

Copyright © 2018 Michael Turk

The right of Michael Turk to be identified as author of this work has been asserted by him in accordance with sections 77 and 78 of the Copyright, Designs and Patents Act 1988.

All rights reserved. No part of this book may be reprinted or reproduced or utilised in any form or by any electronic, mechanical, or other means, now known or hereafter invented, including photocopying and recording, or in any information storage or retrieval system, without permission in writing from the publishers.

Notice:
Product or corporate names may be trademarks or registered trademarks, and are used only for identification and explanation without intent to infringe.

British Library Cataloguing in Publication Data
A catalogue record for this book is available from the British Library

Library of Congress Cataloging in Publication Data
Names: Turk, Michael H., author.
Title: Otto Neurath and the history of economics / Michael Turk.
Description: London ; New York : Routledge, 2018. | Series: Routledge studies in the history of economics ; 208
Identifiers: LCCN 2018002011 (print) | LCCN 2018004377 (ebook) | ISBN 9781315188683 (Ebook) | ISBN 9781351743846 (Pdf) | ISBN 9781351743839 (Epub) | ISBN 9781351743822 (Mobi) | ISBN 9781138732032 (hardback)
Subjects: LCSH: Neurath, Otto, 1882-1945. | Economics--History. | Economics--Sociological aspects--History.
Classification: LCC HB101.N48 (ebook) | LCC HB101.N48 T87 2018 (print) | DDC 330.092--dc23
LC record available at https://lccn.loc.gov/2018002011

ISBN: 978-1-138-73203-2 (hbk)
ISBN: 978-0-367-66671-2 (pbk)

Typeset in Bembo
by Taylor & Francis Books

Contents

Acknowledgments

I would like to thank Cambridge University Press, holder of the copyright, for granting permission to reprint as one of the essays in this work the article entitled, "Otto Neurath and the Linguistic Turn in Economics", which first appeared in the *Journal of the History of Economic Thought,* in September 2016, Volume 38, Issue 3, pages 371–389.

The translation of materials from German into English was performed largely through the work of others, so noted in the lists of works cited. The exceptions occur when the work is cited in the original German, in which cases the translations are my own.

1 Introduction

Placing Otto Neurath in the history of economic thought

In the first decades of the twentieth century a new leading pathway in economics emerged, largely defined and delimited by what has come to be known as neoclassical economics. In the same period Otto Neurath, who wrote extensively about economics, delineated a road in economics not taken by this newly formed mainstream. While more likely lambasted – when acknowledged – than heralded in his time, Neurath nonetheless posed alternatives about how to think about economics that have a not insignificant resonance today.

The Austrian-born Neurath, who was cast in the tradition of the central European polymath, left his mark across an array of fields in the first half of the twentieth century. He is perhaps best known as one of the leading figures among the Vienna Circle of philosophers in the 1920s and 1930s, spearheading what was termed logical positivism and engaging in the quest for the unity of science.

However, Neurath was trained as an economist and engaged in both scholarly pursuits in economic theory and activist applications of it. Even here he is probably best known as a foil in one of the great debates of the twentieth century over the efficacy of economic planning, as he advocated for and promoted coordinated planning, including the replacement of monetary exchanges with in-kind calculation. His calls in the aftermath of World War I for the socialization of the economy, linked to the widespread use of in-kind calculation, were met with strong rebuke from both Max Weber and economists from the Austrian school, as well as from Austrian socialists.

Yet his often unorthodox economic ideas and approach extended further, to include questioning the philosophical foundations of economic concepts; the fuzziness of economic terminology; the unwarranted reduction of economic theorizing to matters of price, including the unreflected acceptance of constructs dependent upon the existence of continuous supply and demand functions; the misplaced reliance upon certain forms of quantification; and the alignment of economics with a mechanical model patterned on physics.

In the long view, what import might be derived from Neurath's work in economics, especially in relation to the evolving canons and conventions of economic thought and the discourse these helped shape and inform? In other words, where might one place Otto Neurath in the history of economic thought? This will entail setting his work in both a historical and a philosophical context. It will also involve considering the imprint of his economic ideas and concerns in more contemporary settings, taking into account where he has been recognized as a precursor, but also where he has not.

Over the last several decades, long after Neurath's death in 1945, his writings on economic theory and economic topics, as well as philosophical questions, have gained wider currency in the English-speaking world – and no doubt more generally – through the efforts most notably of Marie Neurath, his third wife and widow; Robert S. Cohen; and Thomas Uebel.

On the one hand, this has facilitated the exploration of Neurath's ideas about and plans for socialization, as well as his advocacy for 'in-kind calculation', more on his own terms, rather than for them to be viewed as through a mirror from the vantage point of those opposed to them.

On the other, the raft of economic writings by Neurath now more widely available have opened the door to an examination of Neurath's conception and construction of economics more generally, involving a variety of theoretical matters, including the nature of value in economics, and concept formation. It is in this latter area of inquiry that much of what Neurath delved into and saw as central to economics can be characterized as a 'road not taken' in the early twentieth century, as Neurath challenged the philosophical foundations of marginalism and neoclassical economics.

Yet the effort to situate Neurath in the history of economic thought remains very much a work in progress. There are fragments that offer up possible pieces, but are fraught with contradictory elements or curious complexities, and may not sustain a coherent overall picture. Uebel has referred to Neurath as an 'Austrian economist with a difference', in that Neurath placed significant emphasis upon the role of decision theory, likening it to one of the main strands in what has come to be known as Austrian economics. Yet this is belied by the centrality of Neurath's critique of Carl Menger's marginalist construct of utility theory and Friedrich von Wieser's theory of value, let alone Neurath's striking affinity with much of what the German Historical School proposed.

Keith Tribe has identified the paradox in Neurath's model of socialization, built upon the notion of in-kind calculation, as one that essentially eschewed Marxian economics, despite the common link made between socialization and Marxism. Moreover, this took place even as Neurath unabashedly saw himself as a Marxist, writing articles in the Austrian socialist publication, *Der Kampf.* Nonetheless, one would hardly characterize Neurath as an Austromarxist.

Meanwhile, John O'Neill has turned a spotlight on Neurath's interest in 'social happiness' and his assertion of the importance of qualitative measurement in economics to prefigure the ecological economics that would emerge only in the last decades of the twentieth century.

These entries into Neurath's understanding of and approach to economics have often understated Neurath's fluency with the canon and discourse of economic thought as it was constituted in the late nineteenth and early twentieth centuries. Notably, he and his first wife had produced a two-volume reader (*Lesebuch*) of selected texts from political economists and thinkers about economics, beginning with Aristotle and extending through the last decades of the twentieth century. The reader, not surprisingly, provided significant coverage of central European figures and accorded roughly equivalent weight to British political economists, including Adam Smith and David Ricardo.

Neurath's immersion in the discourse proves to be pertinent in grappling with his economic thought, as certain figures highlighted in the reader make recurring appearances in his construction of economics. Aristotle framed Neurath's theory of value, measured in terms of 'social happiness', then refined as 'social epicureanism', drawing further upon his own fondness for comprehending economics from a philosophical standpoint. Nicolas Oresmus and Thomas More would ground Neurath's utopian inclinations, which set as a goal the translation of imagined possibilities into reality. J.J. Becher, the Austrian cameralist, pointed toward a positive role for the state in directing economic activity and guiding economic outcomes; at the same time, he limned the limitations of an unrestrained market.

While critical in certain respects of the assumptions underlying Francois Quesnay's *Tableau économique,* Neurath did adopt Quesnay's proto-macroeconomic framework of matching overall resources and production. On the one hand, this made it possible to comprehend economic activity in terms of relations between different classes of economic agents, rather than solely through monetary transactions and individual exchanges in the market. This would blend, to some degree, the outlook of Marxists and the German Historical School, both signal reference points, if at different moments, in Neurath's thinking. It also laid the groundwork for assessing matters of distribution and for gauging the potential levels of consumption.

On the other, by introducing a broader perspective on what economics ought to take into account, like environmental effects, and especially by melding the natural world and the economic world into one ecosystem, even if the term itself was not used, Neurath was able to apply this framework to what might be regarded as an ecological model of the economy.

Neurath's emphasis upon the need to establish valid philosophical foundations for economics cannot be overstated, as he saw the standard construction of economics as having failed to do so. Here he built upon the conventionalism of Ernst Mach and Henri Poincaré as well as the thesis of underdetermination, with multiple hypotheses comporting with the same set of facts, laid out by Pierre Duhem. Nor did his own effort to limn the logical relations that underlay any 'rational' construction of economics preclude him from recognizing the role of history and the place of institutions in both the study and application of economics.

Did this render him a 'forgotten figure' in the field? To some extent that has been the case. As cast by John O'Neill, "Neurath belongs to the gallery of lost socialists" (O'Neill 1999: 123). His greater visibility as the 'locomotive', to borrow Rudolf Carnap's expression, behind the Vienna Circle of philosophers, in which the social sciences, including economics, tended to be relegated to secondary status, surely played a part. His lack of any academic appointment, following his political engagement in Saxony and Bavaria in the aftermath of World War I, no doubt also had an impact in that regard. Nor, as noted above, did he occupy a role of any significance in the framing of the discourse of Austromarxism in the 1920s and early 1930s. Overall, then, he did not fit well within any particular school of economic thought; not among Marxists or Austromarxists, nor among the latter generations of the German Historical School.

Yet there may be a virtue in Neurath's consummate role as 'outsider' in the field of economics. In time, these seemingly unorthodox ways of thinking about economics might come to be seen as offering insights or directions less obvious or apparent from a conventional perspective. This is evident in Neurath's posing of terms for a 'linguistic turn' in economics decades before any recognizable movement of that sort emerged. It is also the reason that Neurath may well be seen as one of the major precursors of ecological economics.

Moreover, closer scrutiny of Neurath's work reveals affinities with other 'unorthodox' or 'heterodox' thinkers in economics, like Thorstein Veblen, Piero Sraffa, or Amartya Sen, even as their differences are also acknowledged.

And perhaps the one great exception to the lack of any positive consideration of his economic ideas by major economic thinkers in his lifetime offers up intriguing possibilities: Jan Tinbergen's review of Neurath's tract on "What Constitutes Rational Economic Theory" in the logical positivist journal *Erkenntnis* in 1936. Tinbergen appears to accept many of the premises of Neurath's inquiry, including the centrality of economic well-being as the "main problem of the science of economics" (Tinbergen 1936: 70). This was also the moment when Tinbergen put forth his first systematic model of the macroeconomy, based upon natural principles and drawing upon statistical evidence, an approach far more technically advanced but not altogether dissimilar philosophically from that asserted by Neurath.

To uncover the range of Neurath's economic thought I have produced eight self-contained essays in separate chapters, focusing upon different elements of his thought and sources of influence, and also making comparisons with other notable economic figures. In this way I hope to provide a composite picture of his contribution to the history of economic thought.

In the first of these, "Neurath in his Milieu", I have sketched out the Austrian context, both before and after World War I, which largely shaped Neurath's world-view in general and his ideas about economics more specifically. In "Neurath's Vienna" it is possible to see his engagement with the world of Austromarxism and 'Red Vienna', the German Historical School, and the Vienna Circle of philosophers as informing his own, clearly idiosyncratic take on the relation between economics and philosophy, on the one hand, and economics and social life, on the other.

In the second chapter, "The Faulty Philosophical Foundations of Economics", I explore his critique of contemporaneous political economy that marked especially his first major scholarly papers. Here Neurath scored the weaknesses he perceived in the emergent marginalist and neoclassical schools of economics, challenging the too-easy reliance upon basic concepts that obscured more than illuminated and the resort to constructs of price formation within markets in which only 'freely competitive' situations were considered and continuous supply and demand functions were assumed naturally to hold. His reliance upon ordinal measurement and extensive use of combinatorics led him to view as insupportable the restrictive hypotheticals underlying the utility tables introduced by the marginalists like Jevons and Menger, and the indifference curves proffered by Pareto.

In the third chapter I examine the noteworthy overlap in careers of Otto Neurath and Max Weber, both of whom were influenced by, and to a considerable degree, formed their comprehension of economics through the German Historical School. Over time, though, both moved out of the orbit of the school and recast the nature of their intellectual inquiry: Weber's as *verstehende* sociology; Neurath's as 'scientific sociology'. Both sought to blend history and economics, effectively a way of recreating a version of historical economics. At first blush the differences between them may be seen as the tension between Weber's idealism and Neurath's materialism; nonetheless, Neurath's complex embrace of both physicalism and the necessarily intertwined nature of theory and fact rendered his own critique of Weber more problematic.

The fourth chapter takes up the matter of ecological economics and qualitative measurement. Here Neurath's mark on more recent thinking in economics appears most evident, and invites comparisons with Sen. In a pathbreaking paper written in 1917 Neurath challenged the conceptual structure of the foundations of economic theory by systematically linking the most basic concepts used to frame economics to the notion of 'monetary calculation'. This opened the way to considering alternative measures and standards, which for Neurath centered about qualitative assessments of 'life situations' and 'life terrains', all set within different possible 'economic orders'.

Neurath rejected the notion that any subjective 'ethical standard', the term used by Gustav Schmoller and Werner Sombart of the German Historical School, be applied to any economic analysis conducted along those lines, though it is difficult to contend that Neurath's invocation of 'social happiness' and 'social epicureanism' does not rely upon an ethical judgment, however valid it might be.

In the fifth chapter, "Neurath, Sraffa, and the Problem with Prices", I compare and contrast the approaches taken by these two Marxian-influenced economists to contain and delimit the conventional role of prices in economic analysis and construction. Piero Sraffa is widely credited with reclaiming a classical treatment of prices imbued especially with the framework set by David Ricardo. For his part, Neurath emphasized the nature of value in economic activity, expressing concern about the unwarranted reduction of economics to a theory of prices by the marginalists. He put forth a more qualitative and holistic approach to economic decision-making, giving great weight to ordinal rankings and an array of possible outcomes far greater than those presented by the restrictive two-goods models upon which marginalist and neoclassical economics had relied.

Both Neurath and Sraffa would challenge the interdependence of price and quantity that marked the Marshallian construct of partial equilibrium. However, while Sraffa's approach was highly abstracted – in the classical tradition – Neurath's could be characterized as perhaps generalizing, but also grounded more in a historical rather than a theoretical context, and hence ultimately set to a significant degree within the discourse of the German Historical School.

The sixth chapter lays out the case for seeing Neurath as a significant precursor of the "linguistic turn" in economics that occurred in the last decades of the twentieth century. Neurath's concern for the implications of the use of language in economic conceptualizing, description, and analysis, was quite striking, evident throughout his career. Whether it is with regard to categorizing resources as generic factors of production or reducing the measure of everything of value to a monetary amount, Neurath attempted to lay bare the fallacies therein. Moreover, Neurath sought to find a way to cast aside the conventions associated with both ordinary and scientific language and instead create a far less ambiguous form of communication that emphasized the translation of observable statements into a visual language, most notably developed as the Isotype method.

In the seventh chapter the debate over socialist calculation takes center stage. Initially this debate is set in the context of an Austrian crucible regarding discourse about political economy on the eve of World War I. Into this setting Neurath held a unique place, writing extensively about in-kind exchange and calculation, and serving as perhaps the earliest practitioner of socialist planning after World War I. Neurath's case for 'socialist calculation' is examined, then set against the claims of his critics, especially Ludwig von Mises and Frederich von Hayek. Mises focused upon the lack of a requisite form of measurement provided by monetary calculation and a system of prices to make for an efficient, even coherent use of society's resources in shaping the economy. Hayek emphasized the limitations of any form of central planning in ascertaining all the requisite knowledge embodied in more localized 'bits of information' that only a system of prices – or price signaling – might provide.

For his part Neurath stressed the need for coordination, that is, a broad sharing of information across the economy, to avoid contradictory pulls and great inefficiencies in achieving socially optimal outcomes. Moreover, he saw the reliance upon generic categories like capital as illusory, built upon a false foundation of monetary calculation.

What import do these contentions have in an age of computers where 'information' itself has undergone a dramatic transformation? Moreover, in the current moment what mechanisms beyond price-resolving markets might be employed to allow for the efficient use of resources, say, in constructing a railroad, the example raised by Mises?

The last chapter tackles the tension between modernism and postmodernism that may be discerned in Neurath's work and ideas. This tension – even contradiction – in Neurath between the centralized coordination of the 'system' and the necessarily incomplete knowledge embodied in the 'encyclopedia' serves as a launching pad for a more extended discussion of the meaning and implication of modernism and postmodernism, including in economic thought. In Neurath's own writings one might contrast the largely conventional understanding of modernity in his *Modern Man in the Making* with the recognition of the incomplete nature of the scientific structures arising out of, say, the 'relations of order' found in "The Orchestration of the Sciences". One is struck by the fluidity of the terms 'modern', and 'modernism' over the course of the last several centuries, but especially during the twentieth century. This applies as well to the terms 'social engineering' and 'utopianism', associated closely with Neurath's thinking and aspirations.

Finally, one can see in recent decades a pathway created by a renewed interest in the nature of discourse itself, initially in the domain of philosophical and literary inquiry, serving as the vehicle for an inquiry into the discourse of economics and the social – and power – relations that underlie it.

What emerges from this depiction casting Neurath within the history of economics is the need to integrate him and his economic ideas fully into the discourse of the history of economic thought. From there it will then be possible to pursue further the various strands he laid out, whether formulated clearly or fraught with incomplete or contradictory elements, as is invariably the case for economic figures of significance.

References

O'Neill, John (1999) "Ecology, Socialism and Austrian Economics". In E. Nemeth and R. Heinrich, eds., *Rationalität, Planning, Vielfalt*, Vienna: Weiner Reihe, pp. 123–145.

Tinbergen, Jan (1936) "Review of O. Neurath's 'Rational Theory'". *Erkenntnis* 6: 70–71.

2 Neurath in his milieu

As a central European polymath, with an accompanying broad array of interest and activities, Otto Neurath must be comprehended through multiple contexts that nonetheless form a coherent intellectual and historical backdrop to his work and ideas. This emerges most clearly through three major areas of inquiry and influence for Neurath, all affecting his approach to and understanding of economics: (1) the decades-long philosophical inquiry that underlay and informed the thinking of the Vienna Circle; (2) the intellectual currents shaping the thought of the German Historical School and that of other heterodox and utopian thinkers prior to World War I; and (3) an engagement with socialism and Marxism that took hold during the war years.

A brief biographical sketch: to the launching of the Vienna Circle

Otto Neurath might be thought of as a consummate central European of his time. Born in Vienna in 1882, he was schooled at the Hochschule für Bodenkultur in the city, an institution devoted to technical learning and the management of resources, offering up a proto-environmental perspective. It was also the place where his father, Wilhelm Neurath, essentially an economic historian who profoundly influenced his son, taught.

Neurath's academic interests were wide-ranging, and while he sought to pursue advanced studies in which economics and history were joined together, as he confided to Ferdinand Tönnies, he gained a solid background in the physical sciences, logic, and even religion (Vossoughian 2008: 19–25). After the death of his father in 1901, Tönnies effectively served as a surrogate mentor to and correspondent with Neurath over the course of the next two decades. Crucially, Tönnies opened the way for Neurath to seek his graduate studies at the University of Berlin, where the German Historical School of political economists held sway, recommending him to Gustav Schmoller, the leading figure in the school in this period (Vossoughian 2008: 22–23). Neurath completed his doctorate, in the German context his Habilitationsschrift, in 1906, focusing upon the economic history of classical antiquity, with Eduard Meyer serving as his advisor. Meyer was joined by Schmoller in reviewing Neurath's academic work as the requisite preliminary to obtaining his advanced degree. It was while in Berlin that Neurath encountered Gregory Itelson, a rather unique philosophical figure, who impressed upon Neurath the importance of securing the precise meaning of words and the role of language more generally in the formation of concepts and ideas (Neurath 1973a: 7).

Upon returning to Vienna Neurath entered upon two activities that would shape his subsequent thinking about philosophy and economics. He was drawn into what would emerge as a decade-long study of economic life in wartime and its implications for the structure of the economy, as the political instability in the Balkans burst into the two Balkan Wars that ensued on the eve of World War I.

Equally important, he joined with two other Viennese contemporaries, the physicist Philipp Frank and the mathematician Otto Hahn, in forming what has now become known as the First Vienna Circle, with the occasional participation of the physicist and probability theorist Richard von Mises (Uebel 1991). Together they sought to advance a program of scientific inquiry freed of what they saw as the metaphysical cloaking provided by philosophers of various stripes and the conventions of religious thought. They were inspired by the Austrian philosopher of science, Ernst Mach, if also somewhat critical of him, and saw the turn-of-the-century insights of Henri Poincaré and Pierre Duhem as offering up a new pathway in thinking about the nature of science (Frank 1949: 7–8).

This was the world of the Viennese coffeehouse, and the circle of friends and intellectuals was tightly drawn, sometimes remarkably so. In the instant case Neurath, through his interest and work in urban planning, would collaborate with Frank's brother, Josef, a prominent Viennese architect, over the next several decades (see Kapfinger 2016). Within the period of the First Vienna Circle Neurath would also collaborate with Hahn's sister, Olga, on papers exploring new developments in symbolic logic. After the death of his first wife, Anna Schapire, in 1911, following the birth of their son Paul, Neurath married Olga, who by then had become blind. The relationship between Richard von Mises and his brother Ludwig had long been fraught (Margit Mises 1976: 25), but it is nonetheless noteworthy that it would be the latter, ensconced as the leading figure among the Austrian economists in the post-World War I period, whose challenge to 'socialist calculation' and Neurath's ideas about the possibilities of 'natural' or 'in-kind' calculation, would long define the way that Neurath's economic thought would be comprehended.

One additional note: among the Austrian philosophers who influenced this First Vienna Circle was Richard Avenarius, a junior colleague of Mach. Neurath would later reference Avenarius in his paper on "Encyclopedia as 'Model'" in establishing how to construct theories based upon 'observable statements' from ordinary or 'common language' (Neurath [1936] 1983: 150–151). Avenarius' stepson, Wolfgang Schumann, worked closely with Neurath in developing plans for the socialization of the economy of Saxony after the dissolution of the Hohenzollern and Habsburg Empires at the end of World War I (Kranold–Neurath – Schumann plan, see Neurath 1973b: 19–21).

During the war years Neurath served in the Austrian military, but also began his engagement in the increasingly radical environment that gained strength as the war persisted. In 1917 he obtained a junior academic appointment at the University of Heidelberg; the next year he joined the Social Democratic Party.

His exploration of and enthusiasm for the possibilities of establishing a 'natural' form of economic calculation and seeing it instituted through plans to bring about the 'total socialization' of central European economies had life-changing consequences. Neurath headed the central planning office in Bavaria during the period when it was governed as a left-wing, then revolutionary entity in 1919. After that last, short-lived regime was overturned, he was placed on trial for treason. He was able to avoid a prison sentence, but was expelled from Germany and exiled to Vienna. At the same time Heidelberg rescinded his academic appointment, and Neurath never again held a formal academic post, though a generation later he was able to lecture briefly at Oxford University in 1941 (Paul Neurath 1994: 90–91).

The Vienna of the 1920s to which Neurath returned came to be known as 'Red Vienna'. Its political and social life were dominated by Austrian socialists, whose program centered upon far-reaching reforms in housing and education (Gulick 1948: 407–504; Lewis 1983). Broadly speaking, Neurath was in tune with the evocation of the 'new man' by the Austromarxists, as well as their proletarian sympathies, but also had not insignificant theoretical and practical differences with the socialist mainstream. He quickly became active in and soon assumed the leadership of the community garden and settlement organization, involving Neurath in matters of community-based urban planning, including the housing of the homeless. This also put him somewhat at odds with the social housing plans of the municipal government. As Otto Kapfinger put it: "[the movement's] grassroots building and lifestyle reform [in which Neurath played a leading role] … was veritably 'bulldozed' by the dynamic rollout of the five-year residential building program of the municipality" (Kapfinger 2016: 87; see also Vossoughian 2008: 31–42).

In 1925 he accepted the post of head of the new Social and Economic Museum in Vienna. Here he entered into devising the means of broadening communication in the modern era through the use of new visual tools and innovative graphic design. This became the visual language known as Isotype, which was meant to transcend the limitations, ambiguities, and misdirections Neurath saw as characteristic of conventional as well as ostensibly scientific written language. His work on Isotype, as well as his experience in central planning, led him to make annual visits to Moscow to advise the Soviet government on implementing the techniques he had developed.

This was also the period in which the Vienna Circle of philosophers came to the fore. As the 1920s unfolded, the Ernst Mach Society evolved, in part as academic philosophers from Germany, especially Moritz Schlick and then Rudolf Carnap, entered its ranks, but also in part because of the growing impact of pathbreaking developments in physics, namely the emergence of relativity and quantum mechanics, and last, but not least, the dramatic rethinking of the nature and relation of language and thought occasioned by the appearance of Ludwig Wittgenstein's *Tractatus Logico-Philosophicus*.

Within this new Vienna Circle Neurath was often cast as a critical member of its left wing, advocating for a more public, political, and strident role for the circle. In any event, Neurath clearly spearheaded the circle's operations, and served as the main author of the 1929 manifesto that introduced the circle to a wider audience.

Neurath in the Netherlands: Tinbergen's review

During the 1930s the work of the Vienna Circle and the subsequent 'unity of science' movement, within which Neurath played a central role, focused upon matters largely outside the realm of the social sciences. In 1975, when the journal *Erkenntnis,* which had served as the leading publication of the logical positivists between 1930 and 1938, was revived, Carl Hempel, one of the surviving members of the 1930s logical empiricist movement, noted that few pieces about the social sciences were to be found within it. According to Hempel, one of the exceptions was Neurath's work on 'physicalism in sociology' (Hempel 1975: 1–4).

When Neurath was forced to flee Austria in 1934, he was able to settle in the Netherlands. He remained based there until the German invasion in 1940, when he had to flee once more, this time to England. In the Netherlands he was able to establish a working center for himself at the Mundaneum Institute in The Hague, which he had founded the year before. Here the process of gathering statistics continued anew, as the Dutch Foundation for Statistics was set up, under the auspices of the Central Bureau of Statistics (CBS) in the Netherlands, and which made use of the Isotype method of representation that Neurath had helped develop in concert with Gerd Arntz.

A central figure of long standing in the CBS was Jan Tinbergen, who produced in 1936 a general macroeconomic model with empirically-derived variables. Like Neurath, Tinbergen made regular contributions to a socialist party journal on economic matters. For Neurath it was the Austromarxist publication, *Der Kampf;* in Tinbergen's case it was the Dutch publication *De Socialistische Gids*.

It is unclear to what extent Tinbergen and Neurath exchanged ideas about economics, though Uebel has taken note of certain similarities and differences in their thinking about economics (Uebel 2004: 66, 73, 90f175). Tinbergen did review favorably Neurath's 1935 tract on constructing a rational theory of economics in the pages of *Erkenntnis* (Tinbergen 1936). This stands out as perhaps the only occasion in which Neurath's writings about economics – other than when his calls for 'in-kind calculation' and a 'natural economy' were treated as a foil in the debate over socialist calculation – entered the discourse of those recognized as major figures in the field. Tinbergen was awarded the first Bank of Sweden Nobel Prize in Economics in 1969, along with Ragnar Frisch.

The timing may simply be coincidental, but it is intriguing nonetheless. Neurath's 1935 tract gave great weight to achieving a kind of objectivity through a strict reliance upon observable statements, often capable of being formed into statistics. Neurath had already indicated, including in his *Empirical Sociology*, published in 1931, that the royal road to a 'scientific sociology' ran through the use of empirically-derived magnitudes, essentially statistics. For his part, Tinbergen, whose work with statistics had led him to become one of the pioneers of econometrics, launched his 'macroeconomic model' in 1936. Underlying this model was the notion that its grounding in statistics made it possible for it to assume an objective standard hitherto unattainable.

In any event, Tinbergen agreed with Neurath that the central question before the science of economics was "how certain institutions and measures of welfare are effectuated in relation to how their changes affect well-being" (Tinbergen 1936: 70).

Moreover, in offering up the possibility of delineating a general macroeconomic model, Tinbergen utilized econometric methods such that, he contended, the hitherto fuzziness of economic concepts might be overcome (Tinbergen 1951: 5). Crucially, these methods would also be of equal applicability to 'free' societies, employing the term William Beveridge introduced in his sketch of postwar economic policy in Great Britain, and planned economies (Tinbergen 1951: 155–157). While the techniques which Tinbergen developed were far outside the ken of any set forth by Neurath, nonetheless Tinbergen appeared strikingly in accord with Neurath's notion of what constituted the rational grounding of economics.

The importance of place: Neurath's Vienna and the Austrian context

In light of Neurath's involvement with the Vienna Circle and the conscious embrace of Ernst Mach as a guiding figure for it, albeit with certain not insignificant limitations, the philosophical milieu of the intellectual world of turn-of-the-century Vienna stands out as the defining feature of this historical period. This is certainly in accord with Karl Popper's reflection that Neurath, like so many Viennese with whom he held differing, even opposing views about politics, economics, and the state and future course of society, all shared the notion that epistemological matters were primary (Popper 1973: 56). In other words, the theory of knowledge cut through and was decisive for all other fields of inquiry. One might set such a focus within an Austrian tradition in philosophy by taking into account the influence over the previous century of figures like Bernardo Bolzano, who had explored the nature of the infinite, and Franz Brentano, who had emphasized the importance of intentionality. Neurath alluded to such a tradition in the Vienna Circle manifesto.

Austria itself looms large in other, even seemingly contradictory ways. In the realm of political economy one can find favorable treatment by Neurath of the seventeenth-century thinker, J.J. Becher, an Austrian often described as the first cameralist. On the other hand, the staying power of cameralist ideas may have been felt most keenly in Germany over the course of the nineteenth century. Accordingly, the Vienna Circle manifesto appeared to recognize the difference between German and Austrian traditions in economic thought by highlighting the opposition to cameralism and mercantilism in the emergent 'scientific', 'anti-metaphysical' approach of the Austrian economics of Carl Menger.

One other figure from Austrian history should not be overlooked: Count Kaunitz. Operating under the aegis and mandate of the reformist Habsburg emperor, Joseph II, who ruled in the 1780s, Kaunitz proceeded to rationalize the administration of the state. Central to its effectuation was the collection of data regarding both demography and the economy. As an element and manifestation of statecraft, such data represented an early form of statistics, and Kaunitz's program might reasonably be viewed as pathbreaking for its time.

Neurath, who saw the pathway to a 'scientific sociology' through statistics, cited Kaunitz's directives as a precursor, presaging future state efforts to assemble data and forge public policies thereby (Neurath [1926] 1994: 295). Intriguingly, that such administrative actions could be undertaken under the auspices of a hierarchical, if 'enlightened' regime should not go unnoticed in delineating the sources, but also the implications, of Neurath's model of economic planning, where statistics were seen as an essential resource.

To be sure, Neurath was fully aware of this unlikely but evident lineage. In 'Statistik und Proletariat', from 1926, when Neurath had already embraced socialism and elements of Marxist thought for a decade, he noted the following, all italicized for emphasis: "*The first flowering of statistics is narrowly tied with absolutism!*" (Neurath [1926] 1994: 295; emphasis in original).

Later he made explicit the connection between the actions of the reformist Habsburg monarchy in the eighteenth century and the possibilities of attaining a socialist society: "In this as in many other ways the centralized authority of the enlightened monarchy is an undeveloped precursor of the centralized authority of the socialist society" (Neurath [1926] 1994: 295).

An age of cultural efflorescence

To widen the view of what constituted Neurath's Vienna one might turn to a set of cultural associations, essentially a series of impressions about fin-de-siècle Vienna, and, by extension, Austria in the decades just prior to World War I, that has come through both historical reconstructions and literary imaginings. Perhaps foremost among the former are Allan Janik and Stephen Toulmin's (1973) *Wittgenstein's Vienna* and Carl Schorske's (1979) evocation of the cultural and social world of pre-war Vienna, *Fin-de-Siècle Vienna.* What stands out among the latter is Robert Musil's (1953) *The Man Without Qualities,* a multi-volume novel, although writers and artists from the period itself, ranging from Hugo von Hoffmannstahl to Karl Kraus, are also often cited as conveying the essence of the moment and the place.

Of course, it is not surprising to find the appearance of these literary sources in a historical recounting. But what is worthy of further inquiry in this instance is a specific historical construct: the centrality of cultural life and phenomena, whether it is through the efflorescence of literary and philosophical exchanges, the locus of activity centered about the coffeehouse, or other artistic endeavors (say associated with the emergence of the 'Jugendstil' and the Vienna 'Sezession'), set against the evident decline of the political and social world in which it took place. One might even take this contrast between flowering and faltering as the most salient characteristic of pre-war Vienna – and Austria.

Two questions follow from this premise. First of all, to what extent was it also manifested in post-war Vienna as well, since the pertinent setting for both Wittgenstein, the focus of Janik and Toulmin's work, and Neurath would be as much the 1920s, even the early 1930s, as the period leading up to the war? Was there continuity or transformation? Certainly 'Red Vienna' came into its own only in the 1920s, and was an essential part of Neurath's Vienna, if not Wittgenstein's. See, for example, Heinrich Neider's depiction of Neurath upon first meeting him in the 1920s (Neider 1973: 45–49). Janik and Toulmin treat the decades prior to World War I as the decisive context for Wittgenstein's emergence, but Neurath's engagement with the revolutionary fervor of the immediate postwar collapse of the old order and subsequent commitment to 'proletarian' matters and a remaking of society render the question of a possible break or 'coupure' with the past especially pertinent.

Peter Galison takes up the latter approach, emphasizing the role of 'coupure' and situating Neurath in a postwar period of radical change, encapsulated by the evocation of the notion of 'modernism'. This would link new political ideals and policies in Vienna with both new movements in philosophy and architecture, so that the term that resonated throughout this historical moment, 'Aufbau', had literal, philosophical, and metaphorical implications, all rolled into one overarching theme (Galison 1996).

In the event, within what narrative ought the contrast between avant-garde ferment in culture and art and the economic and political backwardness pervading much of the Habsburg Empire in its waning years be fitted? Is this an early twentieth-century version of a 'silver' or 'alexandrine' age? Might it be likened to the metaphor of the overly ripe strawberry at the end of Thomas Mann's novella, "Death in Venice", set on the eve of World War I?

If that is taken as so, then the postwar period, marked by upheaval and the specter of radical transformation, must be regarded as a new era altogether. And if that is the case, then one might rightly note a divergence of significance between Wittgenstein's Vienna and Neurath's Vienna. Wittgenstein spent more time in rural Austria, with effectively only limited contacts with the city itself, often through his family (Monk 1990).

On the other hand, Neurath was fully engaged in the life of the city, working to promote community gardens and cooperative housing at a time when the Social Democratic government of Vienna had placed housing at the center of its program of reform. Neurath advanced the cause of popular education, another mainstay of the reformers in the 1920s, through his work in organizing and running the Social and Economic Museum of Vienna. All of this might be taken as a backdrop to the critical role he played in launching the Vienna Circle of philosophers, at a time when similarly constructed circles of intellectuals and academics, if with rather different frames of reference, interests, and political dispositions, had become the hallmark of intellectual life in Vienna over the course of the interwar period (see, for example, Weibel 2005), at least up until 1934, with the suppression of the Austrian socialists by the chancellor Engelbert Dollfuss, often referred to as 'the events of 1934'.

But it may nonetheless be the case that the mold within which Red Vienna emerged was set in the pre-war period. This would hold for the lively debate engendered by Austromarxism, and for the Vienna Circle itself. Neurath scholars have discerned and examined at some length the First Vienna Circle, a series of meetings that took place between roughly 1907 and 1910 (Uebel 2000, 2004). Moreover, the intellectual wellspring for the Vienna Circle was dominated by such pre-war thinkers as Ernst Mach, Henri Poincaré, and Pierre Duhem, and was broadly affected by what were decidedly Austrian intellectual currents. Second, what might be gleaned as special or unique about this moment in light of the seeming paradox between an era of ferment, a 'golden age' of sorts, and imminent decline and dissolution? Here one might apply Stefan Zweig's nostalgic take upon the changes that had occurred: a 'world from yesterday' that could be seen as lost.

How did this shape Neurath's perspective on the world, as well as form his intellectual outlook? In his writings the advancement of science is often cast against the claims of religion or metaphysics. Religion was seen largely as set in the context of Catholicism, more the institution than anything else, although it was also taken up as the 'spirit of Protestantism' in Neurath's critique of Max Weber. Metaphysics was typically cloaked as philosophy, but could and would surface in a wide array of purportedly scientific disciplines. While Marxism and Catholicism seemed to be posed against the other as opposites, there is an uncanny resemblance between the two, both as institutional forces and as intellectual – or better, ideological – fonts of persuasion (Neurath [1925] 2004: 448). One might posit that this followed generally from a tug-of-war between Marxism and Catholicism in Austria, both during the waning years of the Habsburg imperium and then in the postwar divide between urbanized Vienna and its industrial suburbs, on the one hand, and the rural and agrarian countryside, on the other.

On the influence of Wilhelm Neurath

While the numerous – and continuing – references to Wilhelm Neurath throughout Otto Neurath's career are quite telling, there are other ways to measure the elder Neurath's influence. Otto Neurath's ecological bent can surely be traced at least in part to his training at Vienna's Hochschule für Bodenkultur, at which both Wilhelm Neurath and Oskar Simony taught for many years. Otto's interest in economic history parallels to a significant degree Wilhelm's focus upon economic history.

Wilhelm's influence may also extend to Otto's economic theorizing. In his early critique of the theory of the social sciences, but directed in actuality at political economy, the younger Neurath pointed to the failure of the emerging marginalist and neoclassical economists like Jevons and especially Pareto to take into account the consequences of economic crises, overproduction, unemployment, and cartelization. All of these topics were addressed head on by Wilhelm Neurath in a series of lectures given in Vienna, then compiled into a volume published in 1897 under the title, *Die Wirtschaftskrisen und das Cartellwesen.*

Perhaps even more striking are some of the details laid out by Wilhelm Neurath that can be found in Otto Neurath's 1910 essay on the 'theory of the social sciences'. The younger Neurath refers to the possibilities of price differentiation and the price movements resulting from overproduction. In the process he cites the [Gregory] King rule, complete with the table King developed to demonstrate an apparent paradox in prices set thereby. If one turns to Wilhelm Neurath's 1897 text, one finds the following account: "Gregory King, an English researcher, was likely the first – near the end of the seventeenth century – who attempted to acquaint himself with the peculiar, volatile price movement of harvested wheat" (W. Neurath 1897: 7). W. Neurath included King's table to better illustrate the resultant price movements. In short, Otto Neurath was hewing very closely to the case made by his father, including its historical provenance.

Neurath and the German Historical School

The seemingly incongruous element here was the influence of the German Historical School, which is often contrasted with the contemporaneous world of economics in Austria. Neurath, through the good offices of Ferdinand Tönnies, was able to pursue his graduate studies in Berlin rather than Vienna, studying under some of the leading figures in the German Historical School. At the same time, it is not hard to see the powerful and formative influence and impact of Neurath's father, Wilhelm, who wrote about and taught economic history and had cast recent economic developments in central Europe along lines that appeared congruent with those laid down earlier by Sismondi (see more, below).

Both of these intellectual sources reinforced Otto Neurath's interest in blending history and political economy in some fashion. Yet it is also the case that the Vienna Circle manifesto, calling for the advancement of a 'scientific conception of the world' and largely written by Neurath, adopted the fairly standard notion of a division between Austrian and German economic thinking conjured up by the 'Methodenstreit'. How well does that square with Neurath's intellectual sources – and his earlier writings?

It is perhaps not insignificant, and certainly noteworthy, that while Neurath would routinely list figures, typically historical ones, who influenced his economic thought, neither contemporary thinkers who were Marxists nor who belonged to the German Historical School made an appearance. Moreover, in the Vienna Circle manifesto Neurath did list Carl Menger, the Austrian marginalist.

Hence a central question emerges: to what extent did Neurath's economic thought show an affinity with that propounded by the German Historical School, both in its main outline and more specifically in relation to the work of what was commonly referred to as the school's 'younger generation'?

This warrants careful reflection on a number of grounds. First of all, there is the relatively straightforward matter of inclusion, that is, making sure not to overlook the possible influence the school might have had. There is a significant gap in the treatment of Neurath's economic ideas and outlook, as by and large analysts and commentators upon Neurath's work have tended to bypass the role of the German Historical School.

This can be attributed in turn to a number of factors or considerations, first among them the general lack of inquiry into the formation and evolution of Neurath's economic thought. Second, to the extent that his economic ideas and program are attended to, there is far greater emphasis upon his involvement and engagement with socialism and Marxism, centered about his championing of socialization and the development of what was termed 'Gemeinwirtschaft' (see Vossoughian 2008: 29). It also stems undoubtedly from Neurath's criticism of the general thrust of economic thought in Germany in the 1920s and afterwards as 'metaphysical' rather than 'scientific'.

To take the full measure of the significance of the German Historical School upon Neurath's economic thought it is necessary to explore the content of the school, at least in broad terms, and set it against the central tenets of Neurath's comprehension of political economy. Without question the strongest bond can be identified in Neurath's understanding of the scope of economics. Here he adopted, consciously it would appear, Wilhelm Roscher's view that economics entailed the study of how societies were organized, and, crucially, what alternatives among different economic orders might exist. He also engaged in extensive studies, with an eye to the importance of statistics, of both the economic life of classical antiquity and the contemporary economies of the Balkans beset by wartime conditions. This might be likened to the empirical or historical studies favored by the generation of economists of the German Historical School who were Neurath's contemporaries.

Neurath saw the necessity of comprehending economic experience as a totality, in what he often described as 'Ballungen' or 'clots', which could not be subject to simple disaggregation into individual components (Neurath 1944: 18, 35). Yuichi Shionoya, citing Joseph Schumpeter, notes that among the outstanding characteristics of the German Historical School were "the unity of social life" and an "organic and holistic view of society" (Shionoya 2005: 33). Here one finds both similarities and striking differences. While there is a certain resonance in the notion that totalities were qualitatively different from their individual parts, Neurath would have 'demystified' any of these totalities, so that evocative language intimating or suggesting a mystical unity or referring in any way to society in "organic" or "holistic" terms would be nothing more than metaphysical claptrap.

In similar fashion, Neurath did stress the importance of historical conditions in shaping economic experience and distinguished the notion of satisfying human needs from the price system and the profit motive. Geoffrey Hodgson offers up a striking passage in his description of Werner Sombart, who came to embody the historical school in its last decades, that highlights both the congruence of Neurath's position with that of Sombart in certain critical respects, and yet the deep divide that would separate them:

> Like Aristotle, Karl Marx and Thorstein Veblen, Sombart distinguished between the satisfaction of human needs and the pecuniary pursuit of profit. Under capitalism the profit motive was foremost. Capitalism involved a ubiquity of markets and prices, and the prevalence of a particular 'spirit' and acquisitive culture.
>
> (Hodgson 2001: 130)

Neurath would have been in accord with much of this expression of principles, extending to his setting Aristotle as the initial figure from whom the history of economic thought was launched. Both Sombart and Neurath saw price formation as subordinate to other economic matters. For Sombart this meant "the formation of markets" (Hodgson 2001: 131); for Neurath it had more to do with the "economic order" and "economic terrain", fundamentally an Institutionalist approach.

The alignment of Neurath's views on price formation and the role of non-competitive market structures with that of the German Historical School is quite striking. One further way to capture this affinity is through the contemporaneous observation of Schmoller's treatment of these subjects by the American Institutionalist, Wesley Mitchell, in his lectures at Columbia University. He noted that Schmoller's comprehension of prices differed markedly from that advanced by the marginalists and neoclassical economics more generally. There were both "freely competitive prices" and "regulated" prices (Mitchell 1969: 571). The former resulted largely from the relatively recent emergence of capitalism, while the latter were rooted in the medieval theory and practice of 'just price'. 'Regulated' prices in the modern era could be

> set by government, for instance, for carrying the mails, or such prices as governments allow public utilities to charge, or such prices as two big organized business interests may settle between themselves, not solely with an eye to the immediate profits they are going to make on the transaction, but with an eye to securing a satisfactory flow of goods and satisfactory outlet for prices.
>
> (Mitchell 1969: 570–571)

This latter description comports well with Neurath's notion of 'Verschiebung', with its emphasis upon the 'transfer' of goods instead of a more narrowly conceived price-adjusting mechanism of exchanges, and matches as well Neurath's contentions that economic life was dominated by large-scale entities such that price differentiation might likely occur in consequence, rather than a market-clearing resolution at one – unique – price.

In fact, Neurath was quite explicit in recognizing the similarity in his perspective on the 'transfer' of goods and that of the German Historical School. As he wrote in the 1910 essay on the theory of the social sciences:

> What conditions allow a certain way of transfer of goods at a certain time, by what laws or what customs can one succeed in establishing certain ways of transfer of goods? All those questions are of decisive scientific significance. They become amenable to successful treatment once the theory of price formation [i.e., the marginalist or Marshallian treatment] stops its continuous interference. Conceiving of the transfer of goods as a result of human action was one of the proposals of the Historical School.
>
> (Neurath [1910] 2004: 278)

Moreover, like Schmoller and Sombart, Neurath set the wide sway of money calculation and the dominance of the price system to a historical phenomenon, the rise of capitalism, with attendant losses thereby. Remarkably, one can find a description of this historical setting in a piece Neurath wrote in 1920, at a time when he had ostensibly embraced Marxism and was advocating for the 'full socialization' of the economies of central Europe:

> The general spread of credit and interest destroyed the farmers and in many countries made town dwellers, merchants and money lenders the masters. In the age of the guilds, even later still, money business and trade is felt as something unnatural (Aristotle) or immoral (Catholic Church of the Middle Ages). The money market then set in, broke all fixed relationships, free competition made brother the enemy of brother, the guild and urban economy dissolved: the individual became master of the economy.
>
> (Neurath [1920] 2004: 400)

Mitchell also distinguished Schmoller's notion of demand from the Marshallian version routinized in twentieth-century microeconomics. For Schmoller what mattered was both historical and cultural, emphasizing

> the changing habits of consumers at different stages of culture, going back to ethnological evidence and coming down rapidly through the ages with a series of exceedingly interesting remarks about the increase of supplies of goods available for consumption by people of different classes from century to century.
>
> (Mitchell 1969: 571)

For Neurath as well the demand for goods and the pertinent pattern of consumption associated with it could not be reduced to a simple relation of price and quantity. History and class would matter, though Neurath would differ critically with Schmoller, in that he would not cite 'culture' or 'cultural differences' per se as the underlying basis for establishing such patterns.

On the other hand, he would clearly be in accord with Schmoller about the nature of price formation: "to understand price determination at any given point, one has to recall that the analysis proceeds on the basis of pre-existing prices" (Mitchell 1969: 581). Neurath said much the same in his 1910 essay, noting the importance of addressing the "history of price movements" (Neurath [1910] 2004: 270–271). In turn, all of this laid the groundwork for Neurath's eschewing of the Marshallian demand, and, by extension, supply functions.

However, Neurath would part ways with Schmoller and Sombart over the German Historical School's invocation of 'spirit' and 'culture'. In part this ran afoul of Neurath's philosophical perspective in which all metaphysical accretions and underbrush had to be eliminated from that which might genuinely be regarded as scientific inquiry. In part this followed from Neurath's political outlook, in which nationalist claims of any sort were anathema, and where the evocation of culture and the cultural differences accruing to different nations might be understood as an appeal to nationalist sentiments, even if not made explicit.

Neurath scored any notion of cultural difference that might be placed in the service of a version of 'clash of civilizations', the theme running through Oswald Spengler's *Decline of the West,* which prompted Neurath to write his rebuke in response, *Anti-Spengler,* in 1921.

Neurath and the Marxists

While the lack of any positive reference or listing of pertinent contemporaneous economic thinkers from the German Historical School necessarily affects any reasonable comprehension of Neurath's relation to the German Historical School, it is even more with the case regarding the Austromarxists. One might note how remarkable this is, as Austromarxism served as one of the major intellectual currents in 'Wittgenstein's' and 'Neurath's' Vienna, yet Neurath's primary engagement with the Austromarxists was defensive, combatting their charges against his utopian notions about 'in-kind' or 'natural' calculation and the best pathway toward 'socialization', often playing out on the pages of *Der Kampf,* the journal of the Austrian Social Democratic Party (Chaloupek 1990: 668–670).

This was most striking in the exchanges Neurath had with Helene Bauer, when she challenged the link he had made between the elimination of money calculation (Geldrechnung) and the possibility of forming a socialist economy, in the process questioning his fidelity to Marxism. In the end Neurath laid out his own criteria for being a Social Democrat in 1920s Austria. He accepted the notion that certain basic assumptions about being aligned with the workers' movement bound together all those who espoused the cause of Social Democracy and identified as Marxists. However, as an ideology Marxism did not have a hold on the thinking of those who did so, in contrast to the stance taken by the Catholic Church. Hence,

> Further there is no obligation, none at all, to agree with Marx. Marxism is not the execution of Marx's teaching, but a world-view, which historically was introduced and in large measure founded by Marx. *Marxism can make use of critiques of Marx and deviate from him.*
>
> (Neurath 1924: 288; emphasis in original)

Even before these exchanges with Helene Bauer Neurath had expressed his displeasure with the disdain the Austrian Social Democrats had shown toward the possibilities inherent in utopian thinking. As he wrote in 'A System of Socialisation' in 1921: "Marxists killed playful utopianism, thus saving the unity of the [Social Democratic] Party and 'scientific rigour', but also paralysing the resolve to think up new forms" (Neurath [1920–1921] 2004: 345).

He went on to state: "In place of creative action one pursued detailed analysis of the more accidental forms of the doctrine of surplus value and other parts of the Marxian edifice of ideas" (Neurath [1920–1921] 2004: 345).

Early on in his career Neurath's engagement with Marx and Marxism had seemed quite limited, typically marked by only passing and non-specific references, with evident criticism of Marx's socialist 'economic order' as offering up only one of an array of possible economic orders. When Neurath embraced Marxism he appeared to give far greater weight to Marxian ideas in his writings, and spoke often of and couched the case he was advancing in terms of the class struggle, especially during the 1920s. Yet his references to Marxian thinkers remained remarkably thin. For example, in his 1917 piece assaying the construction of the theory of the social sciences, at a time when his economic and political outlook had taken an increasingly radical turn, Marx alone is listed among the dozen rather eclectic major figures cited, ranging from Carl Menger to Friedrich List to Kropotkin (Neurath [1917] 2004: 340). Moreover, the discussion tended toward the philosophical, that is, on the importance of espousing a materialist framework and perspective. It is notable that Neurath established his most important link to Marx in the realm of philosophical discourse, as he managed to define Marxism as essentially 'social epicureanism' (see p. 27, this volume), an idiosyncratic take, to be sure.

Jordi Cat has tried to set Neurath's theory of knowledge and his ideas about socialization in the context of a broader debate among Marxists about philosophical, especially epistemological, foundations and socialism, citing such figures as Plekhanov and Labriola (Cat 1996: 235–244). Yet even in his most detailed assessment of the role of Marxian ideas, found in his disquisition on the "Economic Plan and Calculation in Kind" (1925), Neurath alluded to Karl Kautsky's plan for socialization only in passing. Moreover, when he praised in brief a close contemporary like Rudolf Hilferding, he noted only in general terms – and without further elaboration – "Hilferding's remarkable predictions of the general cartel and a future order without money" (Neurath [1925] 2004: 425). What, then, was Neurath's relation to Austromarxism and the Austromarxists?

The Viennese crucible of economic thought

In his study of Schumpeter's economic thought and career, Eduard März highlighted the period before the First World War I as one of particular ferment and fertility in Austria in the realm of political economy. März identified two intellectual groupings, with rather large differences in approach, outlook, method, and, to a significant degree, political perspective: the Austrian marginalists, who would lay the groundwork for the Austrian school of economics, and the Austromarxists, who would incorporate matters of current philosophy into their economic concerns and queries and would set out on an independent course sufficient to distinguish them from other Marxists. In this latter grouping Otto Bauer stood out, as did Rudolf Hilferding. März listed Neurath among the members of the younger generation of Austromarxists, though the extent to which this characterization holds is worthy of further examination (März 1991: 99–101).

Two nuances need to be taken into account in this schematic. First of all, the ferment noted above was enhanced by, or perhaps even brought to fruition through a certain fluidity in the exchanges and interactions within the public discourse on political economy in pre-war Austria. Eugen von Böhm-Bawerk, a leading figure in the first generation of the Austrian school and perhaps the second most acknowledged economist of his day, after Alfred Marshall, put forward a major challenge to Marx's economic ideas regarding the relation between value and price, following the posthumous publication of Volume III of *Capital.* Nonetheless, he organized an economics seminar spanning the range of economic views, culminating in a famous debate between Böhm-Bawerk himself and Otto Bauer. Attendees to this seminar included on occasion Ludwig von Mises, Schumpeter, and Neurath.

Moreover, the interplay across contemporaneous schools of economic thought tended to involve Austria and Germany, with regard to discussion and debate over economic ideas and method, as well as career placement and advancement, blurring the discrete lines often placed between differing schools of thought. The 1909 conference of the Verein für Sozialpolitik, the leading academic organization of the German Historical School, was held in Vienna, and Austrian political economists like Friedrich von Wieser and Eugen von Philippovich played major roles at it. Max Weber would be offered a chair at the University of Vienna, succeeding Philippovich, but he instead retained his position at the University of Heidelberg.

März noted that after the war there was a fall-off in the intensity of the intellectual discourse around political economy as many of the major figures so engaged left for elsewhere (März 1991: 100–101). Both Hilferding and Schumpeter took part in the preliminary discussions taking place about the possibilities of socialization in Germany. Hilferding would later serve as Finance

Minister for a time in the Weimar Republic, while Schumpeter would hold a similar post – briefly and disastrously – in post-World War I Austria. They were carrying on the tradition of Böhm-Bawerk, who had served as Austrian Finance Minister at the turn of the twentieth century. However, it might also shed some light on the prominent role accorded economists in other settings in central Europe: first Lujo Brentano in the Kurt Eisner-led Bavarian state and then Neurath's emergence as head of the central planning office in a trio of increasingly radical – and short-lived – Bavarian governments.

All of which brings the question of Neurath's relation to Austromarxism and Marxism more generally back into focus. Brentano saw Neurath's advocacy of 'full socialization' as a kind of wild-eyed radicalism, fueled by Neurath's utopianism (Brentano 1931: 364). Dahms and Neumann, though, suggest that there might have been another possibility, drawing upon Marianne Weber's retrospective account; namely that Neurath had been invited in to temper and modulate the 'ever increasing communist swells' for revolutionary action (Dahms and Neumann 1994: 125–126).

And Neurath's own extensive writings about the possibilities of socialization present a picture of a certain duality, in which both points-of-view appear to have validity. As to the former, Neurath unabashedly embraced Brentano's criticism when meeting before workers councils in Saxony. As to the latter, he called for a peaceful transition to a socialized economy, sought the support and participation of non- or even anti-Marxists, and endorsed in part the plan proffered by Walter Rathenau, a German industrialist.

Should Neurath be considered an Austromarxist? He was Viennese, had joined the Social Democratic Party in 1918, engaged actively in the civic life of the city during the time when the city was run by the Social Democrats and was known as Red Vienna, had strong proletarian sympathies that were always on display, and wrote pieces in Austrian and Viennese left-wing publications. For the greater part of his career he embraced Marxism, and, at the peak of that embrace, sought to meld his case for a 'scientific sociology' with Marxism through their common grounding in philosophical materialism.

Yet there are also striking gaps here. From the various economic thinkers Neurath cites in his economic writings it is clear that he is much more concerned with figures of earlier historical importance and the newly emergent marginalist and neoclassical thinkers than with the Austromarxists.

As noted above, among those figures he does cite Karl Marx looms large, but there are two caveats to this. First, the references to Marx are typically general in nature, rather than an elucidation of specific ideas put forward by Marx or the highlighting of specific texts. The possible exception appears to be his disquisition on the "Economic Plan and Calculation in Kind", where he refers in general terms to Marx's *Capital, The Poverty of Philosophy,* and *Critique of Political Economy,* as well as Engels' *Condition of the Working Class in* England and *Anti-Dühring.* Second, there is little engagement otherwise with Marxist thought as it had evolved over the half-century since Marx's death.

Then there is the matter of content. Neurath did not give any attention to grappling with the labor theory of value, a central concern of leading Marxists of his day, like Karl Kautsky. As F. Peter Wagner put it, "Kautsky in his dispute with [Eduard] Bernstein authoritatively defined the labor theory of value as 'the key for the understanding of the mode of production'" (Wagner 1996: 34). Neurath was dismissive of any such notion, seeing the reliance upon any one standard measurement of economic value, be it labor or money, as deeply flawed, insufficient and incapable of capturing what mattered in economic life. What Neurath put forward in its stead can reasonably be cast as an ecological assessment in which the totality of experience mattered, rather than the individual components out of which it was comprised or any universal unit of measurement into which such experiences might be translated.

But it was also the case that Neurath's view on the purpose of the theory of value, rooted fundamentally in the notion of 'social epicureanism', set him apart from Marx as well as Böhm-Bawerk, gauging less the mechanism, modeled on Newton's laws, through which society was transformed, and more the collective well-being of society: "In striking contrast with Böhm-Bawerk, Marx looks upon the theory of value, not as the means for ascertaining prices, but as the means for discovering the laws of motion of capitalist society" (Wagner 1996: 32).

And on the matter of 'natural economy' and 'total socialization' one might note that their intellectual sources lie essentially outside the field of Marxism. The utopian precursors Neurath was wont to cite were typically not Marxists, in certain respects not even necessarily socialist, as was the case for Josef Popper-Lynkeus. The models upon which Neurath drew could hardly be thought of as Marxian or socialist. The state economy of dynastic Egypt may have achieved remarkable success and longevity, but its hierarchical and hieratic structure was decidedly at odds with a socialist vision of a future society. Neurath's study of the changes wrought by a wartime economy led him to consider the adoption of parts of the Hindenburg plan advanced in wartime Imperial Germany.

Neurath did see the importance of the trend toward cartelization, whereby the dominance of large-scale economic entities was seen as inevitable, whether under private or public auspices. This was an essential element of Rudolf Hilferding's thought as well, but the source for this appears much more decisively to be the work of Neurath's father, Wilhelm.

There is yet another fundamental difference between Neurath and many of his contemporary Marxists, including Hilferding. In the realm of 'epistemological-methodological' inquiry, Hilferding emphasized the social nature of 'commodities', contrasting "the commodity's natural existence and its social existence" (Wagner 1996: 32). "Social relationships" occupy center stage, as one typically finds in Marxist – or Marxian – analyses. This is not at all evident in Neurath's work. 'Goods' did require a broader context to be comprehended properly, but for Neurath such a context involved capturing the 'totality' of experience, at least as much an ecological consideration as a social one.

What may tie Neurath to the Austromarxists as much as anything else is the immersion of philosophy, especially matters of epistemology, in his thinking about political economy and sociology. While the existence of philosophical content in various and varying economic methods, models, and ultimately schools of thought is undeniable, the extent to which the Austromarxists linked philosophy and economics was noteworthy, even remarkable. It was the effort of the Austromarxists to reconcile the thinking of Ernst Mach with that of Karl Marx that prompted Lenin to write a critique of Mach's ideas, under the heading of 'empiriocriticism', to counter and derail the Austromarxists. It should not be overlooked that the precursor to the formal Vienna Circle was the Ernst Mach Society, and Neurath did draw significantly from Mach's philosophy of science. Moreover, Neurath's longstanding opposition to philosophical idealism, extending to that found in Hegel, meant that his materialist outlook was not dialectical.

Keith Tribe has declared that "Neurath was not a Marxist economist; he did not derive is proposals for socialist economic administration from any specific political doctrine" (Tribe 1995: 143). Perhaps one might phrase it a bit differently. Neurath was philosophically inclined toward Marxism, but not especially in his economic thought.

On the formative in history

It may prove to be no exaggeration to set Neurath's utopian vision of a 'natural economy' as arising out of his own formative period, that is, through his exploration of the workings of the economy in the world of classical antiquity in his Habilitationsschrift prepared at the University of Berlin. His continuing references to the experience, hence what one might regard as empirical or, perhaps better, historical evidence, of dynastic Egypt are altogether remarkable, nowhere more so than in his defiant speech before a workers assembly in Saxony, when he embraced Lujo Brentano's criticism of him as a romantic devotee of ancient Egypt (Neurath [1919] 1994: 197–198). The championing of the cause of 'total socialization' in the quasi-revolutionary fervor of postwar Germany by invoking the example of dynastic Egypt appears, on its face, utterly incongruous. Yet it suggests the power of the formative in history on two levels: one personal, the other accruing to the grand sweep of history.

Neurath's study of ancient economic history clearly shaped his way of thinking about ways that economies might be organized. This, one might add, would also strengthen his belief that alternatives to the present state of the economy indeed existed. That being the case, it might help explain the sympathy Neurath held for Roscher's view of political economy as engaged in the study of the organization of society.

As to the influence and impact of the formative on the grand sweep of history, one might note the power accorded precedent. While one might take this to assure the primacy of evolutionary development, as the formative establishes a mold within which future changes will likely occur and hence are delimited thereby, that is not necessarily the case. Radical movements offer what is generally thought of as a break from the past, but in fact they seek to break with the present. Such breaks, or 'coupures', are often set in motion by reaching back into the past, for, more precisely, to be radical is to return or revert to 'roots'. That is, one validates a break with the present by finding a basis for an alternative path or course in the past, and that link is regarded as somehow truer than that which had come to be accepted as the norm connecting past and present.

There is a second element in Neurath's formative intellectual experience that figures significantly as well here. As Nader Vossoughian has pointed out, early on Neurath embraced the idea of 'Gemeinwirtschaft', which Vossoughian suggest, likely reflects Neurath's absorption and reframing of Tönnies' notion of 'Gemeinschaft' (Vossoughian 2008: 29).

Vossoughian contends that Ferdinand Tönnies' famous distinction between 'Gemeinschaft' and 'Gesellschaft' strongly influenced Neurath's embrace of the notion of 'Gemeinwirtschaft'. Vossoughian tries to make the case that Neurath's ideas about urban planning, for example, sought to link 'community' and 'reality' (Vossoughian 2008: 19–25).

I see greater ambiguity here. Neurath does appear to negate any special distinction attached to 'community' or 'society' as a metaphysical impediment, contrary to his physicalist framework (Neurath [1931] 1973: 393). Also, one must be cautious in treating any oppositional pairing, like Tönnies', as falling within the purview of Neurath's way of thinking, as it constitutes a rough-hewn dichotomy that Neurath typically abjured.

Moreover, what does the notion of 'Gemeinschaft' have in common with the 'natural economy' of dynastic Egypt? It is not likely to have emerged as one of the threads unspooled from the economic history of classical antiquity; at the least Neurath, whom one might have expected to do if it had been the case, never cites its historical provenance. Thus, one might reasonably conjecture that the conjoining of 'natural economy' and 'in-kind calculation' with 'Gemeinwirtschaft' represents Neurath's own, perhaps unique contribution to the construction of alternative 'economic orders'.

But as is so often the case, a conjuncture of this sort is fraught with difficulties that may prove insurmountable. It is unclear if Neurath was ever able to join these two formative elements on a theoretical basis. In a way Neurath may have been conscious of at least the tension that existed between the two, as he did assert that the adoption of or adherence to an 'administrative economy', the model drawn ultimately from the administrative state of dynastic Egypt, did not necessarily lead to the formation of a socialist economy.

To achieve the latter, socialist principles, emphasizing egalitarian ideals – presumably – in sorting out matters of acquisition and especially distribution, had to guide the administrative economy. Neurath was able to detail the schematic for the various administrative structures, extending from a central planning office to more decentralized economic councils, that would theoretically make for the broadest representation and allow for wide participation in economic decision-making. Neurath favored inclusiveness: he sought to preserve a place for existing associations like guilds and cooperatives in the new economic councils that would be formed. At the same time, though, one would be hard pressed to find the actual principles that would guide the plans agreed upon.

The examples of 'Gemeinwirtschaft' highlighted by Vossoughian constitute individual or particular moments, ranging across Neurath's experiences in Vienna in the 1920s and early 1930s, the Netherlands in the latter part of the 1930s, and finally in England during the first half of the 1940s. The shift from the general to the particular might be seen as running in parallel with the scaled-down projections of the Austromarxists in the 1920, as plans for the socialization of the Austrian economy faded rapidly and municipal reforms, especially in economic, social, and cultural matters, took center stage in its stead (exhaustively treated in Gulick 1948: 354–543). Yet in Neurath's case the call for a utopian socialism entailed a general transformation; otherwise piecemeal efforts, like those actually undertaken, succumbed more readily to Marx and Engels' original castigation of utopian socialism in the *Communist Manifesto,* standing outside and apart from society as a whole (Marx and Engels [1848] 2011).

The role of the formative also extends to the various forms of inquiry that arose in Neurath's early or earlier education, that is, prior to his graduate work in ancient economic history. I have already noted the importance of Neurath's attendance at the Hochschule für Bodenkultur in Vienna in shaping, among other things, his interest in and perspective on a proto-ecological economics. But it is perhaps of equal significant to point out his study of ancient philosophy, characteristic of the curriculum of the Gymnasium in central Europe in this period. It served as the basis for a certain kind of radicalism, in this instance a divining of the roots of contemporary thought in the groundwork laid by the ancient Greeks and Romans.

Neurath launched his *Lesebuch für Volkswirtschaftslehre,* as well as his history of political economy in *Empirical Sociology,* with Aristotle. According to Paul Neurath, he performed the translation of texts from Greek and Latin for the reader, a work prepared jointly with his first wife (Paul Neurath 1994: 27). Moreover, one cannot overstate the influence and impact of his reading of Epicurus, as Epicurus becomes the touchstone for Neurath's thinking about how economic activity ought to be valued. Further, Neurath then translates his comprehension of Epicurus' central ideas into his own understanding of the import of Marxism as philosophy and sociology: it becomes 'social epicureanism' (Neurath [1928] 1973: 282–290). In the tradition of the Gymnasium education noted above, Neurath seeks to strength the case for deeming Marxism 'social epicureanism' by noting that Epicurus was Marx's favorite Greek philosopher and that Marx wrote his dissertation on Epicurus and Democritus (Neurath [1928] 1973: 284). Neurath went so far as to state that for Marx it would have been "an honour to be called a successor of Epicurus" (Neurath [1925] 2004: 415).

This immersion in Greek philosophy and the intellectual discourse informed by it goes beyond the community of philosophical discourse that existed in Vienna in the first decades of the twentieth century. This is so because it reflects a pedagogical standard about attaining a proficiency and even fluency in classical languages and literatures. Its significance cannot be ignored any more than Adam Smith's training and academic accomplishments in rhetoric.

For the Austrians it may be too simple a catchphrase to say 'philosophy matters', but of course it did, characterizing the Austromarxists, including the various Adlers (Viktor, Max, and Friedrich) as well as Otto Bauer; the Austrian marginalists, most especially second generation figures like Hayek, along with those in close association with them, say, like Karl Popper; and of course all those participating in the movement surrounding the Vienna Circle (which may also include Popper).

The Vienna Circle and political economy

As the elephant was the symbol that Neurath adopted for himself, so the 'elephant in the room' in this inquiry into Neurath's economic thought is the place of the Vienna Circle in shaping, or in turn being shaped by, Neurath's economic ideas and program. In the first meetings of the group that would form the initial core of the Vienna Circle, Frank, Hahn, Neurath, and Richard von Mises, Neurath was identified as an economist, his wide-ranging intellectual interests notwithstanding.

Subsequent references to economics in the workings of the Vienna Circle fell clearly under Neurath's purview. This would include the succession of volumes produced under the auspices of *Erkenntnis*, as well as Neurath's own critique of the theory of the social sciences prepared as part of the unity-of-science project of the 1940s, published by the University of Chicago Press.

Perhaps the themes and goals that would link the study of economics with the Vienna Circle were embodied in the search for what constituted science, or made for scientific inquiry. In recent decades the study of the Vienna Circle has been subject to serious and significant revision, with a greater emphasis upon the different phases through which the group went and the tensions, perhaps even contradictions, that existed in the ideas and work that its various members advanced. Nonetheless, surveying the salient features of the Vienna Circle one might find the following overarching elements:

1 an intense focus upon the relation between language and thought, no doubt influenced by powerful undercurrents in Austrian philosophy and Viennese public discourse in the early twentieth century, and crystallized by Ludwig Wittgenstein's pathbreaking foray into the matter, in his *Tractatus*;
2 a search for greater precision and clarity through the careful use of logical constructions that would eliminate the ambiguities and invariable cloaking associated with the ordinary use of language, aided by the advances made in symbolic logic and the greater attention to mathematical rigor and the philosophical foundations of mathematics by the turn of the twentieth century;

3 the casting out of metaphysical accretions subjected to new scrutiny across the widest possible array of intellectual disciplines so as to unmask their appearance as pseudo-statements and pseudo-rationalizations;
4 the paring down of all superfluous categories in scientific constructs, applying rigorously Ockham's razor, as mediated by Ernst Mach, creating the basis for a kind of conventionalism in assessing concepts and theories; and
5 requiring that all of these elements would serve to establish the terms – and bounds – of that which was 'verifiable'.

Janik and Toulmin cast the program of the Vienna Circle in a somewhat negative light, especially with regard to the group's effort to assimilate Wittgenstein's early work into the framework of a consistent anti-metaphysical understanding of the nature of science and knowledge: "In the *Tractatus,* the basic symbolism of *Principia Mathematica,* as generalized by the truth-table method, had apparently provided positivism with the logical skeleton it had lacked in the writings of Auguste Comte" (Janik and Toulmin 1973: 218).

The result, though, according to these authors, might be characterized as a version of "old wine in new bottles": "Thus was born the hybrid system of logical positivism, which professed to put an end to all metaphysics but succeeded, rather, in rewriting the metaphysics of Hume and Mach in the symbolism of Russell and Whitehead" (Janik and Toulmin 1973: 219).

How well does this case stand up to the scrutiny which the Vienna Circle – and Neurath – have received over the last four decades, in which scholars have attended to both a greater complexity and manifestations of more varied tensions within the various iterations of the group as it explored philosophy, science, and the philosophy of science?

The pathway that Janik and Toulmin present from Mach to the Vienna Circle certainly can be seen, at least in part, in Neurath's work, both generally and in the realm of political economy. These include establishing value on the basis of sensations that can be measured, the behaviorist impulse that Neurath employed in attempting to render sociology 'scientific'. In a similar vein, the reliance upon what were called 'ostensive definitions' was intended to ground and link the observable and the verifiable in all matters that were genuinely scientific. Moreover, 'ethical' statements were accepted only on the basis of their being 'emotive' rather than 'cognitive' (Janik and Toulmin 1973: 213).

Nonetheless, for Neurath 'value' in economics had to be gauged ultimately in terms of satisfaction that could not be separated from broader considerations of the distribution of wealth and poverty across society. This represents the first, but not the only, caution in assessing the infusion of the program of the Vienna Circle in Neurath's economic thought.

Take the matter of 'verifiability'. Neurath, in line with his advocacy of physicalism, especially in contrast to the phenomenalistic approach initially pursued by Rudolf Carnap, translated verifiability into a reliance upon observables, even extending to introducing somewhat awkward phrasing that would render all statements third-person observations, and as such would be fully objective. In the process this would obviate any need to rely upon first-person statements regarded as interior or subjective projections.

But it was also essential to Neurath that economic experience be comprehended as a 'totality' or in 'clots', a notion that appears early on in Neurath's 1910 and 1911 Austrian and German journal articles critiquing the theory of political economy and is laid out full-blown in his late 1944 treatise, produced as part of the unity of science series, also elaborating a broad-based critique of political economy, if couched as one of sociology.

One critical aspect of Neurath's approach was that it offered an explanation as to why economic experience was not subject to strict falsification. In effect, Neurath saw a contrary instance as a 'shaking' rather than an outright undermining or dismissal of a general statement. In his own time Neurath was responding to Karl Popper's critique of the limits of verifiability (Neurath [1935] 1983). Popper had launched his critique as a refutation of the main tack that the Vienna Circle had adopted to establish statements, and combinations of statements, that is, theories, as scientific. Neurath charged that Popper's doctrine of falsification, put forward as the better means to achieving that end, was simply another form of pseudo-rationalization (Neurath [1935] 1983: 123–124; see also Cat 1996: 202–208). Neurath had taken what he called 'pseudo-rationalization' to task as early as his 1913 paper on 'The Lost Wanderers of Descartes and the Auxiliary Motive' (Neurath [1913] 1983).

For all its merits in challenging Popper's ideas, though, it must be noted that the notion of the existence and importance of 'totalities' of experience or 'clots' could also be viewed as a metaphysical accretion and a target of Ockham's razor, and thus seemingly contrary to the ethos of the Vienna Circle.

It is certainly possible to characterize the notion of 'clots' as having some kinship with the outlook of the German Historical School, but also as reflecting the new physics of relativity and quantum mechanics, where 'complexes' would figure more strongly than either disaggregated constituent parts or the action of Newton's laws. Notably Neurath's criticism of Newton's laws of motion as philosophically vacuous not only sets him apart from the mainstream of economists for whom Newton represents a scientific pinnacle, but also aligned him more closely with late twentieth-century mathematicians like René Thom, who pioneered chaos theory. Neurath himself presaged a version of chaos theory in his 1944 treatise on the foundations of the social sciences, characteristically melding the treatment of natural phenomena and human experience in his discussion of "unpredictability within empiricism":

> The aggregation formed by stone, snow, valley, tribes, climate, cosmic rays, etc., may be called unstable if even a small variation in the initial state may bring about a tremendous difference in the state of the whole aggregation in question – 'tremendous' here from a sociological viewpoint.
>
> (Neurath 1944: 28)

References

Brentano, Lujo (1931) *Mein Leben im Kampf um die soziale Entwicklung Deutschlands.* Jena: E. Diederichs.

Cat, Jordi (1996) "Unity on the Earthly Plane" In *Otto Neurath: Philosophy Between Science and Politics.* Cambridge: Cambridge University Press, part 3.

Chaloupek, Gunther K. (1990) "The Austrian Debate on Economic Calculation in a Socialist Economy". *History of Political Economy* 22(4): 659–675.

Dahms, Hans-Joachim, and Neumann, Michael (1994) "Philosophers and Social Scientists in the Munich Council Republic, 1919". *Jahrbuch der Soziologiegeschichte 1992*: 115–146.

Frank, Philipp (1949) *Modern Science and Its Philosophy.* Cambridge: Harvard University Press.

Galison, Peter (1996) "Constructing Modernism: The Cultural Location of Aufbau". In Ronald Giere and Alan Richardson, eds., *The Origins of Logical Empiricism.* Minneapolis: University of Minnesota Press.

Gulick, Charles (1948) *Austria from Habsburg to Hitler.* Volume One. Forward by Walter Federn. Berkeley: University of California Press.

Hempel, Carl (1975) "Introduction". *Erkenntnis* 9(1): 1–4. (New series)

Hodgson, Geoffrey (2001) *How Economics Forgot History.* London: Routledge.

Janik, Allan, and Toulmin, Stephen (1973) *Wittgenstein's Vienna.* New York: Simon and Schuster.

Kapfinger, Otto (2016) "The Art of Urban Architecture from Below". In Christoph Thun-Hohenstein, Hermann Czech, and Sebastian Hackenschmidt, eds., *Josef Frank: Against Design.* Basel: Birkhauser, pp. 86–117. (Dual language edition: in German and English)

Lewis, Jill (1983) "Red Vienna: Socialism in One City, 1918-'27". *European Studies Review,* now *European History Quarterly* 13(3): 335–355.

Marx, Karl, and Engels, Friedrich. [1848] (2011) *The Communist Manifesto,* intro. Marshall Berman. New York: Penguin Books.

März, Eduard (1991) *Joseph Schumpeter: Scholar, Teacher, Politician.* New Haven: Yale University Press.

Mises, Margitvon (1976) *My Life with Ludwig von Mises.* New Rochelle, NY: Arlington House.

Mitchell, Wesley (1969) *Types of Economic Theory,* Vol. 2. Edited, with an introduction by Joseph Dorfman. New York: A.M. Kelley.

Monk, Ray (1990) *Ludwig Wittgenstein: The Duty of Genius.* New York: Free Press.

Musil, Robert (1953) *The Man Without Qualities.* 1st American edn, trans. Eithne Wilkins and Ernst Kaiser. New York: Coward-McCann.

Neider, Ernst (1973) "Memories of Otto Neurath". In Marie Neurath and Robert S. Cohen, eds., *Empiricism and Sociology*; trans. Paul Foulkes and Marie Neurath. Dordrecht: Reidel, pp. 45–49.

Neurath, Otto [1910] (2004) "Theory of the Social Sciences". In Robert S. Cohen and Thomas E. Uebel, eds., *Otto Neurath: Economic Writings/Selections, 1904–1945.* [Multiple translators]. Dordrecht: Kluwer Academic Publishers, pp. 265–291.

Neurath, Otto [1913] (1983) "The Lost Wanderers of Descartes and the Auxiliary Motive". In Robert S. Cohen and Marie Neurath, eds., *Philosophical Papers 1913–1946.* Dordrecht/Boston: D. Reidel Publishing Company, pp. 1–12.

Neurath, Otto [1917] (2004) "The Conceptual Structure of Economics and Its Foundations". In Robert S. Cohen and Thomas E. Uebel, eds., *Otto Neurath: Economic Writings/ Selections, 1904–1945.* Dordrecht: Kluwer Academic Publishers, pp. 312–341.

Neurath, Otto [1919] (1994) "Die Sozialisierung Sachsens". In Paul Neurath and Elisabeth Nemeth, eds., *Otto Neurath oder Die Einheit von Wissenschaft und Gesellschaft*. Wien: Bohlau Verlag, pp. 193–200.

Neurath, Otto [1920–1921] (2004) "A System of Socialisation". In Robert S. Cohen and Thomas E. Uebel, eds., *Otto Neurath: Economic Writings/Selections, 1904–1945*. [Multiple translators]. Dordrecht: Kluwer Academic Publishers, pp. 345–370.

Neurath, Otto [1920] (2004) "Total Socialisation". In Robert S. Cohen and Thomas E. Uebel, eds., *Otto Neurath: Economic Writings/Selections, 1904–1945*. [Multiple translators]. Dordrecht: Kluwer Academic Publishers, pp. 371–404.

Neurath, Otto (1924) "Geld, Sozialismus, Marxismus". *Der Kampf*. Vol. 16.

Neurath, Otto [1925] (2004) "Economic Plan and Calculation In Kind". In Robert S. Cohen and Thomas E. Uebel, eds., *Otto Neurath: Economic Writings/Selections, 1904–1945*. [Multiple translators]. Dordrecht: Kluwer Academic Publishers, pp. 405–465.

Neurath, Otto [1926] (1994) "Statistik und Proletariat". In Paul Neurath and Elisabeth Nemeth, eds., *Otto Neurath oder Die Einheit von Wissenschaft und Gesellschaft*. Wien: Bohlau Verlag.

Neurath, Otto [1928] (1973) "Personal Life and Class Struggle". In Marie Neurath and Robert S. Cohen, eds., *Empiricism and Sociology*. Trans. Paul Foulkes and Marie Neurath; Dordrecht: Reidel, pp. 249–298.

Neurath, Otto [1931] (1973) *Empirical Sociology*. In Marie Neurath and Robert S. Cohen, eds., *Empiricism and Sociology*. Trans. Paul Foulkes and Marie Neurath. Dordrecht: Reidel, pp. 319–421.

Neurath, Otto [1935] (1983) On Karl Popper and pseudo-rationalization. In Robert S. Cohen and Marie Neurath, eds. and trans., *Philosophical Papers, 1913–1946*. Dordrecht/Boston: D. Reidel Publishing Company, pp. 121–131.

Neurath, Otto [1936] (1983) "Encyclopedia as 'Model'". In Robert S. Cohen and Marie Neurath, eds. and trans., *Philosophical Papers, 1913–1946*. Dordrecht/Boston: D. Reidel Publishing Company, pp. 145–158.

Neurath, Otto (1944) *Foundations of the Social Sciences*. Chicago: University of Chicago Press.

Neurath, Otto (1973a) "Recollection of Gregory Itelson". In Marie Neurath and Robert S. Cohen, eds., *Empiricism and Sociology*. Trans. Marie Neurath. Dordrecht: Reidel, p. 7.

Neurath, Otto (1973b) "Autobiographical Excerpts from Otto Neurath". In Marie Neurath and Robert S. Cohen, eds., *Empiricism and Sociology*. Trans. Paul Foulkes and Marie Neurath. *Dordrecht: Reidel, pp. 18–28.*

Neurath, Paul (1994) "Introduction and Biography". In Paul Neurath and Elisabeth Nemeth, eds., *Otto Neurath oder Die Einheit von Wissenschaft und Gesellschaft*. Wien: Bohlau.

Neurath, Wilhelm (1897) *Die Wirtschaftskrise und Cartellwesen*. Wien: Manz.

Popper, Karl (1973) "Memories of Otto Neurath". In Marie Neurath and Robert S. Cohen, eds., *Empiricism and Sociology*. Trans. Paul Foulkes and Marie Neurath. Dordrecht: Reidel, pp. 51–56.

Schorske, Carl E. (1979) *Fin-de-Siècle Vienna: Politics and Culture*. New York: Knopf.

Shionoya, Yuichi (2005) *The Soul of the German Historical School*. New York: Springer Science & Business Media.

Tinbergen, Jan. (1936) "Review of O. Neurath's 'Rational Theory'". *Erkenntnis* 6: 70–71.

Tinbergen, Jan. (1951) *Econometrics*. Trans. H. Rijken van Olst. Philadelphia: Blakiston.

Tribe, Keith (1995) *Strategies of Economic Order: German Economic Discourse, 1750–1950*. Cambridge: Cambridge University Press.

Uebel, Thomas (ed.) 1991. *Rediscovering the Forgotten Vienna Circle*. Dordrecht: Kluwer Academic Publishers.

Uebel, Thomas E. (2000) *Vernunftskritik und Wissenschaft: Otto Neurath und der erste Wiener Kreis*. Wien: Springer-Verlag.

Uebel, Thomas E. (2004) "Introduction: Neurath's Economics in Critical Context". In Robert S. Cohen and Thomas E. Uebel, eds., *Otto Neurath: Economic Writings/Selections 1904–1945*. [Multiple translators]. Dordrecht: Kluwer Academic Publishers, pp. 1–108.

Vossoughian, Nader (2008) *Otto Neurath: The Language of the Global Polis*. Rotterdam: NAi Publishers.

Wagner, F. Peter (1996) *Rudolf Hilferding: Theory and Politics of Democratic Socialism*. Atlantic Highlands, NJ: Humanities Press.

Weibel, Peter (ed.) (2005) *Beyond Art: Third Culture, A Comparative Study in Cultures, Art, and Science in 20th Century Austria and Hungary*. [Numerous translators] New York: Springer.

3 Faulty philosophical foundations of economics

In his economic writings prior to World War I, Otto Neurath laid out a critique of economic theorizing, faulting it for its weaknesses and inconsistencies in concept formation and use of essential terminology. In this Neurath consciously echoed the criticisms voiced by Henri Poincaré about flaws in the construction of science in general. Later, the tension in Neurath's own thinking became apparent between the coherence required to build systems and coordinate life activities and the necessarily incomplete nature of knowledge, with concomitant implications for economics.

For all that his work in political economy would set him apart from the emerging mainstream of twentieth century economics, Neurath's critique sets him well within the world of economic discourse that characterized the turn-of-the-century disputations in the field. His writing in the first decades of the new century is marked by not infrequent references to a host of economic thinkers, both contemporaries and those who flourished over the previous two centuries. From the 1920s until his death in 1945, though, such references appear to be increasingly retrospective, and his engagement in economics substantially more attenuated.

With his work set in high relief, two questions emerge in consequence. How far was Neurath himself able to address and rectify the foundations of economics in his own work? Moreover, how substantial an imprint of Neurath's critique, consciously or implicitly, has found its way into the subsequent discourse of economics, especially as one surveys heterodox treatments?

The scope of Neurath's critique

From the two early papers that Neurath published on the subject of the theoretical foundations of political economy, one can glean the scope of Neurath's critique of what he saw as serious flaws in the emergent and largely preeminent marginalist and neoclassical economics of the early twentieth century. Neurath found these exemplified by their leading representatives. It is in fact possible to read the first of these papers, from 1910, as a challenge to the economic ideas and techniques put forward by Stanley Jevons and Alfred Marshall, while the second, from 1911, appears to be more of a challenge to the Austrian marginalists, most notably Carl Menger, Friedrich von Wieser, and Eugen von Böhm-Bawerk. Both articles have Vilfredo Pareto well in their sights, and sprinkled through them are glancing criticisms of Joseph Schumpeter. Other, later writings of Neurath would flesh out these criticisms further.

Neurath drew extensively upon his knowledge of the canon of the history of economic thought. His comments about various economic thinkers, often presented in passing as a quick, glancing shot, with the greatest detail reserved for footnotes, nonetheless typically provided substantive criticisms of their ideas and techniques.

For example, there may be no better way to set Neurath on the 'road not taken' in economics than to contrast his characterization of Johann Heinrich von Thünen, whose work Neurath had studied early on in his career (Uebel 2004: 10), with that supplied decades later by Paul Samuelson. For the latter von Thünen was the long obscured progenitor of neoclassical economics as it emerged in the late nineteenth and early twentieth centuries. In an article in the *Journal of Economic Literature* dating from 1983 and celebrating von Thünen "at the two-hundred year" mark, Samuelson introduced him as follows: "the economist who … not only created marginalism and managerial economics, but also elaborated one of the first models of general equilibrium and did so in terms of realistic econometric parameters" (Samuelson 1983: 1468).

By contrast, for Neurath von Thünen's construction of the abstracted 'isolated state' was predicated on specific assumptions that informed a particular historical moment and set of accompanying economic and social conditions, as well as a similarly historically grounded theory about the role of prices in it.

> Thunen describes land utilization around a city in an isolated state. Within the innermost circle, vegetables are grown, and then comes forestry (close to town because of transport costs), next comes intensive and then extensive agriculture. All this on the assumption of a specific market economy and a determinate price formation, which is to say, a specific pressure distribution.
>
> (Neurath [1931] 1973: 402)

Neurath's reference to the notion of 'pressure' was based upon an analogy with meteorology, with social groups moving from higher pressure to lower. Neurath grafted this analogy from the work of Franz Oppenheimer. He saw Oppenheimer, like himself, as an economist who also assumed the mantle of historian and sociologist, establishing thereby a kinship of sorts in their conception of the scope, if not necessarily the method, of economics (Neurath [1919] 1973: 129).

The historical moment in question would be characterized as the 'capitalist economic order'. In invoking capitalism in this way, Neurath appears aligned with Max Weber, who saw the dominance of the market system and its attendant price theory as also characteristic of a specific historical moment. However, even before the ascendance of Neurath's Marxist inclinations over the course of World War I, difference in their views about the philosophical grounding of economics were quite apparent.

Principles Underlying Neurath's Critique

Neurath introduced principles he saw as essential to any coherent social science, but especially political economy. A short sketch of the foundations upon which Neurath sought to build a philosophically consistent political economy would include the following:

1. From Friedrich List he took the notion that the economic order, say, the existing capitalist one, should not be treated as a given; instead, it should be analogized to a machine that could be operated in different ways. There were in fact a multiplicity of possible economic orders. Early on in his career Neurath scored Marx and the Marxists for envisioning only one alternative to capitalism (Neurath 1911: 91); later he tended to give singular attention to what he broadly conceived as a socialist alternative.
2. To this view of economic orders as machinery or instruments that could be fashioned in different ways, Neurath incorporated Wilhelm Roscher's expansive view of political economy as a matter of examining "the organization of societies" (Neurath and Neurath [1910] 1913: 100). This gave far greater weight to social circumstances and conditions, as well as the historical moment, in surveying alternative forms or models of 'economic order'. The infusion of historical events and experience would also raise skepticism about the possibility of sweeping or even universal economic laws, including those advanced as laws of economic development.
3. Taken together, these two principles informed Neurath's perspective on what machinery itself entailed. In essence it encompassed technique and technology rather than mechanism. This would play a part in Neurath's rejection of an abstracted notion of generic factors of production, most especially in the case of capital, which he would tie to mistaken efforts by neoclassical economists to make it commensurate with all other inputs by resorting to monetary calculation.
4. These principles also informed the sense in which Neurath would later use the term 'social engineering', especially as it is linked to an exploration of different forms and theories of organization. Here the introduction of different kinds of machinery is seen as launched and even inspired by acts of imagination. As Neurath wrote in the 1911 paper: "*Mechanics gives the builder of machines insight about machines, which have not yet been built, when only their elementary components are known*" (Neurath 1911: 83; emphasis in original).
5. In the 1910 paper Neurath highlighted 'combination problems' regarding consumable goods and the satisfaction, or value, derived from such combinations in the study of organizations. In the 1911 paper he developed extensive tables for these varied and various 'constellations'. The net effect

of these rather long lists of various combinations was to eviscerate the mathematical foundation of marginalism by demonstrating the limitations of the much more restricted – and restrictive – tables that marginalists like Carl Menger had introduced in constructing their cases for measuring utility. Such tables appeared to be based upon arbitrary choices without real empirical backing or substance, giving the appearance of a sort of mathematical precision and insight, while Neurath's tables set forth a dizzying array of possibilities that existed as genuine hypotheticals.

6 At the same juncture Neurath challenged both the use of cardinal measures to gauge economic value through the marginalist notion of utility and the restrictive use of ordinal rankings in the construction of utility or indifference curves as put forward by Pareto. The notion of value itself was challenged, as Neurath emphasized the primacy of measuring wealth and poverty in determining economic value, rather than the sum of individual satisfaction derived from a limited list of and arbitrarily chosen consumable goods. This more global approach to economic value he identified as having deep historical roots in political economy, but was now obscured in the emerging age of marginalism and neoclassical economics.

7 The 'road not taken' was also manifested in Neurath's effort to take into account the non-measurable, that is, from the standpoint of being quantifiable, in gauging economic value. In his 1937 review of Carl Hempel and Paul Oppenheim's volume on 'the concept of type', Neurath cites favorably their attempt to capture the non-measurable, that is, to move beyond the strictly quantifiable to better account for the qualitative (Neurath [1937] 1983: 183), a notion central to Neurath's exploration of a proto-ecological economics. In that regard he quotes Hempel and Oppenheim on the use of topological approaches in mathematics, recalling, among others, Poincaré, but also Oskar Simony, another early topologist, who had taught at the Hochschule für Bodenkultur in Vienna, to achieve that end.

8 Neurath offered a critique of measuring economic value based upon that which was commensurable through monetary calculation. He rejected the use of such forms of measurement to serve in establishing economic proof on the part of Schumpeter, but also even earlier going back to Gossen, like Thunen seen as a critical precursor of marginalist thinking (Neurath [1910] 2004: 278–279).

9 Neurath challenged the use of price curves, as found in Marshall, Pareto, and von Wieser (Neurath 1911: 83). While different prices may be associated with different quantities of certain goods, there are no continuous supply and demand functions as conceived by either J.S. Mill or Marshall, suggesting a different and less interdependent relation between price and quantity.

In this setting it is noteworthy that Neurath introduced the notion of price differentiation to counter the idea that there would necessarily be one price for a good. In consequence, if the relation between price and quantity turns out to be a set of points not necessarily linked or subject to an assumption of continuity and interpolation, then the Paretian and, by extension, the Marshallian microeconomic market construct falls away (Neurath 1911: 83–84f). This would also call into question the nature and range of the appropriate theory of value in economics, establishing a greater distance or disjuncture between value and price.

10 Laws and customs, drawn from historical research, 'condition' the way that goods (and services) are translated (or 'shifted'), suggesting the primacy of historical experience in constructing theory. This imparts an important role to be accorded economic history. Moreover, Neurath's emphasis upon 'Verschiebung' or 'shifting' goods was intended to broaden the nature and scope of economic interactions beyond the conventions associated with exchange, for example introducing the juridical along with the economic.

11 In consequence, sociological laws, built upon scientific statements, should not be conceived as universal, but temporally limited. In *Empirical Sociology* Neurath makes the case that Malthus was wrong to sketch out and posit a universal law of population, but rather, citing the approach taken by Marxists, saw it possible to discern laws of population that hold for a particular historical moment (Neurath [1931] 1973: 384, also 396–397). One is therefore drawn to seeking a comparison of Neurath's treatment of 'sociological law' and the case put forward by the economic historian Paul Bairoch that different times – and historical moments – produce different economic laws (Bairoch 1993: 164–177).

12 Theory and practice did not constitute separate realms of inquiry; rather they were folded into one another. From his 1916 paper on 'the classification of systems of hypotheses' Neurath noted that the "comparative observation of systems of hypotheses … appears to be the foundation of all historical research" (Neurath [1916] 1983: 30), while practice itself is informed by the fact that "historical experiences have made possible abstract theory" (Neurath [1910] 2004: 285).

13 Other elements appear explicitly in later writings. From his 1944 treatise on the 'foundations of the social sciences' Neurath challenged the notion of 'ceteris paribus', the basis for analyzing economic activity through series of partial equilibria, seeing it as "not in harmony" with the different sorts of "aggregations" extant at "different times" (Neurath 1944: 20).

Nature and role of concept formation

One of the most striking moments in Neurath's 1910 paper on the theory of the social sciences is his attack on the looseness and inconsistencies of concept formation in political economy. With Wilhelm Wundt serving as his straw man, Neurath excoriates the wont of political economists to introduce terminology of art, extending even to 'good' and 'price', in cavalier fashion. He contrasted their approach and outlook with that which took place in physics, especially as engaged in by Poincaré and Pierre Duhem, who assiduously traced scientific concepts back to their roots, intending to capture their factual basis (Neurath [1910] 2004: 269).

In exploring how one might go about theorizing about concept formation and the systems of thought that may be constructed from them, Neurath engaged in a critique of the language in which economic concepts were couched, seeking to 'unmask' their actual meaning, if any could be established on a suitably scientific basis, following the conventionalist critique that Poincaré had laid down.

He also drew heavily from the critique of science set forth by Duhem. One can discern a clear pathway from Duhem's notion of a multiplicity of hypotheses that might conform to a given set of facts to Neurath's assertion of the inevitability of the need to select an 'auxiliary motive' or 'auxiliary hypothesis' in any scientific inquiry. (See his 1913 paper on 'The Lost Wanderers of Descartes and the Auxiliary Motive' (Neurath [1913] 1983).) Moreover, he would encapsulate the process of concept formation and system construction through a Duhem-inspired metaphor, an imagined boat under construction while at sea.

Jordi Cat's extended and insightful inquiry into the evolution of Neurath's metaphor of the boat under construction at sea, which came to capture the central thesis of his theory of knowledge, sets its changing nuances fully within the context of philosophy and philosophical discourse, giving special weight to the ongoing discussions and disputations within the Vienna Circle, with some attention as well devoted to a Marxian frame of reference (Cat 1996: 184–244).

At the same time, Cat notes three thematic constants in Neurath's thought: anti-foundationalism, which obviously was crucial to the notion of the 'boat'; pluralism, the notion that multiple theories and theses may be applied to the same set of facts; and a historical frame of reference.

This last principle should garner special attention in any assessment of Neurath's economic thought, as even in his earliest theoretical writings, as noted above, the matter of what a 'historical economics' might entail arises. It was also evident in an early letter to Ferdinand Tönnies, in which Neurath outlined what he felt was his unique interest in combining the study of economics with that of history (Vossoughian 2008: 19–25). Moreover, by the time of his writing of *Empirical Sociology,* in 1931, Neurath was explicitly seeking to meld political economy and history into one discipline, which Neurath would term 'scientific sociology' (Neurath [1931] 1973: 345ff).

But it is in that same work that the limitations of Cat's framework became evident. From its text Cat quotes a significant passage in which Neurath expresses the need to go beyond an anti-metaphysical construction and seeks to establish linkages among pertinent concepts, thereby delving into the matter of concept formation. Neurath speaks of constructing a "pyramid of concepts", likening it to what Rudolf Carnap had laid out in his *Konstitutionssytem* (Neurath [1931] 1973: 390). And so Cat sees this reference as illuminating a turning point within the Vienna Circle: here Neurath appears to continue to embrace the 'phenomenalist' approach advanced by Carnap, only to reject it and make the case broadly for a 'physicalist' language in its stead shortly thereafter. Hilary Putnam viewed this same turning point from a different vantage point, seeing Neurath persuading Carnap to reject the phenomenalist approach he had taken in *Der Logische Aufbau der Welt* and take up instead a more "intersubjective" construction.

This is true within its own terms, that is, in the disputations within the Vienna Circle. However, it must be tempered in a number of crucial respects. For one, it is possible to discover references in Neurath's work on the theory of political economy, appearing two decades earlier, in which the importance of linking concepts and making connections among a common body of principles across seemingly separate disciplines cannot be overstated. For Neurath the question became: how are concepts derived?

Moreover, the text that follows the reference to Carnap in *Empirical Sociology* is also quite telling in that regard. Neurath refers to the seemingly wide differences in the ways that political economy and history are organized in their modes of inquiry and investigation. This is the division between the nomothetic and the idiographic, a central feature in the classification of the various intellectual disciplines as expounded by neo-Kantians like Wilhelm Windelband and Heinrich Rickert (Neurath [1931] 1973: 390–391). In short, Neurath's immersion in the currents of central European thought of the late nineteenth and early twentieth centuries surely helped shaped the bounds of his discourse, even if his main effort and focus were to challenge, refute, or reject some of its central tropes.

The curious case of utilitarianism

What is the place of utilitarianism in Neurath's own construction of economics? The answer is somewhat – and surprisingly – complex. One starting point would be the bridge Neurath attempted to build between utilitarianism and socialism by the early 1930s: "The Epicurean approach, revived mainly by utilitarians like Bentham and Mill, today serves socialism, for, if the principle of the increase of general happiness is to be adopted, wealth side by side with misery cannot be tolerated" (Neurath [1925] 2004: 460).

Jeremy Bentham is an intriguing figure in the history of economic thought. He belongs to a constellation of major thinkers in England active at the turn of the nineteenth century, among whom one might include James Mill, David Ricardo, and Thomas Malthus, as well as Bentham himself. Within the realm of political economy proper, Bentham likely merits only a short passage (see, for example, Stanley Brue's 2000 *The Evolution of Economic Thought*), as he did not weigh in directly on economic matters in his intellectual pursuits. Yet the philosophical doctrine of utilitarianism he espoused, and for which he is taken to be the leading progenitor, would have a profound influence on economic thought nearly a century later. Jevons, one of the first English marginalists, overturned the classical school's notion of value inhering in labor and other factors of production by basing value instead upon utility, drawing from and applying in new ways Bentham's doctrine of utilitarianism. Subsequently, utility – and its negative counterpart, disutility – came to inform standard measures of satisfaction in both marginalist and neoclassical constructions of microeconomic behavior. This extended, at least in part, to Jevons' remaking of the market for labor itself as grounded in the tension between the utility of leisure and the disutility of work.

Therefore, it is more than a little surprising to see Neurath embrace utilitarianism, as the quotation cited above indicates. While Neurath was clearly respectful of Jevons' work in plumbing the science of logic in the 1910 article on the theory of the social sciences (Neurath [1910] 2004: 290), he also distanced himself quite plainly from Jevons' approach to political economy, including his measures of economic value and satisfaction. In *Empirical Sociology* Neurath expressly refuted the use of a pleasure/pain calculus that was aligned with a designated dichotomy between utility and disutility. Nonetheless, Bentham's utilitarianism could be fitted and applied to Neurath's social epicureanism, and thus might be seen as contributing to a Marxian or socialist construction of economic life. Moreover, Neurath also spoke of the utility to be measured by socialist calculation, though understood as 'social' rather than individual utility, and not reduced to any one standard unit of measurement.

However, Neurath's interest in and favorable treatment of Bentham's utilitarianism predates his embrace of Marxism or socialism. The 1910 article contains an extensive footnote, calling for greater recognition of Bentham's work for political economy (Neurath [1910] 2004: 289). Significantly, it is linked to Neurath's initial sketch, developed more fully in his 1911 piece on economic theorizing, of the complexities associated with efforts to measure the satisfaction afforded by different and varying combinations of goods. It is here that Neurath introduces a system of rankings, meant to replace the cardinal measures of quantities of goods then touted by the marginalists. It is also the place where Neurath raised the matter of combinatorics, so that Bentham in effect is appropriated for the task of deconstructing the quantitative mold established by the marginalists as capable of capturing economic value.

It is also the case that Neurath's view of Bentham and the doctrine of utilitarianism was subject to strong crosswinds. In his article on 'An Inventory of Standard of Living', written in 1937 for Max Horkheimer's journal, *Critical Inquiry,* Neurath castigated the principle of 'atomistic utilitarianism'. At issue here was a calculus of pleasure and pain, applied on an individual basis, both by person and perhaps more importantly, by activity.

> The atomistic, utilitarian approach (which we do not accept) would express the matter thus: 'positive' and 'negative', as well as 'indifferent' elements exist side by side. The 'feeling' of a person would then be regarded as constituted of 'pleasure' and 'pain'.
>
> (Neurath [1937] 2004: 515)

Elsewhere Neurath appears to embrace a variant of such a calculus, measuring varying levels of pleasure, gauged, it would seem, on the basis of observable physical sensation. Such a sensory calculus appears derived more from Ernst

Mach than Bentham, or Marx, for that matter. In this form, Neurath's objection is less to utilitarianism per se and more to its 'atomistic' deconstruction. That would be consistent with Neurath's evocation of the centrality of 'clots' and 'complexes' in human experience and scientific inquiry.

Moreover, there is a remarkable and somewhat detailed passage in *Empirical Sociology* in which Neurath extols Bentham's ideas as approximating to a significant degree many of his own ideas and inclinations, but seen indirectly through John Stuart Mill's treatment of Bentham. The passage appears as a subsection devoted to the struggle to eliminate 'metaphysical' content from political economy, and Neurath took up Mill's Bentham as an instrument for that purpose.

> Through his utilitarianism, and through his whole anti-metaphysical tenor Mill has contributed to the overcoming of 'ethics' as a scientific discipline, and to its evolution into a doctrine of the functioning of communal living in society. In his famous essay on Bentham he shows how senseless it is to make much ado about the conscious motives of men and to take their formulation too seriously. What is decisive is their behavior in living together.
>
> (Neurath [1931] 1973: 354–355)

Bentham was characterized as concerned with outcomes, rather than motives, an abiding concern of Neurath, and so did not subscribe to a 'subjective' or idealist interpretation of economic activity and experience. Neurath went so far as to see Bentham embracing a 'class' basis for such activity and experience. "Mill stresses how little Bentham thought of benevolence as a motive in the changing of human affairs … What Bentham himself has, above all, elucidated is the class interest and the class ethics ensuing from it … " (Neurath [1931] 1973: 355).

This, though, seems strikingly anachronistic and likely a product of the kind of enthusiasm Weber saw in Neurath. More generally, it would suggest the underlying appeal materialist philosophy held for Neurath, and his association of such philosophy with progressive politics and ideas, as Carnap, his Vienna Circle colleague, had pointed out (Carnap 1973: 44–45).

Materialism and the role of interpretation

However, this may also serve as a useful entry into assessing the extent to which Neurath was able to align his longstanding effort to eliminate all metaphysics – and metaphysical statements – from science with his embrace of Marxism. The link seems strongest in his reliance upon a materialist philosophy, whose critical forebear appears to be the ancient Greek philosopher Epicurus. Such a philosophy would allow Neurath to make the case for the necessity of using a 'physicalist' language, whereby sociological statements would be cast in terms of stimulus and response, all observables. In this it is important to note that Neurath cited

Epicurus to find common ground with Marx, and was much less likely to make his case through specific Marxist texts, while ignoring altogether commentaries by leading contemporary Marxist thinkers.

But how does this give primacy to economic and social forces in shaping human events and developments? Would not this require a layer of interpretation, about which Neurath appears to assume contradictory positions? On the one hand, the instrument provided by Ockham's Razor, a device heralded by Mach and accepted readily by the First Vienna Circle, was intended to take on in full the manifestations of metaphysical thought, in whatever form they appeared. When pursued rigorously the attack on metaphysics would therefore call into question any intermediate (or mediating) layer, including a Marxist understanding, that is, an interpretation of which circumstances and conditions underlie historical changes of note. In that view, what, after all, are classes but a construction, one that the authors of "The Communist Manifesto" said was central to the comprehension of human history itself.

Yet by linking his materialism with behaviorism in asserting a scientific form to sociology, one can find Neurath challenging even the construct of 'community', set in tension with 'society' (Neurath [1931] 1973: 393). This was the dichotomy that the sociologist Ferdinand Tönnies had set as paradigmatic of the conflict roiling the modern world. As an abstracted dichotomy its elimination might be viewed as consistent with Neurath's Machian anti-metaphysical stance.

However, as Nader Vossoughian has suggested, Tönnies' notion of 'community' may have inspired Neurath's interest in the relation between community and the economy, evident in his longstanding effort to improve urban life, whether in Vienna in the 1920s or in England in the 1940s (Vossoughian 2008). It may also have served as a goad of sorts to his interest as well in 'Gemeinwirtschaft', against which Ludwig von Mises would famously rail in launching the debate over 'socialist calculation'. Was Neurath simply of two minds about the necessity of interpretation and hence the presence of interpretive layers of meaning to mediate immediate experience?

Consider the following: Neurath had already early on taken up the notion that theoretical interpretations were ineluctable, as theory itself was required to establish scientific theories, so that there was no discrete division between the realm of theory and that of fact. Here Neurath was following in the footsteps of Poincaré and especially Duhem, but, for all their differences, also aligning himself with the commonly expressed outlook of Max Weber about the intertwining of theory and fact.

It is also the case, though, that this adoption of what might be termed the necessity of metatheory did not preclude its application to Marxism: to wit, the acceptance of the primacy of economic forces, the role of class, or even the dominance of the class struggle in human affairs. Whether the Marxian view of the sweep of history, a theory of the evolution and transformation of society through 'stages of history', can be similarly situated in Neurath's thought is another matter altogether. Even with its emphasis upon material conditions, the narrative within Neurath's 1939 text, *Modern Man in the Making,* cannot be viewed simply as an exposition of such a Marxian construction of a progression through 'stages of history', and, it might be contended, was not intended to be so. Neurath had prefaced the work by stating that it did not set forth "any social or political theory" (Neurath 1939: 7–8).

On the uses and limitations of dichotomy

Writing in his paper on the "Classification of Systems of Hypotheses", Neurath challenged the validity of establishing oppositional pairings of theories or theses as a way of comprehending and advancing scientific inquiry (Neurath [1916] 1983). His point of departure was the longstanding, but also contemporaneous and heated controversy in the science of optics about the nature of light: was it constituted of particles or waves? However, this led to a broader philosophical disquisition on the nature and use of dichotomies:

> The most primitive form of classification is that of dichotomies of which emission theory – wave theory is one; there is an abundance of such dichotomies in all fields: realism – idealism, tariff – free trade, etc. The corresponding characteristics mostly come about rather haphazardly and independently of each other. The A-theory is characterized independently of the B-theory. If the B-theory were simply the group of non-A theories, there would be no logical objection to this classification; however, it would not be of practical use.
>
> (Neurath [1916] 1983: 15)

He goes on to state:

> In order to obtain a scientifically satisfactory systematization, one must first, willy-nilly, try to give a complete survey of combinations of the elementary notions; by the application of certain principles a selection from the logically possible combinations could already be created. After surveying this totality, one could investigate which of the combinations are realized in 'nature'.
>
> (Neurath [1916] 1983: 15)

In the case of political economy such investigations would require 'historical research'.

Neurath goes on to disparage any reliance upon dichotomies: "Dichotomies, however, are not only crude intellectually, but also the product of scientific pugnacity" (Neurath [1916] 1983: 15). Then, even after allowing for the possibility, argued by some, that dichotomies might "have a stimulating effect on scientific life", Neurath noted, "they would be useful for science perhaps, but themselves unscientific" (Neurath [1916] 1983: 15).

His treatment of dichotomies offers real insight into his thinking about schools of economic thought and the tenets of leading or representatives figures within them. Perhaps the expressions used by mercantilists and thinkers from the classical school overstate the differences between the schools (Neurath [1910] 2004: 271–272).

On the other hand, Neurath was not averse to sketching out thematic threads in the history of economic thought grounded more in philosophical considerations, tracking, for example, the materialist underpinnings of what he saw as the central matter of gauging correctly what constitutes wealth.

It is for that reason that Aristotle and Thomas More anchor his depiction of the evolution of political economy, whether in his *Lesebuch* or in *Empirical Sociology*. What is also notable in this latter work is the extent to which Neurath, in surveying the philosophical dimensions of political economy and sociology, did pose a dichotomy of the sort to which he had alluded in the 1916 paper, namely that which exists between materialist and idealist philosophy, as the fulcrum upon which his case for a scientific sociology rested. Perhaps the disjuncture between these two approaches or perspectives can best be understood as reflective of the tension between two competing, long-held conceptions of his: a way of seeing the world through complexes and 'totalities' analyzed through combinatorics and an adherence to a materialist philosophy as the underpinning of progressive practice, whether economic, social, or political, and scientific advancement.

Inversion of the place of science

One of the more striking ways evincing Neurath's pursuit of the 'road not taken' in economics is his inversion of the place broadly accorded science, but especially the hard or physical sciences, by mainstream economists since the ascendance of the neoclassical school in the late nineteenth century. Here if any model for economics is to be sought, it will be found in the realm of classical mechanics, anchored by the figure of Isaac Newton. And so it is no surprise that the highest accolade that Paul Samuelson was able to bestow upon Leon Walras was that of 'our Newton' (Samuelson [1981] 1986: 343). Nor should it be overlooked that classical economists also did aspire at times to put forth principles and shape a discipline as Newton had been able to do. For example, there are significant Newtonian elements in both Adam Smith and Marx, as in the case of the latter's 'law of motion' of capitalism (see Turk 2010: 489–490).

However, when one turns to Neurath, a rather different picture emerges. In part this follows from Neurath's own study of the physical sciences, references to which abound in his numerous works, often in what might seem unlikely places, a manifestation of his wide-ranging knowledge and interests. One can also find specific works of his devoted to the subject matter of the physical sciences, like his early piece on optics, noted above, translated from lecture to published paper, in which he explored the nature of the formation of scientific hypotheses, advancing a notion that informed his thought throughout his career, whereby the choice of theory and means of theorizing were required to formulate scientific theories.

In part, though, this reflects as well the reliance of Neurath upon the critiques about the nature of science posed by Mach, Poincaré, and Duhem, among others, whose writings and careers centered upon the physical sciences. Their criticism included the need to remove superfluous or unwarranted elements that had become infused in much of conventional science, evident in Mach's strenuous use of 'Ockham's Razor' or Poincaré's conventionalist outlook. From Duhem the variability of scientific explanation was laid bare, as different and diverse interpretations and explanations might be drawn from the same set of facts.

Thus Neurath did not champion Newton as many other political economists did. In the 1930 tract on the 'Ways of the Scientific World-Conception', he challenged Newton's conception of 'absolute space', built upon the unbounded extension and imposition of Cartesian coordinates, as mistaken, whereas Descartes' notion of movement through neighboring areas was seen as a closer approximation of the nature of space in light of the emergence of relativity (Neurath [1930] 1983: 42). Hence, while economics as a discipline appeared to embrace Newtonian physics just as it began to face serious objections among physicists and as physics as a field of scientific inquiry itself was undergoing something of a crisis about its foundations (Turk 2016: 8–24), Neurath stood apart from this.

Moreover, Neurath subjected the matter of the nature of science as a whole to rigorous critique, similar to the approach taken by Poincaré, in his popular writings, including *Science and Hypothesis,* with which Neurath was familiar in its 1906 German translation (Neurath [1910] 2004: 266). At the same time, Neurath inverted the common treatment of the physical sciences as somehow prior, serving thereby as the model for the humanities and the arts.

Instead, Neurath emphasized the importance of and gave priority to the imagination in launching new scientific inquires and approaches. This was of profound importance to Neurath in thinking about the relation of different disciplines, as well as their nature, allowing him to make the case for a greater unity in conception and construction across all sciences. Thus he would contend that 'social engineering', seemingly a St.-Simonian and positivist term par excellence, and one that he embraced as necessary for the advancement of society, could be fitted into the mold of mechanical engineering. This would seem to accord with Neurath's contention in *Empirical Sociology* that "[o]ne might speak of the physics of society in the same way as of the physics of a machine" (Neurath [1931] 1973: 390).

But, according to Neurath, that was because mechanical engineering itself was born out of fantasy, citing Leonardo da Vinci's sketching of lighter-than-air vehicles, an act of imagination only to be realized centuries later. Hence, the imaginative designs for society envisioned by 'scientific utopianism' might also advance from the fantastic to the real, indeed require it.

Furthermore, one might see developments in sociology influence physics, rather than the other way around. "The modern statistical approach, which has become so significant in physics, has its origins in sociological methods that were advocated about the middle of the nineteenth century and even earlier by Quetelet and others" (Neurath [1930] 1983: 44–45).

Needless to say, this nuanced reading of Neurath's conception of science and its significance for history, political economy, and sociology, the areas of inquiry most directly at issue here, might readily be lost or blurred, making Neurath more of a positivist than he ever was. It is also the case that Neurath's own words, a sample of which are noted above, would render that blurring all the easier.

More on machines, mechanical analogies, and mechanisms

As we have seen, central to Neurath's construction of and outlook upon political economy was the notion, drawn expressly from Friedrich List, that the existing economic order not be treated as a given; rather, it is analogized to a machine that could be operated in different ways (Neurath [1910] 2004: 273). In fact, Neurath castigated Pareto in his 1910 essay on the theory of the social sciences for facilely adopting a mechanical analogy for his model of indifference curves (Neurath [1910] 2004: 273–274). But as the citation from List shows, Neurath's rejection of mechanical analogies was not based upon an aversion to likening economic structures or modes of operation to machinery. Instead, what was meant by those comparisons or resemblances sought was at issue.

In part one can see this manifested in Neurath's linkage of engineering feats with acts of imagination. However, there are other striking uses of machinery in Neurath's writings. When Neurath sought to debunk the 'economic theory of factors' of production, he invoked an analogy with machinery to do so. Writing in "The Conceptual Structure of Economic Theory and its Foundations" (1917), Neurath took up the example of the steam engine. What, he asked, would specific knowledge of the boiler bring to an understanding of the overall operation of the steam engine? Here he claimed that it was only through the transformation of the boiler into a monetary figure that it could be identified as an input commensurable with the output provided by the machine; hence, the theory of factors was derived from the mistaken imposition of monetary calculation (Neurath [1917] 2004: 335–336).

There is, though, a second line of reasoning very much at the heart of Neurath's critique of economics. The 'whole' represents a complex that cannot be comprehended by breaking it down into its component parts. It is not so much a matter of the whole being greater than the sum of its parts than it is the whole as qualitatively different from either its individual parts or all of those parts simply lumped together. Instead, it is their integration into a functioning machine and hence the interconnection of parts that is crucial. This is the notion of the precedence of 'totalities' over individual parts or elements.

One can also see its wellspring, or at the least a striking correspondence in framing structures, in the tenets of the German Historical School. As Joseph Schumpeter noted in his contemporaneous characterization of the outlook or perspective of the German Historical School: "[This school] always stressed the fact that economics cannot be split up into an agglomeration of independent economic individuals and that economic phenomena are not merely the resultants of individual components" (Schumpeter [1914] 1954: 179).

If one were to return to the notion of mechanical analogy, one would see that the Irving Fisher model of correspondences between physical or mechanical elements and economic ones, taken up by Leon Walras in his last paper on "Mechanics and Economics" (Walras 1909), was completely alien to Neurath, as such correspondences did not address what had been produced as a whole, that is, a complex or 'clot'.

A foundation provided by Becher and King

Like the grounding of his utopianism in the economic – or proto-economic – writings of Aristotle, Oresmus, and More, so Neurath drew significant elements of his consideration of the nature and direction of political economy from two other early thinkers and practitioners who flourished in the seventeenth century: Gregory King and J.J. Becher. Their appearance may indicate a predilection in Neurath's own economic thought that may predate any specific attachment on his part to identifiable schools of economic thought.

King is often regarded as the "first economic statistician", and Neurath's references to him include both 'King's rule' regarding the relation between changing figures for crop production and the prices obtained for them, along with King's accompanying table (King [1696] 1936). Neurath remained enamored of the use and importance of statistics throughout his career, shaping his construction of visual languages like Isotype and occupying center stage in his historical, anthropological, and economic text entitled *Modern Man in the Making*. Nor should the theoretical role of statistics be understated. In *Empirical Sociology* Neurath makes plain that a scientific sociology must be a statistical sociology. One is reminded in all this of the distance Adam Smith placed between himself and his approach to political economy, on the one hand, and King's approach, on the other. Smith wanted to stay clear of King's "political arithmetic", signaling one of the divisions in method and perspective that has affected and at times roiled economics ever since.

As for Becher, his ideas as the leading Austrian cameralist of his time are treated relatively favorably by Neurath, including concerns about the harm that 'free competition' might cause. Neurath noted that Becher's treatment "of monopoly and perfect competition" pointed to the "detrimental effects of free competition … with remarkable lucidity" (Neurath [1910] 2004: 272).

In a similar vein, the cameralist or mercantilist view accorded more closely with Neurath's critical take on the emerging price theory of his own day, seeing that in exchanges, which Neurath categorized as 'goods transfer', the output was given. This meant that prices did not emerge through an interdependent mechanism requiring the existence of a supply function and a demand function (see 1910 and 1911 articles).

Neurath was also at pains to show that there was at least some convergence of views and method between mercantilism, represented by Becher, and the classical school, rather than a straight-out dichotomy. In part this was through Neurath's account of the accomplishments of the mercantilists, in which he recognized that their blending of theory and practice had to be understood on its own terms. He pointed to the fact that "different types of trade were treated in detail"; moreover, the mercantilists had reasons for "drawing up regulae and axiomata" (Neurath [1910] 2004: 272).

He concluded: "Too much fuss has long been made of these formal issues [involving questions of expression], thus overstressing the distance between the classical school and the mercantilists" (Neurath [1910] 2004: 272).

A further insight into Neurath's view of mercantilism or cameralism can be garnered from the reader that Neurath and his first wife, Anna Schapire Neurath, collaborated on, contemporaneous with Neurath's first major articles on the foundations of economic theory. Among the economic thinkers highlighted in Volume 1 was J.J. Becher. Neurath also included Becher in some of his lists of influences, with the caveat that he did not necessarily accept the views and outlook of those figures wholesale. See, for example, the 1917 article on "The Conceptual Structure of Economic Theory and its Foundations" (Neurath [1917] 2004: 340), at a time when Neurath was moving toward embracing the notion of socialization, or even 'total socialization' of industrialized economies.

It might also be noted in passing that Becher's involvement in an array of disciplines might well have had special appeal to Neurath, who crossed many disciplines himself. Becher delved extensively into chemistry, and is credited with authoring the phlogiston theory of gases, later discredited by Priestly and Lavoisier.

Yet this discussion of the virtues to be found in mercantilist thought only laid the groundwork for a crucial turn from the mercantilist view of the world to what would appear to be, broadly speaking, an Institutionalist perspective, though clearly one that might be rooted at least in part in cameralist thinking as reconstructed and reconfigured by the German Historical School in the nineteenth century.

> Political economists have always been interested in the processes that make people wealthy or poor. As long as this happened by cultivation of land or operating a plant it was treated as basically a technical question, but soon it was realized that it was the system of contracts and of taxes and duties that were of decisive importance; in consequence the systems of organisations themselves became objects of inquiry.
>
> (Neurath [1910] 2004: 272).

It is at this juncture that Friedrich List and Wilhelm Roscher enter the picture. Neurath had already drawn attention to Roscher's ostensibly more inclusive approach to political economy, as he "incorporated problems treated by thinkers like Cournot and Walras into [his] area of research, but also discussed … the life of a society [treated] as a whole" (Neurath [1910] 2004: 270).

What would emerge would be a set of principles, themes, and signposts that conform in many ways to the frame of reference within which Neurath operated at the outset of his career as an economic thinker, still bearing traces of Becher's thought. Among these ideas and approaches were: (1) an emphasis upon an economics grappling with 'society as a whole', hence the need for economics to study the different ways that society might be organized and their effect upon the 'economic order'; (2) a high degree of skepticism toward 'free competition'; (3) a recognition of the role that institutions play in shaping the 'economic order'; (4) a generally positive view of the state's involvement in the economy; and (5) a concern about disparities in wealth and poverty and the prospects for immiseration that appeared to cross ideological lines.

Overproduction, the paradox of plenty, and the theory of value

Neurath contrasted his notion as to how economics is constructed and the theory of value associated with it, with that put forward by the marginalists. In this regard Friedrich von Wieser stood out, at least in part because of von Wieser's own explorations into establishing a theory of value that meshed with the world of late nineteenth-century Austria-Hungary. In his posthumous appreciation of von Wieser, Schumpeter described him as having thought more deeply about the theory of value than any other economist (Schumpeter 1927).

And so it was the case that Neurath took von Wieser to task over the paradox of plenty; that is, how it was that an abundant harvest might result in a lesser value than a more meager harvest. Von Wieser had employed a declining price curve to explain that outcome. Neurath scored von Wieser for mistakenly combining different units of value in constructing the price curve, though implicitly, as discussed in the 1910 article, the idea that any such price curve existed in that form would be subject to serious criticism. In general terms Neurath felt that von Wieser's valuation of price in relation to quantity did not take into account the formative role of the underlying social structure (Neurath [1931] 1973: 394). In the instant case Neurath countered von Wieser with a historically situated approach that appears to draw upon both Sismondi and Marx, but whose proximate source was Wilhelm Neurath's 1892 text on the causes of crises of overproduction (W. Neurath 1892).

The elder Neurath had linked these crises to the increasing place of large-scale economic entities, including monopolies, in late nineteenth-century economic life. Ironically, it was von Wieser who attempted to grapple with the phenomenon of monopoly, and, by extension, oligopoly. Otto Neurath's focus was once again centered upon broad economic structures – the existing 'economic order', as it might have been couched as such by the German Historical School – in contrast to von Wieser's introduction and use of what would come to be treated as the price elasticity of demand, by which the power of a monopoly would be constrained if said elasticity were greater than one. Notably this theory of monopoly so constrained has become the conventional treatment of monopoly as a market structure in standard microeconomics texts.

In taking a position favorable to that of the German Historical School, Neurath contrasted the kind of economic theorizing that generated logical statements, based upon hypothetical principles, that is, the deductive approach asserted by Menger in the Methodenstreit, with an inductive construction, elaborated as follows by Neurath with regard to the study of prices:

> [O]thers hold that only a precise knowledge of reality allows one to establish a system of sentences, which find their application to reality, for instance, by deriving predictions from them. In order to be able to make assertions about the movement of prices – these researchers hold – one has to know the history of prices, one has to know what variations are at all possible, whether these are derivable from the preceding price movements alone, or from other elements, whether the latter maybe could be neglected, how large the error is, etc.
>
> (Neurath [1910] 2004. 270–271)

Neurath's focus upon the possible role of the history of prices in comprehending price movements hints at an analysis that would, at some future date, gauge whether a Markov or a non-Markov chain was in evidence. Neurath's suggestion effectively predates Markov's inquiry into temporal and non-temporal patterns, let alone their formalization and application to economic theorizing, but one may nonetheless connect this suggestion to Paul David's linkage of non-Markov chains to economic situations and patterns in which "history matters" (David 1994).

Overall, Neurath's take on the paradox of plenty relied heavily upon other writings of Wilhelm Neurath. Not only did the younger Neurath reference his father in opposing the tack that von Wieser had taken, but he drew upon the analysis and tables of Gregory King regarding the relation between an augmented harvest and changes in the price of grain (corn in British parlance). From whence did Neurath glean King's table and analysis? It is true that Jevons included it in his discussion of exchanges, found in chapter 4 of his *Political Economy* (Jevons 1892). Moreover, there is ample evidence that Neurath was familiar with Jevons' work, which he cited in challenging Jevons' inability or unwillingness to confront the implications of non-competitive economic situations (Neurath [1910] 2004: 277, 290f).

On the other hand, a fairly detailed discussion of the paradox, building upon King's statement and reproducing King's tables, can be found in Wilhelm Neurath's work entitled *Die Wirtschaftskrisen und das Cartellwesen,* published in 1897 (W. Neurath 1897: 5–8). Moreover, the social and historical perspective to which the younger Neurath brought to this question echoes that of Wilhelm Neurath. The paradox is highlighted as a social matter or 'question', in which the tendency toward overproduction is set against the widespread poverty of workers, and the broader historical context is never lost.

Statistics, generalities, and abstraction

Neurath linked the success of a 'scientific sociology' to an infusion of statistics into the discipline, with Quetelet's evocation of a 'social physics' seen as the precursor or paradigmatic entry across both the physical and social sciences. At the same time, Neurath's embrace of statistics, evident in his development of the Isotype method of visual presentation and central to the construction of the text of *Modern Man in the Making,* resonates in certain crucial ways with the thinking of and studies produced by the German Historical School. One might look to the massive multi-volume study of industry across the various regions of Germany and Central Europe in the years leading up to the First World War to gain a clearer picture of the extent to which the German Historical School laid claim to the primacy of detailed empirical research and its precedence before any effort to impose theoretical structures upon or devise theoretical models from the body of data, replete with statistics, that had been gathered.

At this point one is reminded of the distinction Wesley Mitchell drew between the German Historical School, captured in the thought and work of Gustav Schmoller, and the American Institutionalists, exemplified by the thought and work of Thorstein Veblen. The former, Mitchell charged, engaged in an ultimately unformed amassing of historical data and statistics, while the latter was more selective in his use of such empirical materials, seeking to place them within a theoretical framework (Mitchell 1949: 218–223). What does this portend for Neurath?

Economic or central planning assumes, even presumes, an institutional framing. Neurath was quite explicit about the requirements for coordination across different sectors of the economy, or among the different elements of economic activity. In his writings in the years after the end of World War I, when Neurath wrote extensively about the virtues of – actually the need for – 'total socialization', he laid out a picture of the operations of a central planning office, collecting all pertinent statistics, and even drew up a flow chart depicting the requisite organizational arrangement.

But in this organizational structure could one discern a theoretical mechanism or model at work? Neurath did note the importance of certain principles being established for distribution through some form of representative participation; in the immediate postwar period these would have been workers councils, while later, in the 1940s, Neurath turned to other forms, like the town council in Bilston, England. And Neurath made explicit that such centralized coordination grew out of, and was consistent with, his philosophical perspective on the primacy of complexes or 'clots' that could only function as totalities and were not amenable to disassembly into individual constituent parts or elements.

Yet one is left with the sense that no economic model has taken shape here; rather the statistics gathered will provide the course forward. It is in that regard and context that one might see Neurath's 'scientific utopianism' drawing not only from the league of utopian writers and thinkers whom Neurath often cited, but also from currents within the German Historical School, with its emphasis upon statistics and, with caution, generalities, and its aversion to abstraction.

Implications of the limitations of proof

The matter of what constitutes proof in economics is complicated by Neurath's involvement with the Vienna Circle. The emergence of the group espousing a new and coherent philosophical program could be linked to its adaptation of Wittgenstein's theory of language, as it appeared in the *Tractatus Logico-Philosophicus,* into a standard of verifiability, the notion that statements of fact were verifiable, and all the rest were either tautologies or metaphysics. Even if one leaves aside the distance Neurath felt from what he regarded as the continuing swirl of metaphysics evident in Wittgenstein's early text, one will quickly encounter substantial roadblocks to this first conceptual foray of the Vienna Circle. These range from concerns about whether any such language, meaning, in effect, the language of science, could be constructed on a phenomenalistic basis or a physicalistic one, to the challenges posed by Kurt Gödel's 'incompleteness proof' or Karl Popper's notion of falsification.

While the debate over phenomenalism or physicalism took place largely within the confines of the circle, with Neurath the champion of physicalism, the import of Gödel's work, as well as the critique launched by Popper, played out on a wider stage. Curiously, there are significant strands in Neurath's thought, appearing early on in his work, that address both the challenges posed by Gödel and Popper, the former implicitly, the latter quite explicitly. Neurath had identified the primacy of complexes or 'clots' of experience, representing a 'totality' of the moment that could not be meaningfully be disaggregated into component elements. That formed an essential piece of the case Neurath made against the totality of satisfaction or economic value.

Moreover, as a totality, changes to it tended to be partial, calling forth a remaking of it, rather than a full negation or refutation. Hence, Neurath faulted Popper's notion of 'falsification', intended to account for the limitations and flaws of 'verifiability' on two counts. As an abstracted standard, 'falsification' was yet another manifestation of metaphysics imposed on experience.

Further, Neurath thought that it was hardly likely that the appearance of a counterexample to an existing statement, say, a black swan when all were supposed to be white, would simply negate the statement that 'all swans are white'. Instead, a process Neurath called 'shaking' would occur (Neurath [1935] 1983: 123–124), perhaps revising the statement somewhat, but not discrediting and dissolving it altogether. In general, 'falsification' would be hard to achieve in any event across an array of sciences, including hard sciences.

Neurath saw a commonality in seemingly diverse disciplines like astronomy, geology, and sociology in their shared lack of a suitably scientific basis for experimental testing to 'prove' what Neurath would call their 'statements' (Neurath [1931] 1973: 363–364). The incompleteness of any such science, where knowledge of it comports more with an 'encyclopedia' rather than a 'system', represents a long-held view of Neurath's that nonetheless does not seem inconsistent with the explanatory thrust of Gödel's proof. And, in the immediate context, it is noteworthy that Neurath applied these understandings to economics.

A philosophical critique of political economy: the view from the 1930s

Neurath maintained his critical stance toward the faulty grounding of political economy through his entire career, including in his late work, from 1944, assaying the weaknesses of the construction of economic thought in *The Foundations of the Social Sciences*.

This was also evident in the overview of political economy provided in his 1931 treatise on *Empirical Sociology*. In short order Neurath challenged the terms by which political economy is comprehended by Quesnay, Jevons, and Weber, thereby taking on the Physiocrats, the marginalists, and the sociologists (excepting Neurath himself). Quesnay's cycle of production and reproduction is taken to task for its assumption of inevitability, excluding those forces or elements that might lead to changes in the functioning of the capitalist economic order (Neurath [1931] 1973: 340–345). Jevons' 'sunspot theory' of business cycles was seen as emblematic of the mistaken notion that economic crises are 'accidental' rather than systemic (Neurath [1931] 1973: 359).

Weber's ideas and approach were scored by Neurath in a number of ways. Here Neurath singled out Weber's categorization of events, and hence their differing valuation, as either peaceful or violent (Neurath [1931] 1973: 359). In context one might fold this into a broader critique of Weber's infusion of empathy into sociology, whereby matters of meaning and interpretation, as well as causality, all figure decisively, and all of which Neurath consigned to the non-scientific, or anti-scientific, world of metaphysics. Within the case developed in *Empirical Sociology* Marxism is seen as the counterpoint to these flawed – or failed – approaches. Moreover, the materialism associated with Marxism that he had embraced is quickly transformed into a behaviorism that Neurath saw best expressed as and through physicalism.

One concomitant of this was that Neurath's materialism was not dialectical, which, in light of the Hegelian roots of the dialectic in an idealist philosophy, would have been deemed a metaphysical accretion. Neurath characterized Hegel's oppositional dialectic as having "theological content" (Neurath [1928] 1973: 283). George Riesch has similarly noted that Neurath, as well as Philipp Frank, eschewed the notion of dialectical materialism (Riesch 2005: 144). Carnap framed the issue somewhat differently. "Dialectical logic seemed to us [members of the Vienna Circle], including Neurath, incompatible with modern symbolic logic" (Carnap 1963: 24). Notably Neurath had published short pieces about symbolic logic with his future second wife, Olga Hahn, early on in academic journals.

Neurath also scored the thinking of the German Historical School through its leading later representative Werner Sombart, once again through a philosophical lens and the unmasking of metaphysical concepts. Sombart had divided political economy into three categories: one that judged, one that systematized, and one that understood. Sombart, according to Neurath, had a somewhat favorable view of the first, strong support for the third, but hostility to the second. Furthermore, Sombart embraced Dilthey's division and distinction between the physical sciences and the humanities, into the latter of which political economy belonged. All of this was wrongheaded, as the capacity to systematize was essential for any scientific inquiry, while efforts to 'understand', 'empathize', and 'experience' required both subjective introspection and the creation of metaphysical concepts and structures (Neurath [1931] 1973: 354).

The role of intentionality and interiority: methodological considerations

In his writings from the 1930s it became especially evident that Neurath abjured the use of an ethical standard in any scientific inquiry, including those conducted in sociology, seeing it as a metaphysical overlay and a subjective element, highlighting – mistakenly – a role for intention and motive instead of observable and hence objective outcomes.

Yet the foundation of his proto-ecological economics, discussed more fully in the chapter on 'Ecological Economics', was laid on the basis of what constitutes effectively two value judgments. The first of these entailed his adaptation of epicureanism to society at large, whereby Marxism became 'social epicureanism'. That economic value should be gauged in terms of 'happiness' rather than on a monetary basis represents a significant ethical statement about how individual lives, as well as society as a whole, should be comprehended.

The second might more typically be understood as evoking environmental concerns, though it is by no means limited to them. Neurath spoke of the need to take into account both 'goods' and 'ills', the latter of which had been excluded from view in conventional political economy, largely, Neurath thought, because of the reliance upon monetary calculation. These 'ills' included such things as environmental degradation, while the sustainability of life and natural resources were incorporated into Neurath's calculus of what merited economic value.

Is this simply a contradiction regarding what the German Historical School referred to as the 'ethical standard' that Neurath straddled by not addressing it directly? The answer is a bit more nuanced. In part it appears that Neurath had long reacted to efforts to inject the notion of interiority or intentionality into scientific inquiry of all sorts, which might be taken as a neo-Kantian impulse to make the social sciences, with history included among them, into a 'mental science'. It is noteworthy that on this count Weber and Neurath were in accord in their rejection of this notion, despite the gap to which Neurath pointed in his criticism of Weber's idealism manifested in his theory of 'ideal-types' and his willingness to give primacy to religious ideas and sentiments. In part Neurath could see the ethical standard touted by Schmoller and Sombart increasingly applied as the justification for allowing cultural differences to provide cover for nationalistic zealotry.

But what of this discrete separation of 'motive' and 'outcome'? In certain respects the ethical standard still stands even if one disregards the motives of individual economic agents. One might simply look to the actual impact of certain economic activities on the environment, and in the course of which measure pertinent outcomes. This would hold as well for future developments and consequences, matters of great concern to Neurath, and one in which conventional monetary measures, in his view, fell far short.

However, does this rule out any place for interiority and intentionality in economics? Public policies, by their very nature, engage human consciousness, and the motives and intentions of policymakers clearly matter greatly, as do the ways that the motives and intentions of those economic agents affected thereby. Once again one finds Neurath straddling something of a contradiction. In the model of 'total socialization' that he put forth, it is the decision-making of the economic councils, informing the work of the central planning office, that establishes the principles of distribution and distinguishes an egalitarian socialist form of planning for a more hierarchical one. However, Neurath acknowledged that in the absence of conventional monetary payments to workers it would be necessary to set up a system of premiums to encourage greater productivity on the part of workers. Here the motives of planners have to mesh with the motivations to be induced in the workforce, making the terms of labor, if not the 'market for labor' per se, subject to intentionality.

Neurath's rejection of interior motives makes for strange bedfellows in economics. Adam Smith's passing reference to the virtues of the 'invisible hand' in *The Wealth of Nations*, taken subsequently as a founding principle of laissez-faire economics, set a contrast between the conscious motives of those seeking to do good and the actual workings of the market, with the latter seen as more effective. Such workings may reasonably be interpreted as outcomes.

More recent theorizing in economics has also played upon the tension between motive and subjective intent, on the one hand, and 'objective' outcome, on the other. Milton Friedman (1953) made the case that the motives and intentions of firms notwithstanding, only those that in effect pursued a course of maximizing profit would survive. He also cast the irrelevance of motive in more general terms in his essay on the methodology of economics, in which only outcomes matter. As one might represent Friedman's approach in the manner of a conventional logical syllogism, "If 'p', then 'q'", is reduced to "then 'q'", as 'p' no longer matters.

Paul Samuelson, who took strong issue with Friedman's claims about economic method, nonetheless also turned to a reliance upon outcomes alone to solve, or at least address, the inadequacies of the theory of consumer preference. The thesis (or theory) of revealed preference rested upon the validity of observable outcomes, expressed on the basis of "observed price ratios" (Samuelson 1948: 243), as the best indicators of the intent of consumers. What they actually chose counted, not their thoughts about choosing. In other words, their choices were 'revealed' by their behavior.

This called into question the validity of notions like utility and constructs like indifference curves. Critics might see Samuelson's methodological stance about these notions as contradictory, noting, for example, that 'preferences' and 'behavior' might not be interchangeable (Wong 1978: 67–72). For Neurath the inadequacies of utility and indifference curves as concepts had been marked in his earliest methodological essays. The limitation here regarding Neurath's inquiry, though, is also not insignificant, as he had not tackled the matter as to which combinations of goods would be selected among the array of possibilities, nor the specific bases for such choices.

How fundamental is the tension or interplay between the subjective and objective in economics? One may contend that the construction of partial equilibria through supply and demand functions depends upon just such an interplay, as each function plots a series of counterfactual possibilities, from which one actual outcome emerges. Here Neurath would challenge such a construction, by limiting the economic dynamics to observable statements.

Yet when Neurath asserts a behaviorist stance, he enters somewhat different territory. It becomes a mélange of social utilitarianism, intended to counter Jevons' principle of pleasure vs. pain, and physicalist observation statements. When all matters of consciousness and subjectivity are eliminated, casting if need be first-person consciousness into third-person narrative, interpretation, meaning, and even context are cast aside. This presents a radical program and challenge, to which it is fair to say that Neurath himself could not meet, and for good reason. He cannot avoid making choices that at the least establish context, for which *Modern Man in the Making* provides an excellent case in point, whether it be the statistics selected or overlooked or the narrative episodes treated or not.

Epilogue: on the subjective and objective in economics

There are three possible areas of inquiry to consider. The first involves the somewhat conventional discussion of the distinction between normative and positive economics, where the former entails the introduction of value judgments about the nature and purpose of economic activity while the latter purports to exclude them, offering up instead only a 'science' based on 'what is' rather than 'what ought to be'. Nominally this appears to set subjective elements against objective criteria, but the sources of those criteria follow from valuations or judgments of some sort. For example, among other conditions Pareto optimality is grounded in an acceptance of the existing distribution of income as given.

The second takes up the matter of interiority and motive. To what extent, if any, should fields of inquiry like political economy be understood as an exploration of 'mental states' rather than actual events, experiences, or 'physical states'?

The third leads back to matters of construction and the role of counterfactuals. Does the reliance upon hypothetical conjectures in constructing supply and demand functions, each requiring a logical projection in sequence of 'if's, then's', make them fundamentally subjective in character, or does the notion that an actual resolution exists, or can be found, render them either as objective or transformed from subjective into objective? If, by contrast, no such resolution comes to pass, as in the notion of price differentiation, then does the subjectivity of the counterfactuals used in the construction of such curves stand?

The idea of equilibrium itself appears to depend upon a transformation of the subjective into the objective. The challenge posed by counterfactuals noted above holds for partial equilibria, and hence goes to the heart of a Marshallian analysis and treatment of the interplay of individual markets. Does this extend to the construction of a general equilibrium? On the one hand, in the model advanced by Walras, it would seem to do so. The 'invisible auctioneer', through a version of time-travel, reconciles all of the counterfactual possibilities into a result akin to instant success at a slot-machine. On the other, the notion that the fixed-point theorem might be applied broadly to economic matters and conditions speaks to the possibility that through topological correspondences a transformation of the subjective into the objective may be attainable.

If one now turns to Neurath's economic thought, one is left with the impression that his attention and criticism had been directed at the Marshallian construct, at a time when his call for more qualitative mathematical techniques seemed to have been unheeded. Perhaps coincidentally – or not – some of the critical mathematical developments in reshaping and refining Walras' notion of a general equilibrium into a more topologically-oriented construct took place in Vienna in the interwar period. In part this effort was spurred on by a mathematical colloquium led by Karl Menger, who stood on the fringes of the Vienna Circle.

However, despite the proximity of the mathematical colloquium, nor Neurath's wide-ranging interests in contemporary scientific and mathematical inquiry, as evidenced, for example, by his papers on symbolic logic, nor his own early acquaintance with topology through Oskar Simony, nor, finally, his continuing trumpeting of the virtues of qualitative and topological measures, Neurath did not appear to have been engaged in any new effort or approach to apply topological considerations to matters of economic theorizing or construction.

Instead, Neurath couched his criticism of subjectivity in philosophical terms, evoking and invoking the perquisites and predicates of physicalism and, by extension, behaviorism. This seems a matter apart from the tension between subjectivity and objectivity that I have described above. The latter does, in my view, represent a core problem that emerged more fully only with the rise of neoclassical economics, with its turning away from production as the key to value in economics. In some sense Neurath appears close on the heels of this problem, but he was limited by basing his rejection of subjectivity upon the doctrine of physicalism. He was also caught between his strong anti-metaphysical stance, a version of Ockham's razor, and his recognition of the inexorable intertwining of theory and fact.

References

Bairoch, Paul (1993) *Economics and World History: Myths and Paradoxes*. Chicago: University of Chicago Press.

Brue, Stanley (2000) *The Evolution of Economic Thought*. Fort Worth: Dryden Press.

Carnap, Rudolf (1963) "Intellectual Autobiography". In Paul Arthur Schilpp, ed., *The Philosophy of Rudolf Carnap*. La Salle, Ill: Open Court, pp. 3–84.

Carnap, Rudolf (1973) "From Rudolf Carnap's Intellectual Autobiography". In Marie Neurath and Robert S. Cohen, eds., *Empiricism and Sociology*. Trans. Paul Foulkes and Marie Neurath. Dordrecht: Reidel, pp. 43–45.

Cat, Jordi (1996) "Unity on the Earthly Plane". In Nancy Cartwright, Jordi Cat, Bela Fleck, and Thomas Uebel, *Otto Neurath: Philosophy Between Science and Politics*. Cambridge: Cambridge University Press, part 3.

David, Paul A. (1994) "Why are Institutions the 'Carriers of History'?" *Structural Change and Economic Dynamics* 5(2): 205–220.

Friedman, Milton (1953) "Essay on Methodology". In *Essays in Positive Economics*. Chicago: University of Chicago Press.

Jevons, W. Stanley (1892) *Political Economy*, 4th edn. London: Macmillan & Co.

King, Gregory [1696] (1936) *Two Tracts*. Baltimore: Johns Hopkins Press.

Mitchell, Wesley (1949) *Lecture Notes on Types of Economic Theory*. New York: A.M. Kelley.

Neurath, Anna Schapire, and Neurath, Otto [1910] (1913) *Lesebuch der Volkswirtschaftslehre*. 2nd edn. Leipzig: G.A. Gloeckner.

Neurath, Otto [1910] (2004) "Theory of the Social Sciences". In Robert S. Cohen and Thomas E. Uebel, eds., *Otto Neurath: Economic Writings/Selections, 1904–1945*. [Multiple translators]. Dordrecht: Kluwer Academic Publishers, pp. 265–291.

Neurath, Otto (1911) "Nationalokonomie und Wertlehre, eine systematische Untersuchung". *Zeitschrift für Volkswirtschaft, Sozialpolitik und Verwaltung*, 20: 52–114.

Neurath, Otto [1913] (1983) "The Lost Wanderers of Descartes and the Auxiliary Motive". In Robert S. Cohen and Marie Neurath, eds. and trans., *Philosophical Papers 1913–1946*. Dordrecht/Boston: D. Reidel Publishing Company, pp. 1–12.

Neurath, Otto [1916] (1983) "On the Classification of Systems of Hypotheses". In Robert S. Cohen and Marie Neurath, eds. and trans., *Philosophical Papers 1913–1946*. Dordrecht/Boston: D. Reidel Publishing Company, pp. 13–31.

Neurath, Otto [1917] (2004) "The Conceptual Structure of Economic Theory and its Foundations". In Robert S. Cohen and Thomas E. Uebel, eds., *Otto Neurath: Economic Writings/Selections, 1904–1945*. [Multiple translators]. Dordrecht: Kluwer Academic Publishers, pp. 312–341.

Neurath, Otto [1919] (1973) "Through War Economy to Economy in Kind". In Marie Neurath and Robert S. Cohen, eds., *Empiricism and Sociology*. Trans. Paul Foulkes and Marie Neurath. Dordrecht: Reidel, pp. 123–157.

Neurath, Otto [1925] (2004) "Economic Plan and Calculation in Kind". In Robert S. Cohen and Thomas E. Uebel, eds., *Otto Neurath: Economic Writings/Selections, 1904–1945*. [Multiple translators]. Dordrecht: Kluwer Academic Publishers, pp. 405–465.

Neurath, Otto [1928] (1973) "Personal Life and Class Struggle." In Marie Neurath and Robert S. Cohen, eds., *Empiricism and Sociology*. Trans. Paul Foulkes and Marie Neurath; Dordrecht: Reidel, pp. 249–298.'.

Neurath, Otto [1930] (1983) "Ways of the Scientific World-Conception". In Robert S. Cohen and Marie Neurath, eds. and trans., *Philosophical Papers 1913–1946*. Dordrecht/Boston: D. Reidel Publishing Company, pp. 32–47.

Neurath, Otto [1931] (1973) *Empirical Sociology*. In Marie Neurath and Robert S. Cohen, eds., *Empiricism and Sociology*. Trans. Paul Foulkes and Marie Neurath; Dordrecht: Reidel, pp. 319–421.

Neurath, Otto [1931] (1983) "Sociology in the Framework of Physicalism". In Robert S. Cohen and Marie Neurath, eds. and trans., *Philosophical Papers 1913–1946*. Dordrecht/Boston: D. Reidel Publishing Company, pp. 58–90.

Neurath, Otto [1935] (1983) "Pseudorationalism of Falsification". In Robert S. Cohen and Marie Neurath, eds. and trans., *Philosophical Papers 1913–1946*. Dordrecht/Boston: D. Reidel Publishing Company, pp. 121–131.

Neurath, Otto [1937] (1983) "The Concept of 'Type' in the Light of Modern Logic". In Robert S. Cohen and Marie Neurath, eds. and trans., *Philosophical Papers 1913–1946*. Dordrecht/Boston: D. Reidel Publishing Company, pp. 183–188.

Neurath, Otto [1937] (2004) "An Inventory of the Standard of Living". In Robert S. Cohen and Thomas E. Uebel, eds., *Otto Neurath: Economic Writings/Selections, 1904–1945*. [Multiple translators]. Dordrecht: Kluwer Academic Publishers.

Neurath, Otto (1939) *Modern Man in the Making*. New York & London: A.A. Knopf.

Neurath, Otto (1944) *The Foundations of the Social Sciences*. Chicago: University of Chicago Press.

Neurath, Wilhelm (1892) *Die Wahre Ursachen der Uberproductionskrisen sowie der Erwerbs- und Arbeitslosigkeit*. Wien: Manz.

Neurath, Wilhelm (1897) *Die Wirtschaftskrisen und Cartellwesen*. Wien: Manz.

Poincaré, Henri (1906) *Wissenschaft und Hypothese*. Authorized German edition with explanatory notes by F. and L. Lindemann. 2nd improved edition. Leipzig: B.G. Teubner.

Riesch, George (2005) *Philosophy of Science in the Cold War: Toward the Icy Slope of Logic*. Cambridge: Cambridge University Press.

Samuelson, Paul (1948) "Consumption Theory in Terms of Revealed Preference". *Economica*, 15: 243–253.

Samuelson, Paul [1981] (1986) "Schumpeter's Capitalism, Socialism and Democracy". In Kate Crowley ed., *The Collected Scientific Papers of Paul A. Samuelson*, Vol. 5. Cambridge: The MIT Press, pp. 328–348.

Samuelson, Paul (1983) "Thunen at Two Hundred". *Journal of Economic Literature* 21(4): 1468–1488.

Schumpeter, Joseph (1914) *Economic Doctrine and Method*. Trans. R. Aris (1954), London: George Allen & Unwin.

Schumpeter, Joseph (1927) "Obituary: Friedrich von Wieser". *Economic Journal* 37(46): 328–335.

Turk, Michael (2010) "The Arrow of Time in Economics". *European Journal of the History of Economic Thought* 17(3): 471–492.

Turk, Michael (2016) *The Idea of History in Constructing Economics*. Abingdon, UK: Routledge.

Uebel, Thomas E. (2004) "Introduction". In Robert S. Cohen and Thomas E. Uebel, eds., *Otto Neurath: Economic Writings/Selections, 1904–1945*. [Multiple translators]. Dordrecht: Kluwer Academic Publishers, pp. 1–108.

Vossoughian, Nader (2008) *Otto Neurath: the Language of the Global Polis*. Rotterdam: NAi Publishers.

Walras, Leon (1909) "Economique et mechanique". *Bulletin de la Sociète Vaudoise de Sciences Naturelles* XLV.

Wong, Stanley (1978) *The Foundations of Paul Samuelson's Revealed Preference Theory*. London: Routledge & Kegan Paul.

4 Out of the German Historical School

The divergent paths of Otto Neurath and Max Weber

The pathways of intellectual inquiry pursued by Max Weber and Otto Neurath are remarkably intertwined. Both can be seen as political economists formed within a central European milieu in which the German Historical School played a dominant, if not always decisive role. As their conception about economic theorizing and its philosophical foundations evolved, both would demur from either certain tenets or the approach of the German Historical School, effectively exiting from the school.

Both would attempt to advance a blending of economics and history – one might view this as an effort to restate what a historical economics might be – as a version of what they would call sociology. In Weber's case this led to his formulation of a *verstehende* sociology that came to be recognized as one of the foremost treatments of sociology as an intellectual field of inquiry in the twentieth century. In Neurath's case this led to his formulation of a 'scientific' sociology that hewed to a materialist philosophy and aspired to a substantial, if incomplete congruence with Marxism. In the years after Weber's death Neurath tended to emphasize the differences between them, most notably contrasting his grounding in materialism with the idealist philosophy he scored in Weber's famous shorter work, *The Spirit of Protestantism and the Rise of Capitalism* (Weber 1930). Unlike Weber's sociology, Neurath's rested in obscurity and did not enter academic discourse about the proper relation among the disciplines of history, economics, and sociology.

While the sociology they constructed differed, both figures appeared to be grappling with the problematic aspects of historical economics as it was understood at the turn of the twentieth century. For Weber this task and challenge were explicit, as his pivotal writings about how to conceptualize political economy were entitled, *The Logical Problems of Historical Economics,* which appeared between 1903 and 1906.

One might contend in Neurath's case that the process and project required two steps accomplished over time. In the first of these, laid out in academic papers published in 1910 and 1911, Neurath produced a critique of the foundations of political economy in which historical referents were apparent, and a consciousness of the impact of 'law and custom' in guiding economic affairs had emerged. In the second, after his embrace of Marxism, the earlier critique was melded, to a certain degree, to a Marxian predilection to envision history – and historical consciousness – as shaping economic affairs. In the event, though, it is clear that the first step was the formative one for Neurath.

What this portends is that for both Weber and Neurath their initial inclusion within and even immersion in the German Historical School were crucial in setting forth the central problem of relating history and economics. That both did not remain within the confines of that school, as well as the fact that both moved to what one might regard as a 'default' position, recasting the problem and subsuming the relation as a matter of sociology, is also crucial. Within the context of the evolution of economic thought in central Europe in the first decades of the twentieth century, Weber and Neurath offered up a response to the question: whither historical economics?

In Weber's case, despite the attention and accolades his vast body of writings received as a premier sociologist subsequent to his death in 1920, the matter of historical economics per se got short shrift, revived only a half-century later by Richard Swedberg and Mark Granovetter. They aspired to recreate what Weber had termed 'social economics', effectively an amalgam of economics, history, and sociology (see Swedberg 1998: 189–203).

In Neurath's case the publication of his work through the auspices of the Vienna Circle, including its journal, *Erkenntnis,* as well as through successor entities promoting the unity of science, notably the series launched in the 1940s under the auspices of the University of Chicago Press, did little to draw broader attention to or interest in creating and elaborating upon an intellectual discipline merging history and political economy. In part this was due to Neurath's focus upon the critique rather than the provision of positive examples of what a scientific sociology might illuminate. That said, one might nonetheless contend that his 1939 *Modern Man in the Making,* multi-disciplinary and global in scope, graphical and statistical in presentation, went a fair distance in offering up a case study.

Nonetheless, the efforts of both Weber and Neurath notwithstanding, historical economics became a lost thread in the main body of economic thought in the twentieth century. What might those efforts elucidate if that thread were found once more?

Intertwined paths and careers

Weber's and Neurath's paths crossed at several crucial junctures, even as they belonged to different generations (Weber was born in 1856, Neurath in 1882). References to Weber's work can be found in some of the first pieces Neurath wrote, while still a graduate student. At the time Neurath was in the process of writing his dissertation at the University of Berlin on the economic history of classical antiquity, a subject Weber had explored in his own agrarian economic history of ancient Rome.

Of greater significance was their participation at the 1909 conference of the Verein für Sozialpolitik, the leading academic society representing the German

Historical School, held in Vienna. Dahms and Neumann point to the possibility that this might have been the first direct encounter between the two men. They go on to suggest that Neurath had already crossed paths with Weber's brother, Alfred, probably no later than 1903 at a conference held by the 'Internationale Vereinigung für vergleichendes Recht und Volkswirtschaft', and that they knew each other by the time Neurath arrived in Berlin to pursue his doctorate (Dahms and Neumann 1994: 119).

Perhaps the central topic addressed at the conference was the nature of productivity, launched by a paper delivered by Eugen von Philoppovich. Was economic productivity a technical matter, gauging the economic efficiency of translating inputs into output, or were there external measures that needed to be supplied? In the parlance of the German Historical School, with Werner Sombart referencing Gustav Schmoller, this outside measure was cast typically as an 'ethical standard', valuing the worth of any economic activity by what it was intended to do or its societal impact.

On this matter Weber and Neurath took opposite sides. Neurath thought that it was impossible not to introduce an external measure of some sort, though in contrast to Schmoller and Sombart he challenged its being cast as somehow subjective. Ultimately this would take shape in his referencing of the 'terrain' of capitalism as an 'economic order'. In his later work, infused with a Marxist perspective, Neurath denied the validity of 'ethical or political judgments' in valuing economic activity and experience, since outcomes rather than intentions mattered, but Neurath was clearly relying upon an ethical standard of sorts, with social or collective 'happiness' taken to be what ought to be valued most in economics. For Weber's part, one can find passages in his writings in which he makes clear that the rules of economic behavior conform to a particular historical moment, that of the ascendancy of capitalism (see Turk 2016: 142–143). On this specific count Weber seems to have moved quite close to the position laid out by Neurath, though it might also be taken as a trope of the German Historical School.

Weber's challenge at the conference, in which he was joined by his brother Alfred, brought to light one of his most noteworthy intellectual benchmarks, namely the notion that scientific inquiry had to be 'value-free', and hence the introduction of an ethical or any other external standard constituted a judgment that vitiated the integrity of such an inquiry. Writing about the matter of value judgment in scientific inquiry a few years later, Weber observed that the German Historical School and the 'socialists of the chair' had scored the value placed upon self-interest by the classical school, or what they would term 'Manchester liberalism'. Nonetheless, their substitution of a different standard for valuing economic activity meant that they had indulged in the same flawed approach as the classical school (Hennis 1991:33). This was an argument built upon irony and paradox, but for Weber what was at least as much at issue was the politicization of the classroom by German economists touting nationalist sentiments as somehow falling within the purview of scientific discourse.

There was a second subject that arose in the 1909 conference that foreshadowed major work undertaken by both men. Toward the end of the discussion of productivity and the scope of the ethical standard Neurath raised the possibility that modern economies might make use of exchanges in-kind, rather than through conventional means, that is, money. To buttress his case he cited the economic structures in place in ancient Egypt, with a central or 'giro' bank to facilitate such exchanges, but did note, if only in passing, that this did entail the existence and functioning of a bureaucracy. At that moment Weber interrupted Neurath, declaiming, with a touch of sarcasm, that such a bureaucracy had worked as well as "ours" (Schriften des Verein zur Sozialpolitik 1911: 599–603). As Neurath would come to be known, largely by his opponents, as the leading advocate of in-kind calculation and central economic planning to advance the 'socialization' of the economy, so Weber would come to be known as the sociologist who grappled directly with the problematic aspects of bureaucracy in the operation of the state and the economy.

Neurath's path crossed with that of Weber again in 1917 when Neurath joined the faculty of the University of Heidelberg at the lowest level junior status, where Weber served as a senior member of the faculty. One can trace the relationship between two in this period through Weber's correspondence.

Neurath is first referred to in Weber's letters with regard to Neurath's work on the economic history of classical antiquity. Writing to another colleague Weber noted that Neurath had made a useful contribution in the field ("Er ist kein Null"), but scored him somewhat for not delving sufficiently into the pertinent literature (letter of 2 January 1916, Weber 2008: 242–243).

Shortly thereafter, Neurath's name appears again. This time Weber was discussing with the publisher Paul Siebeck possible authors for an academic piece on the 'war economy'. Weber advanced Neurath as such a possibility, listing him as a second choice and citing his earlier work on the subject (letter of 14 April 1916, Weber 2008: 384–385).

It is also the case, though, that in and around this same moment Weber had begun to take note of Neurath's changing outlook regarding the possibilities of socialism, which had affected his views on economics, both academically and practically. In a letter to Eugen Diederichs Weber says that he "treasures Neurath dearly", but regards his apparently new-found enthusiasm for 'Gemeinwirtschaft' as intellectually perplexing. Weber muses that this is something like a "herring salad", an expression suggesting, one suspects, a mishmash of sorts (letter of 1 September 1917, Weber 2008: 760).

The consequences of Neurath's activism occupy the remaining letters, including, most significantly, one sent to Neurath himself on October 4, 1919, in response to a letter Neurath had sent to him. Two issues are paramount. The first of these involves Weber's attempt to mollify Neurath in light of his removal from his position at the University of Heidelberg by the university's academic senate, along with several other junior faculty members, on account of their political activities, in the year after the end of World War I.

The second pertains directly to Neurath's activities on behalf of the socialization of the Bavarian economy in his capacity as head of the central planning office, which came to an end with the overturning of the Bavarian Soviet Republic by right-wing members of the Freikorps. Here Weber argued strenuously with Neurath that his advocacy for a 'natural economy', administered and relying upon in-kind calculation, would be highly detrimental to the cause of socialism, setting it back a hundred years, and laying out the difficulties posed by the creation and maintenance of a bureaucracy to carry out its program (letter of 4 October 1919, Weber 2012: 798–800).

The other letters from 1919 and 1920 provide a reference point to Weber's last encounter with Neurath: his testimony at Neurath's trial for treason in Munich as a result of his role as head of the central planning office. One takes Weber to have been called as a character witness, and some commentators have described his testimony as both "for and against" Neurath (Schumann 1973: 17). As reported in a local Munich newspaper, Weber emphasized Neurath's role as central planner as professional and technical rather than political, but did point to Neurath's enthusiasm for utopian ideas (Weber 1919: 495). In the end Neurath was able to obtain release through the intervention and good offices of Otto Bauer, then serving as Austrian foreign minister, with the proviso that Neurath be exiled from Germany to Austria. In the meantime, Weber contracted pneumonia, perhaps as a consequence of having been weakened by influenza, and died – prematurely – in June 1920.

A year-and-a-half after Weber's death Neurath wrote to Ferdinand Tönnies, who had long served as both confidante and mentor to Neurath, that Weber had played a special role in nurturing a half-dozen or so 'private docents' at Heidelberg who would assume active roles in the Bavarian Soviet Republic. All lost their faculty posts at the university in consequence. Neurath's description of Weber is quite striking:

> And also Max Weber, who could be called the adoptive father of the council republic, as so many of his private docents from Heidelberg were somehow connected with Munich, Muckle, Salz, Neurath, among others; there were, I believe, 5 or 6.
>
> (letter from Neurath to Tönnies, dated 1/29/1922, in Dahms and Neumann 1994: 116)

Dahms and Neumann were quick to point out that Neurath's characterization needed to be treated cautiously, emphasizing Weber's professional interests in what was taking place in contrast to the political interest and activism on the part of the younger faculty members, Neurath obviously among them (Dahms and Neumann 1994: 116).

Contours of the German Historical School

Both Weber and Neurath can and should be situated in a central European intellectual milieu, evident from their educational background and the philosophical frame of reference within which they couched their inquiries into historical economics and sociology. Yet there are also nuances and differences that are noteworthy.

Neurath was born and came of age in Vienna, whose differences with Berlin and Germany Neurath was quick to point out. Notably, in the manifesto that launched the Vienna Circle of philosophers into the public limelight, Neurath, the manifesto's lead author, distinguished the 'scientific' and 'anti-metaphysical' outlook of Austrian thinkers, influenced by the legacy of such varied figures engaged in philosophy as Bernard Bolzano, Franz Brentano, and Ernst Mach. This was manifested as well in the realm of political economy, in contrast to that which held sway in Germany.

Weber belonged much more clearly to the world of northern Germany, and in his studies, unlike those of Neurath, he followed the path laid out in the German university system, whereby political economy grew out of cameralistics and the standard course of study in economics was subsumed under the faculty of law. Nonetheless, it should not be overlooked that Weber's most well-known short work on the spirit of Protestantism and the rise of capitalism was most likely inspired by his experiences in the Midwestern United States, as he attended the 1904 World's Fair in St. Louis, a cynosure for highlighting and celebrating the achievements of international scientific endeavors at the turn of the twentieth century.

For all that, one can and should note the affinity of both Weber and Neurath, at the outset of their careers, for a conception of the scope and state of political economy that had arisen with the rise to prominence of the German Historical School in the latter half of the nineteenth century. The school had assumed a more formal status by that time, but had its roots in the mercantilist or cameralist thought going back to the seventeenth century, with the work and writings of J.J. Becher. In the 1830s Friedrich List's focus upon the distinctive role of the state in the economy, and the importance of distinguishing among differences in national economies, set the broad terms of the inquiries undertaken by the German Historical School as it emerged, especially under the tutelage of Wilhelm Roscher, Karl Knies, and Bruno Hildebrand.

The German Historical School, in its early days, presented itself as an alternative, or 'third way'. On the one hand, it stood in opposition to the laissez-faire liberalism of the classical school, which adherents to the German Historical School labeled 'Manchester liberalism', intending to lay bare its nature as 'English economics' rather than a construct built upon universal principles. On the other, it stood apart from the socialism advanced by Marx and Engels, which was seen as too disruptive and did not allow for a state-run and directed reform of the economy and society in the face of changing economic circumstances and conditions, an approach that had been the hallmark of Prussian reformism since the days of the successful Napoleonic invasion.

What emerged was an interest in comprehending the economy within a broader social and cultural context. This could mean taking into account the organization of society, a favorite trope of Roscher, including the role of institutions within it. It might also mean paying attention to and highlighting the differences in culture, and the history underlying such differences, that marked the experiences of individual nation-states. This, of course, was an invitation to examine the histories of these nation-states, and it would lead to an interest in gathering statistics about them to gain a clearer picture of the individual, even unique, character, of those nation-states.

At the same time, though, such an inquiry might lead to an evocation of the special qualities of those states, so that the seeds of a strongly assertive or extreme nationalism were also planted within and by the German Historical School. While the school was always tinged with German nationalism, by the 1920s some of the leading figures in the German Historical School, like Eduard Meyer and Werner Sombart, would be increasingly swept up in an extremist and nationalist fervor. This would place Neurath deeply at odds with those, like Meyer, with whom he had worked two decades before. In the end, in the 1930s and 1940s, this last element would result in its discrediting and dissolution as a school of economic thought.

In the period just before and after the turn of the twentieth century, though, the specter of extreme nationalism might have seemed a bit more distant. For all that, it is noteworthy that Weber's first major research project to gain recognition as a substantial academic achievement fell within the orbit of German nationalism, in that he explored in careful detail the impact of a Polish labor force upon the agrarian economy of eastern Germany, assessing its implications upon the labor market from a German perspective. At the same time, Weber's challenge to the ethical standard put forward by Gustav Schmoller was intended to address the open politicizing of lectures by German political economists.

Nationalism of this sort was alien to Neurath, and did not appear in any of his writings. Instead, what the German Historical School offered him was a setting for expanding upon his interest in economic history and an institutional context for economic inquiry that was most likely rooted in the early influence provided by his father, Wilhelm Neurath.

However, it is also the case that the younger Neurath drew upon sources and ideas that fell well within the orbit of the German Historical School. He took up as a central theme in his own work Roscher's dictum that the main subject of political economy was the study of societal organization. He also gave substantial weight to the ideas of the mercantilists, especially J. J. Becher, and saw their work as equally valid as that of the representatives of the classical school. The lineage in political economy that Neurath traced in his reader of important economic texts, as well as in his subsequent writings, tended to enhance the role of continental and central European figures and temper the treatment of figures seen as dominant from a British standpoint. For example, in *Empirical Sociology*, written well after Neurath had left the orbit of the German Historical School, he outlined a substantially larger role for Becher and Francois Quesnay in his sketch of the history of political economy than that accorded Adam Smith.

Test case: the nature of exchange

One measure of the influence of the German Historical School upon the economic thought of both Weber and Neurath can be found in their treatment of the notion of exchange. While one may trace the centrality of this notion to the emergence of the classical school in the latter part of the eighteenth century, encapsulated in Smith's pithy expression of the primacy of "truck, barter, and trade", nonetheless it assumed even greater importance in the marginalist conception of political economy. Here exchanges between economic agents became the central mechanism underlying the formation of prices, thereby rendering price theory both fundamental and essential to any economic analysis.

The German Historical School stood apart from this. One certainly must posit an important role to exchange in the constructions of the mercantilists and cameralists, often so dependent upon the imbalances in international exchanges in determining the economic advantages or disadvantages accruing to nation-states. But the nature of exchange itself was seen as something more diffuse than monetary transactions, and was likely subject to broader social conditions. These concerns were reflected in the ways that Weber and Neurath handled the concept of exchange.

Weber advanced a culturally determined notion of exchange, elaborated in the 1904 essay that launched the *Archiv für Sozialpolitik und Sozialwissenschaft* in which he sought to remake – and broaden – the framework for comprehending and analyzing economics and economically related matters. The critical passage in the text runs as follows:

> The analysis of the *general* aspects of exchange and the technique of the market is a – highly important and indispensable – *preliminary task*. For not only does this type of analysis leave unanswered the question as to how exchange historically acquired its fundamental significance in the modern world; but above all else, the fact with which we are primarily concerned, namely the *cultural significance* of the money economy … we are concerned with the analysis of the *cultural significance* of the concrete *historical* fact that today exchange exists on a mass scale.
>
> (Weber [1904] 1949: 77–78; cited in Hodgson 2001: 122)

For his part, in his early essays from 1910 and 1911 on the theory of the social sciences Neurath emphasized the importance of 'Verschiebung' rather than the exchange of goods (Neurath [1910] 2004: 274–278). 'Verschiebung' refers to a shifting or, more generally, a transfer of goods, introducing thereby a linguistic aspect to his economic critique, which remained an abiding consideration in his treatment of concept formation in economics. On the one hand, Neurath took the notion of exchange to be a somewhat fuzzily constructed concept, like most concepts in economics. On the other, the notion of exchange was delimited to a more narrowly conceived set of conditions and circumstances, hence not unlike the version laid out by Weber, seen as a product of the existing capitalist economic order but without any specific references to the 'culture' of capitalism. Neurath, it should be noted, abjured such references, a sharp line of distinction with the main thrust of the German Historical School.

The monetary piece is not unimportant in this context as well. Weber focused upon "the *cultural significance* of the money economy" in framing his analysis of exchange. By contrast, Neurath would take it as a springboard for introducing 'natural' or 'in-kind' calculation as an alternative to the 'money economy' altogether, and lead to a stark division between Weber and Neurath over the implications of pursuing such an alternative.

The pivot afforded by a conceptual critique

One can detect the shift away from the framework of the German Historical School at decisive moments in the work of both Weber and Neurath. In Weber's case it is evident in his pathbreaking work from 1903–1906, when in a series of lengthy essays he challenged the philosophical foundations of economics as espoused by the lead figures of the first generation of the German Historical School, Roscher and Knies (Weber [1903–1906] 1975). More to the point, both Roscher and Knies served as springboards for Weber's own reconceptualization of how one ought to categorize political economy. Weber's text took to task the distinction in classifying different scientific disciplines between the nomothetic and idiographic, which had insinuated its way into the thinking of the German Historical School.

While Yuichi Shionoya sees Weber's assumption of this task effected with "one foot in German historical economics and the other foot in neo-Kantian philosophy" (Shionoya 2005: 34), the interrelation of these two intellectual currents in his thinking was quite nuanced and complex. For example, in contrast to the leading neo-Kantian figures of the day, Wilhelm Windelband and Heinrich Rickert, Weber saw the tension between the generalizing sciences and those based upon particulars as a false dichotomy; rather it was a matter of how meaning and causality were attached to the content of any science.

It is also evident that Weber's rethinking of historical economics in these essays, that is, by seeking to establish the philosophical foundations for the proper relation between political economy and history, set him on a course that led to his development of what he termed *verstehende* sociology. But it was as much a reformulation of what historical economics ought to be that took shape finally in his *General Economic History* (Weber 1923). Drawn from Weber's last lecture notes and published posthumously, this work has garnered relatively little attention, despite its translation into English by Frank Knight in 1923. Nonetheless, it blends salient historical detail with a broad sweep of the emergence of capitalism and an outline of changes associated with it, thus attempting to bridge the divide between the nomothetic and the idiographic

Of no small significance in these essays, Roscher and Knies essentially took a back seat to the central figure around whose ideas Weber had fashioned his critique, Wilhelm Wundt, whose text on the logic of the sciences, and the appropriate divisions that followed from it, had become a highly influential work in central European intellectual circles at the turn of the twentieth century.

The evolution of Neurath's economic thought

One need look no further than Neurath's early critique of the theory of the social sciences, published in 1910, to see how formidable a figure Wundt was. While Neurath's essay should be read as critical, broadly speaking, of marginalist and neoclassical economic theorizing about the primacy of price theory, the central figure about whom Neurath's case revolves is none other than Wilhelm Wundt. Neurath was even more direct than Weber in criticizing Wundt, as he lambasted the lack of an in-depth examination of concept formation in political economy by Wundt, characteristic of the cavalier way in which political economists in general dealt with such matters (Neurath [1910] 2004: 268–269). In Neurath's eyes the elevation of the role of price theory was linked to the unacceptable narrowing of the focus of political economy to what was readily quantifiable (Neurath [1910] 2004: 274).

At this stage Neurath's concern for a historical reckoning by which price movements, but also phenomena like unemployment, overproduction, cartelization, and economic crises, appeared to fall neatly within the general terms of the research projects and outlook of the German Historical School. Neurath's favorable treatment of the views of mercantilists, especially J.J. Becher, reinforced this affinity with the tenets of the school.

Hence, it is of interest to capture the evolution of Neurath's thought in plumbing the philosophical foundations of the social sciences two decades later, when these concerns were subsumed by and under his work advancing the Vienna Circle of philosophers as a broadly scientific, anti-metaphysical movement.

In the manifesto that publicly launched the Vienna Circle, Neurath, its main author, discussed the mission underway or awaiting the various scientific disciplines, all of which needed to address their philosophical foundations. And so, in the case of the social sciences, Neurath wrote the following:

> As we have specially considered with respect to physics and mathematics, every branch of science is led to recognize that, sooner or later in its development, it must consider an epistemological examination of its foundations, a logical analysis of its concepts. So too with the social sciences, and in the first place with history and economics.
>
> (Neurath [1929] 1973: 315)

The case that he then proceeds to make appears targeted directly at the German Historical School, especially as the views of its leading figures in the 1920s were increasingly inclined toward the rising tide of extreme nationalism and mysticism. He goes on to state:

> It is not too difficult to drop concepts like 'folk spirit' and instead to choose, as our object, groups of individuals of a certain kind. Scholars from the most diverse trends, such as Quesnay, Adam Smith, Ricardo, Comte, Marx, Menger, Walras, Müller-Lyer, have worked in the sense of the empiricist, anti-metaphysical attitude.
>
> (Neurath [1929] 1973: 315)

This list of economic thinkers is worth examining more closely. No figure from the German Historical School is mentioned, nor any from its precursors. The only individual listed who would have been known within the confines of central Europe, but not elsewhere, was Franz Müller-Lyer, who had advanced a version of a scientific sociology to which Neurath referred, if typically only in passing, on numerous occasions in his own work.

That said, Müller-Lyer's influence should not be overlooked. Neurath infused his case for a scientific sociology by grounding it in a materialist philosophy. As such his approach echoed closely the philosophical tack taken by Müller-Lyer in his 1910 work entitled, *Der Sinn des Lebens und die Wissenschaft: Grundlinien einer Volksphilosophie*:

> Thus these last observations might awaken the belief that they had their source in an old error, which earlier to be sure very great thinkers (like Turgot, Condorcet, Comte, Hegel, Buckle, and others) committed, which however was opposed by Marx and Engels; namely the error that the world is ruled by 'ideas'; while we now are of the insight, that the course of culture will not be determined by conscious ideas, but overwhelmingly through economic life, and that the (philosophical, religious, scientific, moral, aesthetic) ideas are not the cause, but much more the consequence of economic development.
>
> (Müller-Lyer 1910: 140)

Among other economic or sociological thinkers highlighted by Neurath in the manifesto, Quesnay had always loomed large in his thinking about economics. The Neuraths had translated portions of Quesnay's *Tableau économique* in their 1910–1911 reader of historically important economic texts, while his *Empirical Sociology*, dating from 1931, contains an extended exposition and critique of Quesnay's model of the circular flow of production. Meanwhile Auguste Comte represented the well-spring for sociology as a science, which had become the discipline Neurath conceived as providing the necessary unification of history and political economy, as well as taken as the one who had initiated positivism. As noted elsewhere, in this period Neurath saw himself in general terms as a Marxist.

Instead, it is the inclusion of Walras and especially Menger that is especially noteworthy. Neurath had long opposed the program of the marginalists, yet Menger (meaning Carl Menger, the elder), the father of the Austrian school, was always cited with approbation, even as Neurath noted the divergence in their views about political economy.

There is a larger question to be addressed here. Had the need to rally the 'anti-metaphysical' forces across scientific disciplines, the rallying cry of the manifesto, transcended the importance of incorporating the historical into the economic or maintaining the primacy of the statistical? A certain ambiguity arises in this context that may not easily be resolved.

Totalities vs. aggregations

While it is essential to take account of the extent to which both Weber and Neurath exited the orbit of the German Historical School, it is equally important to see where tenets of the school continued to inform the thinking of both of them. One of the most striking similarities between Weber and Neurath is the notion they share of a 'totality' qualitatively different from its constituent parts and consequently subject neither to aggregation from such elements nor the converse process of disaggregation. As we shall see, the uses to which they put and applied this notion are quite different, yet one senses a common origin in the thought of the German Historical School, which divined the importance of the 'totality' of culture in order to understand the economic experience of each nation or country.

First, one ought to take note of Weber's resort to the notion of totality in the groundwork he laid in his challenge to the standard treatment of historical economics in pivotal essays written between 1903 and 1906 critiquing ostensibly the tensions and contradictions in the work of Roscher and Knies. The foundation of Weber's analysis rested upon the following: "Clearly the economy is not a mere aggregate of single economic organizations, no more than its analogue, the human body, is 'simply a mixture of chemical phenomena'" (Weber [1903–1906] 1975: 80).

As I have described this set-up stage in *The Idea of History in Constructing Economics,* Weber is here rethinking "the nature of economics ... by conceiving the 'institutions of economic life' as the result of a qualitative transformation of their constituent elements" (Turk 2016: 129).

Moreover, as he explored the nature of causality in history and developed his case for distinguishing between the natural and the social sciences, Weber saw as crucial the necessity of infusing the latter with interpretations in which 'historical meaning' of some sort was inscribed. Here again, Weber separated the overall understanding of historical events from any aggregating of the elements that entered into those events: "However, the fact that we ascribe historical 'meaning' to each of these events cannot be deduced from the circumstances of their causation" (Weber [1903–1906] 1975: 108).

He elaborated as follows:

> On the contrary, in each of these cases, the meaning we ascribe to the phenomena – that is, the relations which we establish between these phenomena and 'values' – is a logically incongruous and heterogeneous factor

> which cannot be 'deduced' from the 'constitutive elements' of the event in question.
>
> (Weber [1903–1906] 1975: 108)

When one turns to Neurath, it is impossible not to see the notion of 'totality' qualitatively different from the sum of its constituent elements at work in his economic thought throughout his career. His challenge to the emerging theory of consumer behavior set forth by the marginalists was at least in part based upon the idea that the totality of consumer satisfaction could not be derived from a simple calculus of monetary units associated with different quantities of possible consumables. Instead, what was required was to gauge the 'quality of life' provided, and this was a qualitative matter that could not be captured through the aggregation of parts. Through this approach Neurath sought to highlight a real-life complexity missing from the marginalist or neoclassical constructs.

Similarly, Neurath rejected the marginalist and neoclassical categorization of inputs into production as generic factors, contending that, say, in the case of capital, the machinery in use could not be measured through a valuation of the parts required for its construction or maintenance. He chose the example of the steam engine, whose value in production could not be calculated on the basis of the value of the sum of its parts, like the boiler (Neurath [1917] 2004: 335–336). As such, it seems remarkably akin to Weber's dismissal of the idea that the human body was the aggregation of mixing certain chemicals.

Perhaps most notable in Neurath's work was his continuing evocation of the importance of complexes or clots, essentially 'totalities' of experience that could not be comprehended through a process of disassembly, which led him to find scientific advances occurring more along the lines of an 'encyclopedia', always incomplete and in some flux, than a full-blown and fully consistent system. One might recognize traces of other influences upon Neurath in this notion of 'clots', among them Duhem, yet without question it also bears the hallmark of the German Historical School's embrace of the notion of qualitatively based totalities.

Blending political economy and history

In *Empirical Sociology* Neurath spoke of joining political economy and history into one discipline (Neurath [1931] 1973: 345). Certainly one can see versions of such a claim or goal in both the German Historical School and Marxism, but was the case laid out by either school in the manner that Neurath chose?

As to his own execution of this project, one might look to his *Modern Man in the Making,* published in 1939, with its extensive use of statistical graphs to provide 'economic' content to a sweeping treatment of human history that blends what might typically be thought of as anthropology, demography, and sociology, as well as what might more narrowly be conceived as history. Neurath began with a global perspective, identifying common features of the empires that had dominated world history into the nineteenth century. His main focus, though, was on the experience of the last few centuries, highlighting those broad trends that marked the rise of what in the early twentieth century would have been regarded as 'modern' and exploring the state of the distribution and use of global resources, including the tension between the aggregated wealth of different societies and the import of its unequal distribution within them. Neurath also made the claim, hardly without controversy, that the facts presented, regularized through the use of Isotype-based statistics, would speak for themselves (Neurath 1939: 7–8).

Neurath also juxtaposed the depiction of sweeping historical trends, often in graphical form via the Isotype method, with carefully selected details. For example, he illuminated broad changes in average life expectancy over the course of the Industrial Revolution in industrializing countries, yet also homed in on the incidence of tuberculosis in the poorer districts of Brooklyn, New York, in the 1920s.

In its popularized form this work might bear comparisons with – and contrasts too – with Weber's *General Economic History*. One of these differences can be found in the evocation of an ecological economics in *Modern Man in the Making,* where the relationship between resources and consumable goods takes center stage, providing a kind of economic geography with political implications conforming to varying 'economic orders' (Neurath 1939: 65–79). Another, to be sure, is Neurath's reliance upon statistics, presented largely in graphical form, which Neurath saw as underpinning a 'scientific sociology'.

The case for such a sociology was laid out most fully by Neurath in *Empirical Sociology*. This text was written at a time when his association with Marxism was at or near its peak and his role in spearheading and sorting out the major themes and approaches of the Vienna Circle of philosophers was fully on display. These can be seen in evidence in the text through Neurath's emphasis upon a behavioral approach to and understanding of sociology, grounded in a 'physicalist' language of 'physical facts', and resistant to any 'metaphysical' intrusions that might insinuate themselves into any sociological analysis (Neurath [1931] 1973: 349–353, 358–364). Neurath asserted that Marxism represented the best form of a scientifically-based empirical sociology.

Materialist and idealist tensions

One might let this version of Neurath's inquiry into political economy and history stand in certain regards in his critique of Max Weber's sociology. While treating the body of Weber's work with a certain admiration, Neurath scored Weber's resort to metaphysics in placing the religious pronouncements and statements of Calvinism at the center of – indeed the spur for – an emergent capitalism rather than seeing the rise of capitalism resulting from economic and societal changes. Elsewhere, in his paper on "Universal Jargon and Terminology", Neurath decried Weber's 'ideal-types' as extraneous and hence metaphysical (Neurath [1941] 1983: 225), standards that should be removed, in part through the use of Ockham's Razor, one of Ernst Mach's favorite philosophical tools.

On one level Neurath's materialist philosophy was posed against Weber's idealist philosophy.

A closer reading, though, of Neurath's text reveals a more complex, layered, and perhaps even contradictory comprehension of the intellectual currents in central Europe at or about the turn of the twentieth century that affected both Neurath and Weber. Neurath challenged the neo-Kantian notion of a fundamental division between the natural sciences and the humanities or cultural sciences. Evocations of this division appeared in the work of Dilthey and extended through that of Windelband and Rickert. Neurath then associated Weber with this notion as well, citing a passage in Weber's work on the logic of historical economics, in which he highlights the importance of Rickert as an influence upon him.

The full text of Neurath's critique of Weber's philosophical stance is worth citing:

> Max Weber more than anyone else has endeavored to treat sociology empirically but nevertheless he also has always striven for an anti-behaviorist attitude in principle, he who time and again has ascribed a moving power to the spirit of the age.
>
> (Neurath [1931] 1973: 356–357)

He then challenged the philosophical path underlying Weber's *verstehende* sociology:

> He tries, like Rickert, to carry out a division in the pursuit of science, which makes impossible any universal connection of all lawlike features that are required by the empirical sciences in their forecasts. With Weber, time and again, the empathic immersion appears in place of science. Over this poetic activity there is no test, no control, nor does it belong in a scientific account. From Dilthey the path leads through Windelband and Rickert to Weber, who is clearly conscious of his own outlook: "It is a purpose of this essay [on Roscher and Knies] to test the applicability of Rickert's thoughts to the methodology of our branch of research."
>
> (Neurath [1931] 1973: 357)

While it is certainly the case that Rickert loomed large in Weber's thinking, and Weber laid out some of his own rethinking about matters of concept formation in correspondence with Rickert, Weber did not adopt the neo-Kantian formulation about the division of the sciences, opting instead for distinctions based upon meaning and purpose (Turk 2016: 130–131, 138–139).

Moreover, for his part Neurath began his discussion of the necessary integration of political economy and history, which here, once effected, will assume a largely Marxian cast, by seeking to overcome the metaphysical trappings of all sorts that had beset both disciplines. But then adds that this is insufficient, as there is also the matter of how concepts are formed in both fields. He then frames the difficulty involved by positing the ideographical character of history and the nomothetic character of political economy (Neurath [1931] 1973: 390–391), a distinction that was a central feature of the conceptual apparatus advanced by Windelband and Rickert.

Thus, Neurath's resolution of this difficulty appears incomplete. The nuances in Neurath's thinking about the philosophical foundations of political economy or sociology can be elucidated further through an exploration of Neurath's critique of Weber's theory of ideal types. In one of his later short philosophical pieces Neurath took Weber's theory to task, characterizing it as an unnecessary imposition set upon empirically-based observations (Neurath 1941: 142–143). Herein appears to be one of the bright lines separating Neurath's sociology from Weber's, with all statements deemed 'scientific', whether they be particular or general, grounded in observation and comprehended as observable behavior, even gauged as sensations. In Neurath's own parlance the theory of ideal types introduced a superfluous layer of theorizing, which rendered the theory as 'metaphysical', constituting an idealist overlay. Yet if one probes more deeply, the clarity of this opposition as well gives way to something much murkier.

On the role of history and consciousness

Neurath stated that "[h]ow we think about historical events ...significantly affects those events, whereas astronomy cannot significantly affect the course of the stars" (Neurath [1920/1921] 2004: 346). Here Neurath acknowledges that consciousness of history, and hence how history is understood, will affect, that is, change history itself, whereas sciences like astronomy are impervious to matters of consciousness and understanding. This notion appears rooted in what had become an emerging strand of Marxist thought after World War I, though Neurath did not cite any specific source or text.

However, what does this portend for the typology of science? Neurath, it appears, invariably likened aspects of the treatment of the natural sciences and the social sciences, making the case for an underlying 'unity of science'. On occasion he explicitly linked sociology and astronomy, highlighting their similarities (Neurath [1931] 1973: 363). In this instance, though, consciousness and understanding pertain to history, but not to astronomy. While cast in terms of the Marxian version of historical agency, this division also does appear to partake of the neo-Kantian elements that Neurath had found wanting in Wundt's *The Logic of Science*. And though it is important to state that Neurath spoke of 'consciousness' rather than 'understanding', his reference to 'conscious realization', derived from "[h]ow we think about historical events", implies both consciousness and understanding.

To that extent, Neurath's efforts to distinguish 'scientific sociology' from Weber's *verstehende* sociology may fall short. Even if 'consciousness' is not meant to convey 'empathy', it does appear to place history and – in light of the framework in which Neurath has cast political economy – political economy as well, into a separate realm from the natural or physical sciences.

One might distinguish Neurath's position from Weber's in that Neurath appears to engage with a 'consciousness of history', while Weber focused upon the construction of meaning. Yet there may be common ground to be found between them, as it is difficult to imagine the emergence of consciousness without the need for or presence of interpretation, nor can one separate the infusion or attachment of meaning from the interpretation that follows thereby. Moreover, this common ground had already surfaced in the intermingling of theory and fact that both saw at work in any scientific inquiry. Weber liked to cite Goethe in that regard; Neurath, while also fond of Goethe, was more likely to turn to Poincaré and especially Duhem to support a similar supposition. Indeed, Neurath prepared a lecture, then turned it into a paper published in 1916 on the necessity of making use of systems of hypotheses to create or establish scientific theories (Neurath [1916] 1983).

Pivoting on the 'spirit of Protestantism' and the role of ideas

The broader charge of metaphysical interpolation by Weber has to do with his celebrated, though controversial, thesis about the transformative effect of the 'spirit of Protestantism', most especially Calvinism, on the rise of capitalism as an economic system (Weber 1930). Fernand Braudel, the great economic historian from the French *Annales* school, saw no foundation for Weber's thesis in the history of the evolving European economies from the Renaissance through the seventeenth century, where business practices associated with capitalism were developed first and fully in Catholic states before being taken up by Protestant ones (Braudel 1977: 65–67).

Neurath's reproach was more philosophical than historical. He asserted that this thesis accorded far greater power and efficacy to the words of religious speakers, among other flaws in Weber's case (Neurath [1931] 1973: 356–358, 384). As a materialist Neurath posited that economic changes and developments drove ideas, rather than the other way around.

One way to explore Neurath's contention in this instance is to weigh his critique of Weber on this subject in relation to his treatment of the impact of Catholicism, especially as Neurath often paired Catholicism in opposition to Marxism.

This does come with a twist. In 1931, in a review of J.B. Kraus's *Scholastik, Puritanismus, und Kapitalismus,* which appeared in the socialist journal *Der Kampf,* Neurath made the case that a Catholic Jesuit like Kraus was able to see through the claims made by Weber or Sombart for the priority of ideas, in this instance Protestant ones, in reshaping economic life. The article was encaptioned "Marxismus eines Jesuiten" (P. Neurath and Nemeth 1994: 271–276).

A preliminary matter needs to be taken up in this regard. When Neurath refers to Catholicism and the Catholic Church, and the historical role of each, to what extent does the former refer to the words of theologians and a set of beliefs, and the latter to an institution? The intermingling of the two might prove problematic, including in the oppositional pairing of Marxism and Catholicism. Here one might think of the propaganda wars launched by the Catholic Church through the Counter-reformation, on the one hand, and the 'agit-prop' of the Soviet Union in its early days, on the other. After all, the term 'propaganda' itself first appeared as a major offensive weapon in the Counter-reformation, with the creation in 1622 of the 'Congregation for the Propagation of the Faith'.

Does in some sense Neurath acknowledge a blending of sorts of Catholicism, as a system of beliefs propagated by the words of theologians, and the Catholic Church as an institution? If a case can be made that this is so, then Neurath's critique of Weber's ideal types, or of any other similar formulation melding ideology and institution, itself must be subject to review. It is clear that for all his emphasis upon behaviorism as an essential feature of 'scientific sociology' and his determination to limit the body of scientific statements to those that met the physicalist criterion of being based upon observation, Neurath was enamored with the 'power of ideas'. How else is one to explain his continuing effort to cast Marxism as a form of social epicureanism and to highlight the high regard with which Marx held Epicurus, noting specifically that Marx had written his doctoral dissertation on the philosophy of ancient Greece, and had identified Epicurus as his favorite philosopher (Neurath [1928] 1973: 282–290). By contrast, idealist philosophy, whether espoused by Hegel or others, invariably appeared to Neurath to assume a reactionary bent.

Moreover, and this is clearly germane to the tendency on Neurath's part to cast Marxism and Catholicism as mirror opposites, Neurath also took pains to point out that Catholicism had attempted to squelch epicureanism as an unwanted materialist philosophy (Neurath [1925] 2004: 415).

And that does introduce a question of intellectual and social milieu that may have informed Neurath's oppositional pairing. The refashioning of an Austrian state in the wake of the dissolution of the Habsburg Empire at the end of World War I produced a small country that was not altogether homogeneous. The two major political parties that emerged out of this transformation were the Social Democrats, exponents of Austromarxism, and the Christian Social Party.

The base of the former was the city of Vienna, with its industrial environs surrounding it; the base of the latter was the new Austria, essentially rural countryside, dotted by a few small cities. From 1919 to 1934 Vienna was known as 'Red Vienna', and its leading political figure was Otto Bauer, a socialist who had served as foreign minister and, as noted above, had played a crucial role in extricating Neurath from Munich in 1920 in the follow-up to his trial for treason. For most of this period, though, the post of Austrian prime minister was held by a cleric, Ignaz Seipel, leader of the Christian Socials. Might one see a congruence of sorts between Neurath's oppositional pairing and the general perception of interwar Austria as riven between a progressive Marxism and a conservative, if not reactionary Catholicism?

Neurath, Weber, and the fate of historical economics

Both Neurath and Weber drew upon the notion that economics encompassed a broader social world, consistent with the general outlook of the German Historical School. In Neurath's case this called for an attunement with the organization of society and the different possible economic orders arising out of the varieties of social organization that might occur. In Weber's case this meant linking the examination of individual behavior with that of social behavior, as Richard Swedberg has couched the bases for Weber's 'social economics'. Moreover, it is striking that even at the time of Neurath's closest association with Marxism, he strove to remake Marxism on his own terms as 'social epicureanism', linking the formulation of 'scientific sociology' with the teleology of maximizing 'social happiness', even as he denied invoking any teleology.

As both Neurath and Weber confronted the question of the relation of history to economics, hence addressing, explicitly or not, the nature of historical economics, they faced the problem of categorization, as the then dominant treatment of economics and history followed from the neo-Kantian division of the former as nomothetic, or law-making, and the latter as idiographic, or constructed from the accumulation of factual detail. Could a bridge be built between the two so that a philosophically grounded and sustainable foundation for some version of historical economics might go forward?

One finds Neurath wrestling with the matter of categorization a generation after its peak influence, appearing to distinguish his own 'scientific sociology' from Weber's *verstehende* sociology by placing Weber squarely in the tradition of the idealist neo-Kantians, drawing a line from Dilthey through Windelband and Rickert, then on to Weber himself.

It seems to me that Neurath misstated Weber's position, as the latter's effort to place the need to establish meaning and engage in interpretation as the key to comprehending the human or social sciences was meant to circumvent and transcend the neo-Kantian division between the nomothetic and the idiographic.

Moreover, after emphasizing the centrality of an anti-metaphysical conception of the world in advancing any and all scientific inquiry, Neurath also saw the need to structure the concepts of political economy and sociology on a consistent basis. This would prove to be somewhat problematic, as the conflict between the generalizing aspects of economics and the particular aspects of history had to be surmounted.

Of what significance does all this have on the fate of historical economics? From Swedberg's perspective one might take note of a certain affinity between Weber's effort at shaping a 'social economics' in the 1910s and the emergence of the New Institutional Economics in the 1980s. One might look as well to the acknowledgment of the value of the accomplishments of Douglass North and Robert Fogel within the field of economics through being awarded the Bank of Sweden's Nobel Prize in Economics.

Yet one must also be cognizant of the critique of the New Institutionalists by Paul David, who saw their work as largely framed by the subordination of history to existing neoclassical economic theory. Criticized as a self-justifying process, this approach left open the question whether, in Paul David's words, 'history matters' as an independent form of inquiry. Neurath would have decidedly objected to this role for history in economics, inverting, if not subverting, the approach taken by the early influences upon him, the German Historical School and Wilhelm Neurath, and once more elevating price theory to the core of economic theory.

By dint of their association with the German Historical School and their absorption in the intellectual cross-currents pervading central Europe at the turn of the twentieth century both Neurath and Weber were situated and poised to take on the problem posed by historical economics, whether logical or otherwise. However, it is rather in the matter of the bridge itself between the nomothetic and the idiographic that Neurath's and Weber's efforts to join economics and history in some fashion assume more contemporary relevance. While the neo-Kantian distinction between the nomothetic and the idiographic appears to have long since passed its heyday, it remains, a century later, a central factor in the difficulty of sustaining historical economics as a field of inquiry. Economists continue to struggle with how to incorporate historical evidence into economic analysis, if they attempt to do so at all, or even envision any role whatsoever for history in economics.

It was still possible for the economic historian Carlo Cipolla to write at the close of the twentieth century that the gap between economics and history constituted a chasm, placing even economic history "between two cultures", as he borrowed the phrase C.P. Snow had used in 1960 to characterize the seemingly wide division between the sciences and the humanities (Cipolla [1988] 1991). For Cipolla that chasm bore all the traces of the neo-Kantian division between the nomothetic and the idiographic. It was also still possible in the late 1980s for the economist Robert Solow (1985), in addressing the American Economic Association, to lament the lack of connection economists in general had to history, overtaken instead by the notion that economics ought to model itself upon the hard sciences, especially physics.

In *The Idea of History in Constructing Economics* (Turk 2016), I have suggested that Fernand Braudel's notion of establishing a general typology or grammar of history, however incomplete and imperfect (Braudel 1982: 21), might prove a not insignificant step in bridging the gap that has persisted over the course of the twentieth century.

References

Braudel, Fernand (1977). *Afterthoughts on Material Civilization and Capitalism*. Trans. Patricia M. Ranum. Baltimore: Johns Hopkins Press.

Braudel, Fernand (1982). *The Wheels of Commerce*. Trans. Sian Reynolds (1992). London: Collins.

Cipolla, Carlo [1988] (1991). *Between Two Cultures: An Introduction to Economic History,*. Trans. Christopher Woodall. New York: W.W. Norton.

Dahms, Hans-Joachim, and Neumann, Michael (1994). "Social Scientists and Philosophers in the Munich Council Republic". *Jahrbuch für Soziologiegeschichte 1992*: 115–146.

Hennis, Wilhelm (1991) "The Pitiless 'Sobriety of Judgement': Max Weber between Carl Menger and Gustav Von Schmoller – The Academic Politics of Value Freedom". *History of the Human Sciences* 4(1): 27–59.

Hodgson, Geoffrey M. (2001). *How Economics Forgot History*. London; New York: Routledge.

Müller-Lyer, Franz Carl (1910). *Der Sinn des Lebens und die Wissenschaft:Grundlinien einer Volksphilosophie*. Munchen: Lehmann.

Neurath, Anna Schapire, and Neurath, Otto [1910] (1913). *Lesebuch der Volkswirtschaftslehre*. 2nd edn. Leipzig: G.A: Gloeckner.

Neurath, Otto [1910] (2004). "Theory of the Social Sciences". In Robert S. Cohen and Thomas E. Uebel, eds., *Otto Neurath: Economic Writings Selections, 1904–1945*. [Multiple translators]. Dordrecht: Kluwer Academic Publishing, pp. 265–291.

Neurath, Otto [1916] (1983). "On the Classification of Systems of Hypotheses". In Robert S. Cohen and Marie Neurath, eds. and trans., *Philosophical Papers 1913–1946* Dordrecht/Boston: D. Reidel Publishing Company, pp. 13–31.

Neurath, Otto [1917] (2004). "Conceptual Structure of Economic Theory and Its Foundation". In Robert S. Cohen and Thomas Uebel, eds., *Otto Neurath: Economic Writings Selections, 1904–1945*. Dordrecht: Kluwer Academic Publishing, pp. 312–341.

Neurath, Otto [1920/21] (2004). "A System of Socialisation". In Robert S. Cohen and Thomas Uebel, eds., *Otto Neurath: Economic Writings Selections, 1904–1945*. Dordrecht: Kluwer Academic Publishing, pp. 345–370.

Neurath, Otto [1925] (2004) "Economic Plan and Calculation in Kind". In Thomas E. Uebel and Robert S. Cohen, eds., *Otto Neurath: Economic Writings/Selections 1904–1945*. [Multiple translators]. Dordrecht: Kluwer Academic Publishers, pp. 405–465.

Neurath, Otto [1928] (1973). "Personal Life and Class Struggle". In Marie Neurath and Robert S. Cohen, eds., *Empiricism and Sociology*. Trans. Paul Foulkes and Marie Neurath. Dordrecht: Reidel, pp. 249–298.

Neurath, Otto [1929] (1973). "Wissenschaftliche Weltauffassung der Wiener Kreis". In Marie Neurath and Robert S. Cohen, eds., *Empiricism and Sociology*. Trans. Paul Foulkes and Marie Neurath. Dordrecht: Reidel, pp. 299–318.

Neurath, Otto [1931] (1994). "Review of J.B. Kraus". In Paul Neurath and Elisabeth Nemeth, eds., *Otto Neurath oder Die Einheit der Wissenschaft und Gesellschaft*. Wien: Bohlau Verlag.

Neurath, Otto [1931] (1973). *Empirical Sociology*. In Marie Neurath and Robert S. Cohen, eds., *Empiricism and Sociology*. Trans. Paul Foulkes and Marie NeurathDordrecht: Reidel, pp. 319–421.

Neurath, Otto [1941] (1983) "Universal Jargon and Terminology". In Robert S. Cohen and Marie Neurath, eds. and trans., *Philosophical Papers 1913–1946*. Dordrecht/ Boston: D. Reidel Publishing Company, pp. 213–229.

Neurath, Otto (1939) *Modern Man in the Making*. New York & London: A.A. Knopf.

Neurath, Otto (1941) "Universal Jargon and Terminology". *Proceedings of the Aristotelian Society* 41 (New Series): 127–148.

Neurath, Paul and Elisabeth Nemeth, eds. (1994) *Otto Neurath oder Die Einheit der Wissenschaft und Gesellschaft*. Wien: Bohlau Verlag.

Schriften des Verein der Sozialpolitik. 1911. Bd. 132. Leipzig: Duncker & Humblot.
Schumann, Wolfgang (1973) "Memories of Otto Neurath". In Marie Neurath and Robert S. Cohen, eds., *Empiricism and Sociology*. Trans. Paul Foulkes and Marie Neurath. Dordrecht: Reidel, pp. 15–17.
Shionoya, Yuichi (2005). *The Soul of the German Historical School*. New York: Springer Science and Business Media.
Solow, Robert (1985). "Economic History and Economics". *American Economic Review*, 75(2): 328–331.
Swedberg, Richard (1998). *Max Weber and the Evolution of Economic Sociology*. Princeton: Princeton University Press.
Turk, Michael. 2016. *The Idea of History in Constructing Economics*. Abington, UK: Routledge.
Weber, Max [1903–1906] (1975). *Roscher and Knies: The Logical Problems of Historical Economics*. Trans. with introduction by Guy Oakes. New York: Free Press.
Weber, Max [1904] (1949). *The Methodology of the Social Sciences*. Ed. and trans. Edward A. Shils and Henry A. Finch. New York: Free Press.
Weber, Max [1919] (2012). 'Bericht uber Webers Testimonie'. In *Gesamtausgabe, Abteilung I: Band 16*. [Multiple editors]. Tubingen: J.C.B. Mohr, p. 495.
Weber, Max (1923). *General Economic History*. Trans.Frank Knight. London: George Allen & Unwin.
Weber, Max (1930). *The Protestant Ethic and the Spirit of Capitalism*. Trans. Talcott Parsons, with a foreword by R.H. Tawney. New York: Scribner.
Weber, Max (2008). *Briefe: 1915–1917*. Eds. Gerd Krumeich and M. Rainer Lepsius. Tubingen: J.C.B. Mohr. Letters of 2 January 1916, 14 April 1916, and 1 September 1917.
Weber, Max (2012). *Briefe: 1918–1920*. Eds. Gerd Krumeich and M. Rainer Lepsius. Tubingen: J.C.B. Mohr (Paul Siebeck). Letter of 4 October 1919.

5 Ecological economics and qualitative measurement

What is the nature of economic value, and how might it be measured? The challenge posed by these questions to economic theory and analysis, in which the quantifiable is taken as the point of departure, informs the rise of an ecological economics integrating both human experience and the natural world into a comprehensive economic structure. It was a challenge central to Otto Neurath's inquiry into political economy.

Backdrop: the rise of ecological economics

Through the 1970s and 1980s the notion that an ecological perspective on or within economics ought to be forged more deeply gained momentum, finding its expression in works by Kenneth Boulding (1978) and Joan Martinez-Alier (1984), among others. With the launching of a new academic journal in 1989 devoted especially to it, ecological economics came into its own as a formal subfield in economics. In the first issue of *Ecological Economics* Robert Costanza took on the task of describing what this new subfield entailed and, perhaps more importantly, what gap it filled in the various areas of inquiry that had hitherto defined the bounds of economic discourse.

In effect, Costanza presented a manifesto for ecological economics. He began as follows:

> Ecological Economics addresses the relationship between ecosystems and economics systems in the broadest sense. These relationships are the locus of many of our most pressing current problems (i.e. sustainability, acid rain, global warming, species extinction, wealth distribution) but they are not well covered by any existing discipline.
>
> (Costanza 1989: 1)

He elaborated as to why that was the case:

> Environmental and resource economics, as it is currently practiced, covers only the application of neoclassical economics to environmental resource problems. Ecology, as it is currently practiced, sometimes deals with

> human impacts on ecosystems, but the more common tendency is to stick to 'natural' systems.
>
> (Costanza 1989: 1)

Hence, ecological economics would emerge to "extend the modest areas of overlap. It will include neoclassical environmental economics and ecological impact studies as subsets, but will also encourage new ways of thinking about the linkages between ecological and economic systems" (Costanza 1989: 1).

One might make the case that more than a half-century earlier Otto Neurath had advanced an inchoate form of ecological economics. Neurath did not comprehend consciously the notion of ecology, formally conceptualized only decades after Neurath was active. However, he did "encourage new ways of thinking about the linkages" between society as an ecosystem, though he described "the world … as one enormous factory", blending the human with the natural (Neurath [1931] 2004: 487). This terminology was obviously more in keeping with contemporaneous currents of thought, in which the possibilities but also the unfavorable consequences of scientific management and Taylorism were seen as holding sway, and as increasingly large-scale economic entities were taken to be both the norm and the likely wave of the future.

This in turn may give rise to an ancillary but not insignificant inquiry into the relation between ecological economics and socialism, a subject explored by John O'Neill in his own examination of the pioneering aspects of Neurath's economic thought. As O'Neill expressed it, "[m]ore than any other socialist theorist of [the twentieth] century, Neurath offers an account of socialism that is sensitive to our current ecological problems" (O'Neill 1999: 145).

It may also call for a glimpse into the relation between ecological economics and evolutionary economics, as both partake in some measure of the foundational notion of the economy as a living system, directly as such or by analogy, and the extent to which Neurath relied upon such a notion may prove central to an understanding of his version of ecological economics.

In addition, Neurath's vigorous assertion of the lack of commensurability across different forms of economic activity and experience, as well as his championing of the unity of science, has provided some scholars of ecological economics, including O'Neill, further grounds in seeing Neurath as an essential figure in the early history of ecological economics. According to O'Neill, Martinez-Alier, and Giuseppe Munda:

> Neurath has been recently claimed, with reason, as one of the founders of ecological economics, not only for his part in [the] debate [about natural or in-kind calculation] of the 1920s and 1930s, but also because of his work on the 'unity' – or rather, the 'orchestration' – of the sciences in the study of specific issues in social, economic, ecological history.
>
> (Martinez-Alier, Munda, and O'Neill 1999: 38)

Ecological economics: the divisions within

In revisiting Costanza's declaration one might think of ecological economics in two distinct ways. First of all, there is the construction of an economy as a natural or ecosystem, where the limitations of the national economy may be readily transcended into a global setting. Here the measure must be taken of all that flows in and out, requiring a reckoning of the availability and use of resources, the outputs produced, whether the proximate aim of production or by-products of it, and all the other consequences, however indirect or circuitous, that follow from the economic paths pursued. While on one level it might be possible to categorize these flows within the context of resource economics, where one applies the full measure of the externalities involved, with a special emphasis upon social costs and benefits, this misses the central point. That which is external to the conventional treatment of production occupies center stage, that is, the broad impact on the ecosystem as a whole.

If the ecosystem is taken to be a living system, then biological analogies or metaphors become germane. Of these the notion that such systems evolve, and hence come under the purview of evolutionary biology, stands out, rendering the economic ecosystem subject to concerns and treatment found in evolutionary economics (or at least some versions of it). The decades-long work of Kenneth Boulding, challenging the premises upon which economics had been constructed, exemplifies this blending of the ecological as the evolutionary.

Second, there is a rather dramatic reinterpretation of the nature and value of economic activity. Indices that have gained favor over the last century as the most reliable measures of economic wealth, like national income and gross domestic product, have been subject to sharp criticism, seen as either inadequate and insufficient or outright misleading, as to what they say about the well-being of individuals in different societies or about the quality of life in those societies. One might place in this category the qualitative elements and alternative measures that inform the United Nations index of quality of life or other similar reconstructions of a national standard of living. Here one finds front and center average life expectancy, rate of infant mortality, level of education, and state of the health care system as essential indicators of human welfare. Other critics have sought to gauge well-being on a seemingly more subjective basis, through the introduction of 'happiness' indices, which do have the advantage of attempting to capture expectations about well-being, but which face somewhat daunting problems in assembling such information.

How well do these two versions of or approaches to ecological economics comport with one another? On the surface, it would seem, not necessarily all that well. The first approach subsumes economics under the natural world, even as it seeks to comprehend human activity in relation to it, or, perhaps better, in tension with it. The second attends much more to the social world that humans have constructed. Thus, in this largely heterodox field (or subfield) within economics, the pull of the natural versus the pull of the social, a critical trope in the theorizing about economics, has not vanished. Instead, it appears to have reasserted itself, only in transmogrified form.

In his depiction of the proper subject matter of economics, Neurath gave great weight to both versions. As noted above, in a thumbnail sketch in one of his many pieces on socialization, he compared society to a factory, arguably a 'closed system', to borrow from a later era, requiring an accounting for all inputs and outputs contained within. I would take the popular text Neurath later produced in the 1930s, *Modern Man in the Making,* as guided significantly by an ecological ethos within what might be deemed a cross between economic geography and social anthropology. Note how he introduced the section of the text devoted to 'The State of the World':

> Man's daily life, his happiness and unhappiness, depends upon old and new customs and institutions, upon a great many agencies. The modernity of living-conditions depends, first of all, upon technical equipment and natural resources. A bird's-eye view of the interconnexions between all parts of a society in action makes it possible to analyse the state of the world or the structure of a single country.
>
> (Neurath 1939: 65)

What followed was an 'Economic Scheme' worthy of Quesnay, going from "the Use of natural resources" to the "Distribution and service" (Neurath 1939: 65).

But it is also the case that Neurath's early critique of marginalism and neoclassical economics was grounded in his view that the new mainstream in economics, as it had emerged, had pursued a mistaken notion about economic values, hemmed in by their elevation of price theory and an exclusive reliance upon monetary calculation. Instead, Neurath sought to associate the notion of value with the satisfaction found across varied constellations of goods and services; effectively, this was an effort to gauge quality of life or the expectations of it. Neurath would go on to elaborate a tripartite schema, presented in some detail in his theoretical pieces from the mid-1930s, in which 'life terrain', 'life situation', and 'economic order' assume central place (Neurath 1935: 45–46).

Ecological economics and socialization

Hence, both strands of ecological economics are evident in Neurath's thought. I would contend that these two strands arose early on in Neurath's inquiries into the sciences as well as political economy. I take as a reasonable supposition that Neurath's interest in the availability and use of resources was stimulated, if not initiated, by his acquaintance with Vienna's Hochschule für Bodenkultur. At the same time, Neurath's embrace of what he would later describe as 'social epicureanism' (see Neurath [1928] 1973: 282–290) was already evident in his focus upon an economic standard of 'satisfaction' and 'happiness' separate and at far remove from marginalist price theory in his first major publications about the foundations of political economy and its concept formation.

Yet these two strands are woven together only when Neurath began to espouse a Marxian socialist point of view, especially as he laid out the case for the socialization of the economy. The replacement of a monetary economy by a natural one, where in-kind calculation supplanted monetary calculation, advanced the proto-ecological standard of overall happiness as the proper measure of economic value. However, the administrative economy that would serve as the vehicle for socialization would require the broad coordination of national economic activity, across both production and consumption, through a form of central economic planning. This in turn would require the gathering of statistics to identify the availability of resources and the extant needs of the population. Neurath pointed to a model for constructing such tables in the pioneering work of Josef Popper-Lynkeus. Neurath made clear that this sort of construction could not be considered as simply socialist or capitalist (Neurath [1943] 2004: 529).

Here is a sample of the case that Neurath made in advancing the possibilities of a socialized economy, whereby only a comparison of the requirements for and impact of a total plan offered a valid form of measurement:

> In the traditional economic order one decided the question whether to build a mill or a foundry in terms of the net profit yielded by one or the other enterprise ... What then will replace net profits in a socialized economy? The greater or lesser economic efficiency of a system of measures can be ascertained only by comparing total plans. The central office for measurement in kind would for instance have to design an economic plan on the assumption that a generating plant is to be built and agriculture is to be improved in certain ways, and a second plan on the assumption that a canal is to be dug and a foundry built.
>
> (Neurath [1919] 1973: 146)

He goes on to state:

> Then the economic central office and above all the people's representatives have to decide whether they prefer one or the other shaping of living standards: better supply of electricity and food with attendant effects, or better supplies resulting from enhanced imports and increased production of iron. There are no units that can be used as the basis of such a decision, neither units of money nor hours of work. One must directly judge the desirability of the two possibilities.
>
> (Neurath [1919] 1973: 146)

What may be drawn from Neurath's 'socialist ecological' economics? As it exists at the level of possibility rather than any fully realized state, one might see it as an idealized conception. Critics would challenge and deride it as either impossible to achieve outright or fraught with a host of unforeseen complications and consequences. There is also a certain tension remaining between the two approaches noted above. The second is immersed in a world of statistics, consistent with Neurath's advocacy in the 1930s of the royal road to a 'scientific sociology' being paved by observable magnitudes, namely statistics (Neurath [1931] 1973: 358–364).

Yet the effort to gauge satisfaction and happiness, the first approach to ecological economics, lies in a different mathematical realm, in which qualitative measures and topological considerations assume a far more central role, and specific results, as opposed to arrays of possible combinations, are hard to come by, let alone pin down. In short, Neurath's ecological economics offers more a vision than a roadmap to a fully constructed model, even with Neurath's caveat about the necessary 'incompleteness' of any model taken into account.

Thus, there may be a number of reasons why Neurath's ecological economics, if accorded its full dimensions, does not inform, broadly speaking, more recent excursions into ecological economics. Neurath's intertwining of socialism and ecological economics, even if regarded as idiosyncratic by many of his socialist contemporaries (see below), may have less appeal to those who live in an age where the ferment of socialist ideas in an earlier period has been largely disregarded, often because it is unknown or thought of solely in the context of twentieth-century 'socialist' states.

It is also noteworthy that the tension between the two approaches that Neurath was unable to dissolve might make the case for developing two different and rather discrete versions of ecological economics, which is essentially where things stand today. That separation, though, has not made it possible to surmount the resort to qualitative judgments characterizing the second approach. The difficulties or limitations Neurath encountered in that regard a century ago remain present and evident today, so that contemporary ecological economists often find themselves putting forward an idealized conception rather than an operational model, or the data gathered is drawn from subjective opinion surveys on general states of happiness.

Of course, one should not overlook perhaps the most obvious basis for Neurath's lack of direct influence in this field upon later generations: the lack of knowledge of the work he had done in exploring the subject in a way that does presage future forays in the field. As rediscovery can often lead to reassessment, the act of bringing Neurath's ideas and overall conception, as well as the tensions and limitations that arose in the process, to light may help rewrite this piece of the history of economic thought.

Of goods and ills

Signs of what would emerge as one of the hallmarks of environmental economics, an effort to gauge social costs as distinct from private costs, appeared in Neurath's early piece on the theory of the social sciences:

> Until now the introduction of negative magnitudes into the theory of value has not succeeded either. The development of the theory of ills has been entirely unsatisfactory until now, one tries to leave it aside if at all possible. The reason for this is probably that money is used to buy 'goods', not 'ills'.
>
> (Neurath [1910] 2004: 280–281)

He expanded his case by venturing into and critiquing marginalist theory in that regard:

> Similarly the theory of marginal disutility corresponding to the theory of marginal utility has received little consideration. Should one want to characterize the state of an individual person, however, one has to mention goods as well as ills, since there can be no question of adding the two magnitudes as long as one has not set up a calculus for that.
>
> (Neurath [1910] 2004: 281)

In an ecological economics the problem posed by 'ills' has been addressed in two ways. The first, following the lead of Arthur Pigou, elaborating upon a Marshallian construct, was to identify at the microeconomic level a divergence between private output and social output, later translated into private costs and social costs (Pigou 1924: 155–163). Here the 'ills' are associated with the negative impact of economic activity upon third parties, potentially a proxy for the immediate neighborhood or community but just as easily might encompass society as a whole. The second, more in line with the country 'silhouettes' that Neurath would later create, established standards in designated areas of human experience and activity that would allow for cross-country comparisons. This approach thus proceeded on a macroeconomic level.

But Neurath's critique had raised concerns about the possibility of calculating the gains and losses experienced by individuals, questioning the possibility of interpersonal comparisons (see Lessman 2008), a matter falling under the realm of consumer economics. How well would the theory of revealed preference, as laid out by Paul Samuelson, respond to Neurath's criticism? It should be recalled that Neurath had directed such criticism at Vilfredo Pareto, the leading contemporaneous exponent of a marginalist treatment of consumer behavior, and that Samuelson's theorizing about the subject was intended to clarify and rectify earlier treatments of consumer behavior, like Pareto's. In its favor the theory of revealed preference measured consumer choices via rankings, introducing a form of qualitative measurement. On the other hand, the theory of revealed preference, beyond its conflation of 'preference' and 'behavior' (Wong 1978: 70), also depended upon the efficiency of prices and monetary calculation, a position Neurath rejected, both because of the limitations of price theory in monetizing value and because it required the introduction of an auxiliary hypothesis about the efficiency of the price system.

Delineating an ecological economics in the conceptual structure of economic theory

Neurath delineated the terms for an ecological economics more fully in his essay on "The Conceptual Structure of Economic Theory and its Foundations", written in 1917, in retrospect a pathbreaking piece in the prefiguration of ecological economics. This paper was produced during wartime, and a not insignificant part of it was devoted to the implications, both theoretical and practical, of a wartime economy. Here Neurath had undertaken to expand upon the notion of 'in-kind calculation' in lieu of monetary calculation and its role in an 'administered economy', with the model of a wartime 'command' economy firmly in mind.

Despite this, or perhaps, oddly enough, on account of this, significant elements of an 'ecological economics' are limned thereby. Broadly speaking they are made manifest through Neurath's continuing invocation of the need to employ a qualitative standard to gauge what it is that an economic life provides. There is a certain measure of subjectivity in this, as Neurath notes that the pleasure that one individual might derive from an individual good might not be the same as that of another, objectified to some degree by casting this within a broader set of circumstances, say with regard to the different hours of labor required to be able to acquire the good.

In at least two areas, though, Neurath's economic calculus prefigures that of environmental economists a half-century or more later. Among the concepts Neurath introduces are 'positive increases' and 'negative increases', both associated with economic activity. According to Neurath the blanket acceptance of any new economic activity contributing to an overall economic advance is mistaken. Some activities constitute actual improvement, but others detract from overall well-being, and should therefore be comprehended as subtractions rather than additions. It is a short step from this to an environmental accounting in which, say, pollution or other forms of environmental degradation are treated as losses in an economic balance sheet rather than simply ignored or shunted aside as 'by-products' of production or consumption.

Moreover, Neurath addresses directly the notion of human cost. While economics has typically and conventionally only measured losses, if at all, with regard to the objects of production, Neurath suggests in a somewhat impassioned way that the "destruction of [human] existence" (Neurath [1917] 2004: 338) should account for more than the destruction of objects made or structures built. In other words, activities that may indirectly affect the quality of life, if not life itself, should be central to what might later be termed an ecological calculus. One might think of this as well in terms of negative externalities, a notion that would come to occupy center stage in environmental economics, as a means of capturing social cost.

It is also noteworthy that Neurath listed a set of conventional economic concepts, all of which he attempted to show are derived from, and hence are limited by, their foundation in monetary calculation. One of these is 'national income' or 'wealth'. Writing in 1917, Neurath did acknowledge that 'national income' was not explicitly expressed in monetary terms, but conceptually did rest upon a form of monetary measurement (Neurath [1917] 2004: 336). Here one might take Neurath to be prescient, in that the pioneering work especially of Simon Kuznets, starting in the 1920s, as well as other economists, like Colin Clark in the 1930s, did lead to the formulation of a set of key macroeconomic measures, including 'national income', 'gross national product', and ultimately 'gross domestic product', each of which depended upon and was composed through a monetary calculation. Much of the purpose of ecological economics was to challenge the explanatory power of these measures and to posit alternatives that might better capture the phenomena contributing to a better, rather than worse, quality of life.

Neurath laid out a detailed case that most of the standard measures used in economics were not 'natural' choices but rather were the product, or as he preferred to call it, 'derivatives of money calculation', and hence were accorded their role as standards only because they conformed to the terms of a specific economic order. While Neurath set these monetary measures against other possibilities that might obtain in a socialist economic order (Neurath [1925] 2004), these alternative measures or indices were typically conceived as gauging 'happiness' (or 'social happiness') and the 'quality of life'. These alternatives would most likely be raised in more recent times as the means of measuring, to the extent possible, the value of economic activity or the state of development of various countries from an ecological standpoint, and not necessarily informed by a socialist perspective like Neurath's (but not precluding it either).

Neurath began by casting the "adequacy" of "money calculation" as illusory, describing "how extraordinarily crude the basis is on which the money order is founded as a matter of fact", whose origins and prominence can be attributed to "tradition and accidents of history" (Neurath [1917] 2004: 339) He then proceeded to walk through a number of examples to elaborate upon this contention.

The first term Neurath took up was 'cost accounting', which he saw as linked to the marginalist construct of utility and disutility, corresponding to a calculus of pleasure and pain. "Cost accounting ... sees in the opposition of pleasure and pain the very essence of all economic accounting" (Neurath [1917] 2004: 335). Neurath challenged specifically the treatment of work that informed the model devised by Jevons, in which labor is measured as the disutility of pain, and leisure, the absence of work, the utility of pleasure. Neurath noted: "There may be work that is performed with pleasure, and results of work which cause pain. Should now the pleasure of work be added to utility, the pain of result to cost?" (Neurath [1917] 2004: 335) One is reminded here of Veblen's critique of the marginalist construct of labor, including his evocation of the "instinct for workmanship" that would accord with Neurath's view of the pleasure that work might provide.

As a 'derivative of money calculation', cost accounting devolves into the following: "[C]ost then corresponds to expense, utility to income, the difference either gain or loss" (Neurath [1917] 2004: 335). This in turn is tied to a false notion of efficiency: "[R]eal life often behaves differently from money. Sometimes it can be more economical to undertake something which according to cost accounting would cause a negative difference, namely, if in other cases the negative differences would be even larger" (Neurath [1917] 2004: 335). It was Neurath's contention that money calculations only countenanced economic actions to be efficient if a "positive difference" could be produced, as he sought instead to advance a calculus capturing "phenomena of higher and lower pleasure" (and no oppositional pairing of pleasure and pain, another of those commonly constructed dichotomies, was necessary). Thus, the mathematical structure Neurath employed was, once again, an ordinal system of ranking.

The second term Neurath took on was 'factors of production', or the theory thereof. Here the challenge centered upon questioning the validity of valuing a 'totality' or 'complex' as the sum of the value of its component parts. Neurath proceeded by an analogy with machinery: "Such procedure is reminiscent of the attempt to apportion the performance of a steam engine to boiler, pistons, valves, etc." (Neurath [1917] 2004: 336) He then added:

> But the theory of factors becomes intelligible at once when we think of it as applied within money calculation and as charged with the task of establishing relations between money prices of parts of the condition of life with money prices of partial causes of the condition of life, or of investigating the distribution of money sums to profit-making enterprises.
>
> (Neurath [1917] 2004: 336)

Neurath then tackled the subject and measurement of consumption. He announced his basic premise at the outset:

> Given our own approach to economic efficiency, it seems appropriate to comprehend also work and illness under the concept which covers food, clothing, housing, theatre visits, etc. These things, however, are not part of the [current] concept of consumption and real income, which covers only what appears as a reflection of money income.
>
> (Neurath [1917] 2004: 336)

As was his wont, Neurath posited hypothetical examples, here putting forth numerical combinations of different wages and levels of consumption in order to demonstrate the disjuncture – Neurath called it a "contradiction" – "between real income and quality of life" (Neurath [1917] 2004: 336)

In light of Neurath's firm conviction of the centrality of statistics in constructing a scientific sociology, it does seem worthwhile to ask why these examples, so crucial to his case for turning to alternative measures and advancing an inchoate version of ecological economics, were not drawn from real life. Might it be possible that Neurath's embrace of combinatorics, which served him well in his critique of marginalism's narrow focus upon price theory and its transformation of economic experience into utility, does not square all that well with his equally enthusiastic embrace of statistics? One might not unfairly contend that this represents a translation of the often revisited tension between the abstracted and the empirical.

In the event, Neurath ended his disquisition on the flaws in the "current concept of consumption" by leaping from the microeconomic to the macroeconomic: "What can be said about the real income of the individual also applies to national income" (Neurath [1917] 2004: 336).

His critique then centered upon what would emerge as perhaps the most fundamental measure of the macroeconomy as the twentieth century unfolded: national income. Curiously, Neurath would argue that a shift from monetary to in-kind measurement of national income would not require "alter[ing] … the theoretical structure" (Neurath [1917] 2004: 338–339). Yet one might well conceive of national income and wealth differently, that is, constructed in a substantially different way, as indeed it appears Neurath set out to do quite cogently. He began with a conceptual reformation:

> We need the concept of the totality of conditions of life, which is not identical with the national income during a period; nor is the concept of the basis of life at a certain moment identical with the national wealth at this moment.
>
> (Neurath [1917] 2004: 337)

He elaborated as follows: "Among liabilities, national wealth recognizes foreign debt, but not swamps causing disease; among assets a quarry will figure, but not the power of invention" (Neurath [1917] 2004: 337).

This was then linked to a second conceptual reformulation or transformation, this time with regard to the nature of economic efficiency:

> The computation of national wealth and national income in money terms is always a questionable affair from the viewpoint of our treatment of economic efficiency, since money prices stand only in an indirect relation to the quality of life and mainly serve to express the distribution of purchasing power and the money order as such.
>
> (Neurath [1917] 2004: 337)

Neurath introduced the notion that the disjuncture noted above "becomes especially obvious" when the state intervenes in the setting of prices, vitiating the attachment of "uniform purchasing power" to the "money unit". At first blush, this appears to be a self-referential construction, where money's role as a standard measure for accounting and exchange has been weakened, owing to the state's superseding it in crucial areas of economic activity; how could this be otherwise?

However, it is clear that Neurath saw this in relation to actual changes that had occurred in the more industrialized countries by the early twentieth century, with increasingly large production entities, cartelization, and dominant financial institutions, setting the stage for a new role for the state (Neurath [1920] 2004: 372–374). With the advent of war, the command economy came to fruition in quite powerful ways, and offered a model that Neurath embraced in the postwar period. This, I suspect, was intended less to be a hypothetical projection than a picture of the present as it seemed likely to unfold into the future.

From the study of 'Bodenkultur' to 'multidimensional classification'

There is a biographical strand worth exploring in assessing Neurath's affinity for ecological economics. It might be possible to trace Neurath's interest in this field to his familiarity, at an early age, with the Hochschule für Bodenkultur in Vienna. The school, now a university, had been founded in 1872 and had a practical and technical bent in its curriculum, and, one suspects, a somewhat more popular appeal or outlook than more established academic institutions in Vienna. It emphasized the natural sciences and engineering, as well as the social and economic sciences, all with the goal of managing natural resources. The name 'Bodenkultur' actually translates as 'soil culture', so that natural resources, both in terms of their availability and their use, remained front and center, even if a more contemporary connotation of 'ecology' would no doubt be anachronistic.

Neurath's father, Wilhelm, taught at the Hochschule für Bodenkultur for many years, as did the mathematician and physicist Oskar Simony. Among the four figures listed as special influences upon Neurath's intellectual formation in the acknowledgment to his 1906 dissertation on the economy of classical antiquity are Wilhelm Neurath and Simony (Neurath 1906: 34). Wilhelm Neurath is cited extensively in Otto Neurath's writings, either with regard to a more historical approach to political economy or as one of several figures found in a listing of Neurath's major influences, a common feature in many of his writings. By contrast, references to Simony are few and far between, but when they do appear, they highlight Simony's work on topology and the avenue topology opened up to deploying qualitative forms of measurement and bases for comparison in economics (see, for example, Neurath [1921] 1973: 188).

These influences are reflected in the ecological framework underlying the thesis of Neurath's 1939 text, *Modern Man in the Making,* recapped in his brief critique of James Burnham entitled "Planning or Managerial Revolution".

In seeking to create a "multidimensional classification" of economies and societies, "[Neurath] started in all such cases with 'silhouettes'. We select a multiplicity of qualifications, each of which may be presented in different degrees. We so get a rich field of colour with many hues and shades" (Neurath [1943] 2004: 531).

To what extent should Neurath's advocacy of "multidimensional classification" and his championing of "topological orders of classification" (see especially his 1937 piece on the logical theory of types) be seen as contributing to and informing an ecological economics? By one measure one might view it as an essential feature, in that it gives much wider berth to the qualitative and at the same time diminishes in certain crucial respects more conventional quantitative measures. As constructed in *Modern Man in the Making* the 'multidimensional classification' of economies and societies presented a picture that hews closely to those more recently devised by those seeking alternative indices to measures like GDP and national income. How "rich [a] field of colour" is produced may remain an open question, but it is undeniable that Neurath's approach is grounded in logical or mathematical consistency, that is, that a qualitative version of multiplicity follows from the multiple possibilities derived from combinatorics.

Of course, one should not overlook Neurath's alignment of this multiplicity with his theory of economic value and his express goal of realizing the greatest 'social' happiness. In *Modern Man in the Making* Neurath introduced a country-wide 'profile of happiness', which he contrasted with the capacity of a nation to produce or its aggregate level of consumption.

> How different are the 'silhouettes' of various nations! For good or evil, rich and poor states form the international background with its periods of prosperity and depression, with its production and destruction, with its war and peace. These rough contrasts do not present an adequate 'profile of happiness' within a particular nation.
>
> (Neurath 1939: 93)

He went on to posit the role of social conflict in shaping the "social environment in which modern man grew up" and the consequent 'profiles of happiness' (Neurath 1939: 93).

It is worth asking if latter-day ecological economists have shunted aside or effectively dropped the logical or mathematical grounding which Neurath had provided. Certainly much of environmental economics is built upon the notion of giving externalities, that is, negative ones, and social costs their full due. At the same time, this comes with an acceptance of the conventional approach and framework found in microeconomics, arising out of the paradigm launched by Alfred Marshall, and elaborated upon as a matter of 'economic welfare' by Pigou. By contrast, Neurath did not work within that paradigm, challenging its assumption and construction from the outset in his 1910 and 1911 critiques of the foundations of and the nature of concept formation in political economy.

However, it also must be noted that Neurath's multidimensional classification is based upon selected statistical measures, so it is not strictly qualitative. Instead, its qualitative nature is to be found in the selection of particular statistics as noteworthy; hence, these are the product of an external process, as they cannot be taken and accepted outright except by a convention of some sort or another. In effect one is saying: why these statistics and not those?

Moreover, the choice is limited to available statistics. Neurath saw the royal road to a 'scientific sociology' running through statistics. Here a contradiction, or at least a tension, may arise. Statistics constitute quantifiable measures, gathered typically by the state (hence the origin of the term) or by other institutional sources, like church records of baptisms and deaths. Qualitative judgments – and goals – may accordingly be relegated to secondary status, and so the construction of a richly hued, qualitative silhouette may face significant limitations.

One statistic in particular of which Neurath availed himself in *Modern Man in the Making* highlights the problem. Neurath took as an index of the increasing secularization of Western societies the rise in the suicide rate over the previous two centuries. He based this contention on the notion that Christianity, through its institution of the 'Church', had enjoined against the practice. Hence, an increase in the suicide rate reflected a weakening of the hold of the Church – and religion more generally – on the populations of Western nations that were overwhelmingly Christian (Neurath 1939: 54–56). This must be regarded as more assertion or inference than validated social fact. It also brings to the fore the complications associated with assessing the impact of changing ideas or even changes in customary practices. Has the emphasis upon the observable become simply too reductionist or perhaps not even all that pertinent?

In addition, if the statistical and the topological are seen as proceeding along separate tracks, how exactly will a bridge be built that allows for their merger? Or, will one necessarily take precedence over the other?

The nature of ecological measurement

When one probes Neurath's notion of measurement more deeply, it appears that it not only sets him apart from the marginalists, who, early on, received the brunt of his criticism, but also many socialists.

What, in his view, is the nature of measurement? In place of monetary units Neurath turned to indices or judgments about the quality of life. These, though, are not all of a piece. His construction of complex combinations or constellations of goods and services represents a critique of marginalism from within. Here Neurath proffered his own tables of preferences serving in stark contrast with those put forward by Jevons and Carl Menger. Neurath's tables emphasized ordinality and ordering (or ranking) rather than any form of cardinal measurement. This was consistent with his longstanding interest in and exploration of qualitative measurement and mathematics.

But at least as significant was his emphasis upon complexity, producing a far wider range of possibilities for satisfaction and presumably consumption than that suggested by the marginalists. In itself this complexity would call into question the capacity to construct indifference curves or utility curves, even where the ordinality of preferences had superseded the use of cardinal measurement, as Pareto had shaped them (Neurath 1911: 77–79).

Lurking deeper in Neurath's critique, and separate from his grappling with marginalism from within, was the notion of price differentiation. While alluded to in only a limited way in the early essays, price differentiation, among other things, was intended to sunder the relation between price and quantity as it emerged in and through the Marshallian price adjustment mechanism. For Neurath different levels of output were associated with different prices. No interdependence of price and quantity that could be captured in conventional supply and demand curves could be accepted as a foundational assumption. Thus one can see Neurath's approach to measurement and political economy, already formulated to a significant degree by 1910, in philosophical terms as more generally an assimilation of crucial elements from the German Historical School – and his father Wilhelm Neurath – with his epicurean take on materialist philosophy.

Moreover, Neurath's consciousness of the economy and economic life as part of an ecosystem emerges clearly in his efforts to distinguish his understanding of the nature of measurement with that put forward by socialist thinkers. He begins by shaping and refining the notion of 'utility' as it obtains in a socialist setting: "The socialist economy, by contrast, is concerned with 'utility', with the interest of the social whole and the welfare of all of its members with regard to housing, food, clothing, health, entertainment, etc." (Neurath [1931] 2004: 468).

Such utility must be comprehended as if it were to be measured in what later would be called a 'closed system'. So Neurath states:

> Right at the start it must be determined what this is, the 'interest of the social whole.' Does it include the prevention of the premature exhaustion of coal mines or the karstification of the mountains or, for instance, of the health and strength of the next generation? Once that has been determined at least in outline, it makes sense to ask what is the best use of the existing raw materials, machines, labour power, etc. One has to find the best way to achieve a non-wasteful exploitation of the coal mines, to ensure the health of the next generation, etc.
>
> (Neurath [1931] 2004: 468)

This then spurs the inquiry into the matter of measurement and calculation, or, as Neurath put it: "Now how can this 'best use' be calculated in a socialist economic order?" (Neurath [1931] 2004: 468).

No single unit, according to Neurath, can be found that is suitable, and this includes any reliance upon a labor theory of value.

> For such a socialist calculation there does not exist a unit of the sort which capitalism finds in money. Some had the idea to introduce a certain amount of labour as a unit. But how could this make it possible for the excessive exploitation of a coal mine to figure as a negative entry in the balance? How could a quantity of electricity which a river provides use with be entered as an increase in amounts of labour units? Or the increase in wind power used in the running wind mills?
>
> (Neurath [1931] 2004: 468)

Neurath sharpens his critique of the flaws inherent in the use of a single-unit form of measurement to undergird 'socialist calculation':

> Again and again consideration is given to one or another type of socialist economic calculation with a single unit in order to show, for instance, that the type of economy I is less advantageous than the type of economy II, for I provides 1000 but II provides 1500 units. No author has yet devised a calculation for the entire economy (as Popper-Lynkeus did schematically for his economic plan), instead they rest content with abstract formulations or with a very partial calculation without showing how the calculation of the whole would proceed. This should make us suspicious: let us consider the matter in detail.
>
> (Neurath [1931] 2004: 468–469)

Joan Martinez-Alier has cast the matter of calculation, or the lack of commensurability in assessing the value of economic activity that involves consequences to humans as well as the natural world, in terms of at least two fundamental difficulties. One concerns the limitations of making use of externalities to capture what might be described in the Pigovian treatment of economic welfare as the 'divergence of social cost', in short a critique of the conventional folding of environmental matters in particular into a neoclassical economic framework devised largely by Marshall. Notably Neurath did not pursue this path.

The other is the inability to account for future or intergenerational developments for which unforeseen or unexpected changes by definition cannot be known. Here Martinez-Alier inverts Neurath's utopianism from enthused speculation into rational insight, through his recognition of the necessity of not having one standard unit of measurement. As a result, he characterizes his approach under the oxymoronic title, "ecological economics and concrete utopias". The case he makes translates and updates Neurath's understandings about ecological economics to a host of contemporary ecological issues:

> We must not only decide, therefore, on a rate of discount and on the time horizon but also guess the evolution of technology (use of solar energy, use of water power, use of nuclear power, to which we would add considerations on global warming, on acid rain, on radioactive pollution, which Neurath could have mentioned). Because of this heterogeneity, a decision on which plan to implement could not be reached on the basis of a common unit of measurement. Elements of the economy were not commensurable, hence the need for a *Naturalrechnung*.
>
> (Martinez-Alier 1992: 41)

Martinez-Alier, joining with Munda and O'Neill, took the further step of challenging traditional economic methods of reaching a common measure to value the environment, broadly understood to be "a site of conflict between competing values and interests and different groups and communities that represent them" (Martinez-Alier, O'Neill, and Munda 1999: 37). They cast traditional economic methods of doing so as, curiously, "utilitarian", intent on balancing gains and losses through a series of trade-offs, allowing for the internalization of such calculations through a system of "interpersonal compensability". They contended that such methods, whether through cost-benefit analysis or cost-efficient accounting, failed to "provide adequate principles for rational environmental choices" (Martinez-Alier, O'Neill, and Munda 1999: 38), and saw Neurath as the first figure to lay the groundwork for an ecological alternative.

Neurath and Sen on welfare and measurement

One of the best ways to grasp the presaging role played by Neurath in matters now common to ecological economics and social measurement is through a comparison of the ideas and approach put forward by Neurath about consumption, economic value, and, effectively, economic welfare, with those set forth by Amartya Sen. Through a series of papers and articles written especially in the 1970s and 1980s, many gathered in a compilation entitled *Choice, Welfare and Measurement* (Sen 1982), Sen laid out a detailed challenge to prevailing notions in economic theory about how consumer preferences were comprehended and how economic inequality might be measured, posing an alternative vision of economic welfare.

In their respective work one can mark broad areas of mutual concern and note striking similarities in the framing of the major questions to be addressed. At the same time there is a dramatic difference in the body of economic thought and applicable techniques within and through which each of them shaped their program, extending on occasion to the language employed. Without question Sen's approach is far more detailed, and accordingly it enabled him to engage in dialogue and debate in the contemporary discourse of economics, but Neurath's insights hold their own in laying out many of the essential issues involved. Unlike Neurath, Sen paid more specific attention to matters linking legal constructions, like voting, with economic welfare, as one might analyze the scope and limitations of the Arrow 'Impossibility Theorem', and made a conscious effort to address economic issues in terms of moral philosophy.

First to the areas of mutual concern: at the outset both saw their work as a challenge to the prevailing orthodoxy in economics, which were rooted in the foundational assumptions underlying it. And so Neurath presented his first major essays about economic theory as 'critiques' of the theory of the social sciences. He specifically called into question the theoretical foundations of economics in the 1917 essay from which his criticism of the conventional language of measurement, discussed above, was drawn in some detail. For his part, Sen spoke of the shortcomings of the commonly held assumption of 'rationality' in economics as narrowly conceived, the central subject of an essay entitled

"Rational Fools: A Critique of the Behavioural Foundations of Economic Theory" (Sen 1982: 84–106).

Sen made extensive use of the language of 'choices' and 'preferences', a reflection of the state of microeconomic consumer theory by the second half of the twentieth century, while Neurath, not surprisingly, did not. Nonetheless, both saw the standard view held in their own time of consumer choices, whether through simple tables of marginal utilities, as configured by Jevons, Menger, or Pareto, or through convex sets and the axioms of revealed preference, as hypothesized by Samuelson, as failing to capture the vast array of possible choices actually available.

This was so even if the typical – if limited – schema of preferences were attributed to situations arising out of competitive markets. To this they both introduced the greater complexity associated with distinguishing between market and non-market settings, as well as that which arose as a result of the inclusion of non-competitive situations.

In general terms Neurath appealed for consideration of 'quality of life' as the appropriate benchmark of consumer satisfaction; this extended to the maximization of 'social happiness' as the true measure of national wealth. Sen's frame of reference was similar, though his inquiry into the economic perquisites of human behavior was substantially more detailed than that of Neurath. Sen framed the matter of consumer satisfaction as going beyond the bounds set by what was presumed to be rational behavior. Other life events and issues routinely intervene. For example, how ought one take into account "[d]ecisions regarding work ethics, job choice, where to live, whether to strike, etc." (Sen 1982: 6)? What about the problem posed by "the interdependence between different people's welfare" (Sen 1982: 6)? Moreover, one should not overlook the importance of 'sympathy' and 'commitment' in limning human behavior (Sen 1982: 7–8). Sen, like Neurath, challenged what has come to be a central notion in welfare economics, namely that "social welfare … [is] a function of individual utilities only" (Sen 1982: 328), where, moreover, its construction is limited to 'utility information', narrowly conceived at that (Sen 1982: 336).

Both Neurath and Sen viewed the extant standard theory of consumer behavior as informed by a superfluous set of psychological assumptions intended, as Sen would put it, to flesh out the model of the 'rational' consumer or economic agent. For Neurath this represented the mingling of the psychological with the economic, where he saw the price theory of the marginalists as effectively a 'purely psychological theory'. It also could be comprehended as an example of the 'auxiliary motive' or 'auxiliary hypothesis' that Neurath posited as an essential element in the construction of models, including economic ones. For his part, Sen saw the necessity of positing a far more complex psychology underlying economic behavior to make it explicable and subject to genuine economic analysis.

One can also discern a community of interest between Neurath and Sen in matters of measurement, though with certain cautions. Neurath devoted much of his efforts to overturning the use of and any reliance upon 'monetary calculation', making a 'natural' form of calculation an essential element in his case for and the construction of alternative forms of measurement. By contrast, Sen did not.

Nonetheless, both sought to develop ways of measuring economic value that challenged reigning versions. Neurath spoke in terms of maximizing 'social happiness', arising out of social choices regarding 'life situations'; Sen spoke of effectuating forms of 'social measurement'. This took place on a macro-economic plane, and extended to gauging matters of wealth and poverty. Better measures were required, affording deeper insight into the implications of wealth and poverty in everyday economic life. Thus he proposed to devise an appropriate measure for 'real national income' and called for an 'ethical measurement of inequality', to gauge more precisely the nature and scope of poverty. For Neurath the focus upon wealth and poverty represented the original course upon which political economy was first built. Consequently marginalism and neoclassical economics had deviated along a mistaken path. Notably both sought to increase the reliance upon ordinal measurement or scaling systems to gauge economic value.

Furthermore, both placed great weight on capturing and accounting for that which was observable. This entailed questioning the standard approaches used for empirical verification. In Neurath's hands this meant adopting a physicalist comprehension of the observables, making all scientific statements be in accord with a Machian measure of observable sensations. For Sen it was a matter of recognizing the limited nature of any actual testing of what were in reality only hypothesized outcomes of consumer choices, and thus remained theoretical suppositions.

'No teleology, no imperative'

Yet it is also the case that Neurath's theoretical framework for his ecologically-minded economics may complicate matters somewhat. In his 1935 tract laying out what is meant by a 'rational theory of economics', Neurath boldly asserted that the constitution of it barred the introduction of an underlying teleology or imperative (Neurath 1935: 10–11). Such a theory, he added, was a logical construction unencumbered nor limited or shaped by historical circumstance. Both of these claims require substantial and substantive scrutiny, as they go to the heart of Neurath's scientific project, yet appear to raise elements and assumptions that are at odds with, or even contradict, other notions, largely philosophical in nature, that were essential to Neurath's program and outlook, and nowhere more so than in what constitutes an ecological economics.

First, there is the challenge raised to the notion that a rational economic theory might be driven by an imperative and guided by a teleology. At the outset of the tract Neurath made the case that what economics measured as a science was human 'welfare', gauging matters of wealth and poverty. He had long taken that position, contending in his 1910 essay on the theory of the social sciences that it had occupied the thinking of the earliest economists.

Now in the 1935 tract he went further. He began by noting a metaphorical correspondence, identifying the origins of the term 'welfare' (Wohlstand) in the realm of public health, then applied more broadly, and thus extended to political economy (Neurath 1935: 9). Here Neurath's attunement to the nature and role of language in shaping economic concepts is once again evident.

Then, he turned to address the difficulty posed by choosing human welfare as the proper subject of economics. Did not such a choice mean that there was an underlying teleology associated with economics? Elsewhere, Neurath had spoken of maximizing social happiness, so that it would seem to provide a goal that might guide economics, one which was intended to counter the notion of maximizing individual utility via exchange, the view that had become dominant in the marginalist and neoclassical schools of thought. To this one might apply the paradox noted by Max Weber in the controversy over value-judgments in economics: was the rejection of the goal – and teleology – of marginalist and neoclassical thought merely replaced by a different goal – and teleology, and hence was subject to the criticism that it too represented a particular and limited worldview?

Neurath demurred. He claimed that the strenuous adoption and use of the physicalist construction of language, with 'carefully formed definitions', could establish observable states of affairs without requiring the acceptance of any specific goal regarding the nature or purpose of economics.

But was this defensible? Did not any choice of framework, in and of itself, call forth an act of consciousness, informed by the need to interpret (and thus to rely upon the meanings of terms and concepts)? Moreover, was it not motivated by an ethical standard of some sort? In fact, this latter consideration in particular may be seen as underlying the ecological economics that Neurath helped set in motion. Hence, was it possible for a physicalist construction to override, obviate, or circumvent any such act of consciousness and choice, so as to produce a non-ideological framework or structure? In that regard, how far might the 'naturalistic' approach to the foundations of scientific inquiry emphasized by Jordi Cat, among others, lead to that result?

One must also consider the curious possible linkage between Neurath and the Austrian school of economics raised by Thomas Uebel and Cat through a shared reliance on some form of 'decision theory' (Uebel 2004: 10; Cat 2014). While there is good reason to question the firmness or even existence of such a link, should it hold it would strengthen further the case that an economic teleology was very much in play, as it placed conscious acts at the center of any framework, where presumably there were a multiplicity of possible alternatives.

This notion of an Austrian-school connection may well turn out to be mistaken. See, for example, the review of *Otto Neurath: Economic Writings 1904–1945,* especially Uebel's lengthy and detailed introduction, by Giandomenica Becchio (2008). Cat, it should be noted, took up the theme of Neurath's being an 'Austrian economist, with a difference', in an extended piece delineating Neurath's economic thought from a philosophical standpoint, in the *Stanford Encyclopedia of Philosophy* (Cat 2014).

A second concern arises, this time with regard to the very existence of a teleology in economics. When economics is likened to evolutionary biology, it is suggested that the teleology associated with 'natural selection' might somehow be applied to economic change and development, or that an inherent process of change and development, ultimately transformative, might be found, corresponding to 'natural selection', say through pathways of greater efficiency. The problematic nature of such a correspondence was explored by Elias Khalil (1990), Khalil and Boulding (1996) and later taken up by Turk (2009).

By contrast, Neurath seemed to focus less upon the possible pathways and more upon the ends, that is, the state and scope of social happiness, for which different and differing processes might be evaluated as to their capacity and efficacy in achieving these ends. Nonetheless, his pairing of the idea of an 'imperative' with that of 'teleology' points to his understanding that the internal mechanisms driving toward the ends described were also at issue. Neurath's 'instrumentalist' approach, built upon the work and ideas of Mach, Poincaré, and Duhem, would serve to mitigate the need to identify such mechanisms.

What was Neurath trying to achieve? Did he think that a physicalist construction of all pertinent statements about 'social happiness' and 'wealth and poverty' would provide an objective picture or account of the framework for economics such that it was no more subjective, ideological, or even purposeful than physics, as he stated in the 1935 tract? Would accepting or embracing a teleology of social epicureanism, or any other teleology for that matter, undermine the cause of the 'unity of science', as it would produce a division across the sciences between the teleological and the non-teleological disciplines, a revisiting of sorts of the neo-Kantian division very much in evidence in central European thought at the turn of the twentieth century? And, as Ernest Nagel, a philosopher of science within the broader orbit of the logical empiricist movement, has pointed out, biology – and evolutionary biology – might prove to be exemplars of a teleologically based science, but quite distinct from any proffered teleology that might surface in the social sciences (Nagel 1961: 531–535).

Philosophy of science and ecological economics

I have focused primarily on the content of what I have described as Neurath's inchoate ecological economics, a precursor to the formal subfield that would emerge in the last decades of the twentieth century. In this it has been necessary to attend to the assumptions underlying such content, like Neurath's emphasis upon the importance of qualitative forms of measurement, as well as to the framework in which it is set; for example, capturing both positive and negative effects and outcomes of economic activity, widely cast.

Neurath's role in laying the intellectual groundwork for a set of ideas that would assume substantive shape in the independent subfield of ecological economics, though, may be extended to matters of methodology by embracing concerns about the pertinent epistemology that ought to inform the discipline and, more generally, the philosophy of science appropriate to its advancement.

In a series of articles appearing in the journal *Ecological Economics,* Clive Spash (2012) has presented a challenge to prevailing notions of methodological pluralism or neutrality that have come to dominate the subfield and the appropriation by it of the concepts, techniques, and assumptions of neoclassical economics. In Spash's view, ecological economics has mistakenly been taken to be a combination of existing and by now conventional resource economics and environmental economics. Moreover, Spash is explicit about the social and political implications of pursuing this line of inquiry, hewing to convention as well, and, by the same token, the imperative of changing course.

Spash's critique is rooted in a vision of logical empiricism, advanced by the 'left wing' of the Vienna Circle, that he sees as nuanced in its approach to achieving the necessary unity of the natural and social sciences, critical to the joining of economic inquiry and analysis to the comprehension of ecosystems.

As Spash himself noted, the 'left wing' of the Vienna Circle has traditionally been taken to include Philipp Frank, Hans Hahn, and Otto Neurath, with Rudolf Carnap a later addition. Without question, though, the figure among them that stands out in Spash's case for adopting a methodology and a philosophy of science drawn from this nuanced version of logical empiricism is Otto Neurath. That is evident in the conclusion to Spash's 2012 article entitled, "New Foundations for Ecological Economics" (Spash 2012: 36–47). "The continued support for mathematical formalism and quantification as providing the sole means to scientific rigour and validity is damaging to an alternative vision for ecological economics" (Spash 2012: 45). He then elaborates upon the terms on which such an alternative would be based:

> After over two decades the time for a more progressive stance on the philosophy of science appropriate for ecological economics is overdue. Ecological economics has an empirical aspect and some possible intellectual roots amongst members of the left Vienna Circle.
>
> (Spash 2012: 45)

One might add to this Neurath's rejection of many of the assumptions, concepts, and constructions that have shaped neoclassical economics, thereby bringing to bear not only Neurath's philosophy of science, as Spash has done, but also his economic thought in grounding a twenty-first century ecological economics.

Spash's article presents yet another matter of contention and controversy regarding Neurath and the Vienna Circle. In this piece Spash fought a rear-guard battle over the nature of logical empiricism, noted above in brief, taking up concerns raised by Neurath scholars like Cat, Uebel, and O'Neill, among others. On the one hand, the claim has been made that logical positivism, associated closely with the Vienna Circle, forms the basis in the philosophy of science for neoclassical economics, supposedly because it relies solely upon observation statements and logical formalism. On the other, the Neurath scholars cited above would characterize that understanding of logical positivism as lacking nuance or even representing a gross caricature. Uebel, for example, produced a lengthy study with the insightful title and thesis that Neurath had "overcome" logical positivism from within (Uebel 1992).

The contemporary philosopher Hilary Putnam has introduced yet another vantage point in this debate. Drawing in part upon the work of Vivian Walsh, Putnam contended that a 'fact/value' dichotomy posited by the logical positivists held sway over many "influential economists" of the mid-twentieth century (Putnam 2011: 284–285, 290).

From the perspective of the history of economic thought it would be nothing short of remarkable if Otto Neurath, an unorthodox economist (who in more contemporary parlance would clearly be thought of as 'heterodox'), whose work in political economy has long been obscured and largely neglected, had somehow played a leading part in shaping the underpinnings of neoclassical, that is, mainstream economics in the latter half of the twentieth century. Would the caricatured version of logical positivism fill – and fulfill – this role?

In the manifesto that launched publicly the Vienna Circle, for which Neurath was the prime author, he did list both Karl Marx and Carl Menger as the two economic thinkers who supported a 'scientific conception of the world' and sought to eliminate metaphysics from science. I have my doubts about any such major role for logical positivism in underpinning mainstream economics, certainly as it was espoused by Neurath. For one, as the references to Marx and Menger show, he took note specifically of the diversity in views, approaches, and perspectives of those engaged in the study of political economy who adhered to a 'scientific conception of the world'. Second, and this may be crucial in considering the long arc of the history of economic thought, clear statements of philosophy – let alone coherent or consistent ones – seem generally to be lacking among practitioners of economics, as distinct from its methodologists, who have typically been cast apart.

References

Becchio, Giandomenica (2008) "Review of Otto Neurath: Economic Writings/Selections, 1904–1945." *Journal of Economic Behavior and Organization* 66(2): 440–444.

Boulding, Kenneth E. (1978) *Ecodynamics: A New Theory of Societal Evolution*. Beverly Hills: Sage Publications.

Cat, Jordi (2014) "Otto Neurath". https://plato.stanford.edu/archives/spring2014/entries/neurath/, first published August 15, 2010.

Costanza, Robert (1989) "What is Ecological Economics?" *Ecological Economics* 1(1): 1–12.

Khalil, Elias L. (1990) "Entropy Law and Exhaustion of Natural Resources: Is Nicholas Georgescu-Roegen's Paradigm Defensible?" *Ecological Economics* 2(2): 163–178.

Khalil, Elias L. and Boulding, Kenneth E., eds. (1996) *Evolution, Order, and Complexity*. London: Routledge.

Lessman, Ortrud (2008) "A Similar Line of Thought in Neurath and Sen: Interpersonal Comparability". In Elisabeth Nemeth et al., eds., *Otto Neurath's Economics in Context*. Dordrecht: Springer, pp. 115–130.

Martinez-Alier, Joan (1984) *L'ecologisme i l'economia: historia d'unes relacions amagados.* Barcelona: Edicions 62.

Martinez-Alier, Joan (1992) "Ecological Economics and Concrete Utopias". *Utopian Studies* 3(1): 39–52.

Martinez-Alier, Joan, Munda, Giuseppe, and O'Neill, John (1999) "Commensurability and Compensability in Ecological Economics". In Martin O'Connor and Clive L. Spash, eds., *Valuation and the Environment.* Cheltenham, UK: Edward Elgar Publishers.

Nagel, Ernst (1961) *The Structure of Science.* New York: Harcourt, Brace & World, Inc.

Neurath, Otto (1906) *Zur Anschauung der Antike uber Handel, Gewerbe und Landwirtschaft.* Jena: G. Fischer.

Neurath, Otto [1910] (2004) "Theory of the Social Sciences". In Robert S. Cohen and Thomas E. Uebel, eds., *Otto Neurath: Economic Writings Selections, 1904–1945.* [Multiple translators]. Dordrecht: Kluwer Academic Publishing, pp. 265–291.

Neurath, Otto (1911) "Nationalokonomie und Wertlehre, eine systematische Untersuchung". *Zeitschrift für Volkswirtschaft, Sozialpolitik und Verwaltung* 20: 52–114.

Neurath, Otto [1917] (2004) "Conceptual Structure of Economic Theory and Its Foundations". In Robert S. Cohen and Thomas E. Uebel, eds., *Otto Neurath: Economic Writings/Selections, 1904–1945.* [Multiple translators]. Dordrecht: Kluwer Academic Publishers, pp. 312–341.

Neurath, Otto [1919] (1973) "From War Economy to In-Kind Economy". In Marie Neurath and Robert S. Cohen, eds., *Empiricism and Sociology.* Trans. Paul Foulkes and Marie Neurath. Dordrecht: Reidel, pp. 123–157.

Neurath, Otto [1920] (2004) "Total Socialisation". In Robert S. Cohen and Thomas E. Uebel, eds., *Otto Neurath: Economic Writings/Selections 1904–1945.* [Multiple translators]. Dordrecht: Kluwer Academic Publishers, pp. 371–404.

Neurath, Otto [1921] (1973) *Anti-Spengler.* In Marie Neurath and Robert S. Cohen, eds., *Empiricism and Sociology.* Trans. Paul Foulkes and Marie Neurath. Dordrecht: Reidel, pp. 158–213.

Neurath, Otto [1925] (2004) "Socialist Utility Calculation and Capitalist Profit Calculation". In Robert S. Cohen and Thomas E. Uebel, eds., *Otto Neurath: Economic Writings/Selections 1904–1945.* [Multiple translators]. Dordrecht: Kluwer Academic Publishers, pp. 466–472.

Neurath, Otto [1928] (1973) "Personal Life and Class Struggle". In Marie Neurath and Robert S. Cohen, eds., *Empiricism and Sociology.* Trans. Paul Foulkes and Marie Neurath. Dordrecht: Reidel, pp. 249–298.

Neurath, Otto [1931] (1973) "Empirical Sociology". In Marie Neurath and Robert S. Cohen, eds., *Empiricism and Sociology.* Trans. Paul Foulkes and Marie Neurath. Dordrecht: Reidel, pp. 313–421.

Neurath, Otto [1931] (2004) "The Current Growth in Global Productive Capacity". In Robert S. Cohen and Thomas E. Uebel, eds., *Otto Neurath: Economic Writings/Selections 1904–1945.* [Multiple translators]. Dordrecht: Kluwer Academic Publishers, pp. 475–505.

Neurath, Otto (1935) *Was bedeutet rationale Wirtschaftsbetrachtung?*Wien: Verlag Gerold & Co.

Neurath, Otto (1939) *Modern Man in the Making.* New York & London: A.A. Knopf.

Neurath, Otto [1943] (2004) "Planning or Managerial Revolution?" In Robert S. Cohen and Thomas E. Uebel, eds., *Otto Neurath: Economic Writings/Selections, 1904–1945.* [Multiple translators]. Dordrecht: Kluwer Academic Publishers, pp. 527–538.

O'Neill, John (1999) "Ecology, Socialism and Austrian Economics". In E. Nemeth and R. Heinrich, eds., *Otto Neurath: Rationalität, Planning, Vielfalt.* Vienna: Weiner Reihe, pp. 123–145.

Pigou, A. C. (1924) *Economic Welfare*. 2nd edn. London: Macmillan.
Putnam, Hilary [2011] (2012) "The Fact/Value Dichotomy and Its Critics". In Mario De Caro and David Macarthur, eds., *Philosophy in an Age of Science*. Cambridge, MA: Harvard University Press, pp. 283–298.
Sen, Amartya (1982) *Choice, Welfare, and Measurement*. Cambridge, MA: Harvard University Press.
Spash, Clive (2012) "New Foundations for Ecological Economics". *Ecological Economics* 77: 36–47.
Turk, Michael (2009) "Economics Pursuing the Mold of Evolutionary Biology". In Pierre Pontarotti, ed., *Evolutionary Biology: Concepts, Modeling, Applications*. Heidelberg: Springer Publishers, pp. 379–392.
Uebel, Thomas E. (1992) *Overcoming Logical Positivism from Within*. Amsterdam: Rodopi.
Uebel, Thomas E. (2004) "Introduction: Neurath's Economics in Critical Context". In Robert S. Cohen and Thomas E. Uebel, eds., *Otto Neurath: Economic Writings/Selections 1904–1945*. [Multiple translators]. Dordrecht: Kluwer Academic Publishers, pp. 1–108.
Wong, Stanley (1978) *The Foundations of Paul Samuelson's Revealed Preference Theory*. London: Routledge & Kegan Paul.

6 Neurath, Sraffa, and the problem with prices

Otto Neurath and Piero Sraffa, both of whom could be identified as having strong associations with Marxism, if in unorthodox fashion, offered up two of the most important critiques of the conventional understanding and treatment of the role of prices in economic thought over the course of the twentieth century. At first blush one might cast both of these critiques within the context of their criticism of capitalism as an economic system. Yet the differences in their approach to the 'problem with prices' are perhaps as striking as their commonly held depiction of a diminished place for prices in analyzing the operation of the economy. How they made their distinctive cases is the subject of this chapter.

A brief retrospective on prices in economic thought

How central a role should prices play in the construction of economic structures intended to describe the maintenance and stability of economic systems, large and small? The answer might seem obvious, as conventional models set prices as the means for attaining the resolution of markets, reduced at times to the basis for settling the interplay of supply and demand through establishing the going or equilibrium price.

One might see this expressed in a variety of ways, reflecting not insignificant differences in the approaches and perspectives put forward by major schools of economic thought. The neoclassical school, adopting the somewhat curious format laid out by its perhaps most seminal figure, Alfred Marshall, sets the price as the independent variable depicted along a vertical axis that adjusts between projected imbalances between quantity supplied and quantity demanded, producing – instantaneously or through a process of convergence – the diminution of any such excess to a nullity. For Marshall these were also independently determined microeconomic markets, set in isolation from one another through the adoption of ceteris paribus conditions, and hence represented separate partial equilibria.

A variant of this notion has been advanced especially over the course of the twentieth century in which prices are treated as embodying all pertinent information from and about the market, so that market prices necessarily reflect an efficient outcome of market forces. This is commonly known as the 'efficient market hypothesis', and it has gained support both from within and without the neoclassical school by those economists who have set store to price theory as the core of economic theorizing.

However, if one were to step back farther in time, one would have to contend with the classical school's treatment of prices, which even at first encounter appears to be quite distinct from that put forward by the neoclassical school. Adam Smith spoke of both a 'market price' and a 'natural price', where the former represented a resolution of current market arrangements, more loosely thought of as supply and demand (but not necessarily as the supply and demand schedules formalized more than a century later by Marshall), while the latter captured the costs of production, what might be taken to constitute effectively supply conditions (Smith [1776] 1976). It was Smith's hope and expectation that the short-term variations in market prices would, in the end, tend toward the natural price, a sentiment not shared by the next generation of classical economists, most notably, David Ricardo, nor, obviously, even later by Karl Marx.

Nonetheless, Smith's conception of prices linked it closely to the classical school's labor theory of value, but also cast prices in a way that made it possible to subsume them under a related economic notion, that of productivity. Indeed, an exhaustive study of centuries of historical data about costs, prices, and standard of living by the twentieth-century French economist Jean Fourastié placed productivity at the center of any assessment of economic activity and development over time, and relegated prices to a dependent variable of it (Fourastié 1958).

There are other strains in the primacy accorded prices in either the classical or the neoclassical treatment of them. Marshall's graphical diagram of microeconomic markets, with quantities measured along the horizontal axis and prices along the vertical, seemed to defy the common logic of the disposition of independent and dependent variables in analytical geometry. Marshall's contemporary, Leon Walras, reweighted the role of quantities and prices, privileging the former over the latter, so that Walras' schema for a general equilibrium laid out first the quantities of inputs and output in each sector of the economy and then introduced equilibrating prices through the device of an 'invisible auctioneer', somehow able to telescope a temporal process of convergence across all markets into an instant (known as "tâtonnement"). In Paul Samuelson's hands the process of reducing excess demand in individual markets could be applied, writ large, to the economy as a whole, thus melding the price adjustment mechanism to the macroeconomy.

Hence, criticisms of these approaches to the nature and role of prices might range from challenges to the theoretical assumptions upon which each of these constructs rested to the broader context in which they were placed. For example, Marshall's supply and demand curves might be viewed as projections that did not actually exist, but rather served as hypothetical counterfactuals. The going price might instead be taken to be given and visible, while supply and demand curves were introduced as a theoretical support to explain why that price ought to be understood as the result of a market equilibrium. This then allowed for price changes as these curves were projected to shift with changes in the underlying determinants of supply and demand.

But it would also be the case that these critiques would raise contextual matters. For one, how tenable was Marshall's claim that microeconomic markets could and should be treated separately, in isolation from one another? If this contention was cast in doubt, and the notion of ceteris paribus was voided, what would remain of these microeconomic markets?

Second, to what extent was the neoclassical understanding of the nature and role of prices tied to the wider social setting in which economic activity took place, or even to the economic system in which prices were seen as fulfilling certain economic functions? Where the notion of social setting was invoked, one might see the hand of Institutionalist critics. Simon Kuznets, for example, contended that markets could not be isolated or set apart from their social setting and framework. Kuznets in fact put forth the notion that the social meaning ascribed to markets was far more significant in understanding their functioning than any mechanical rules applied to their generic operation (Kuznets 1941: 3–8).

This Institutionalist frame of reference has its own affinity with a Marxian perspective, in which market prices are set within the framework of the capitalist system. As was often the case, Marxist economists would recast economic theorizing that purported to describe or explain economics in general to one that characterized capitalist economies. So, for example, Paul Sweezy (1942) wrote a treatise entitled, *The Theory of Capitalist Development,* as counterpoint to the tome produced by his mentor, Joseph Schumpeter, entitled *The Theory of Economic Development* (Schumpeter [1912] 1934).

However, Marxists were not the only economic thinkers to highlight the centrality of situating economic theory within a specific economic order. One would find a similar point of view in the thinking of the German Historical School, for whom the study of economic organization and hence of different possible economic orders served as the main task of political economy, as Wilhelm Roscher, one of the school's earliest leading thinkers would have put it (see Neurath [1910] 2004: 270; also Neurath, A. and O. 1910–1913, Vol. 1: 100).

Neurath and Sraffa: 'prelude' to a conceptual critique

It is with this backdrop that it is now possible to turn to the thought and writing of Otto Neurath and Piero Sraffa and their treatment of the role of prices in constituting economic structures and analyzing the economy. There are two common strands that run through their critiques of the mainstream in economic thought prevailing in the time when they were active. Both of them focused critically on the concepts typically employed in economic theorizing, and both of them explored what they saw as a serious disjuncture between price theory, elevated in mainstream thought with the emergence of marginalism and neoclassical economics, and the theory of value, which they identified as the more central matter to be resolved in economics.

Accordingly, Neurath and Sraffa stand apart from the mainstream of economic thought in the twentieth century. Sraffa is often characterized as a leading "heterodox" economist by dint of his work in reformulating and reinvigorating the classical school, setting it more firmly apart from the neoclassical school and in the process providing it with a more contemporary cast, commonly identified as neo-Ricardianism.

Neurath, for a variety of reasons, may prove somewhat more elusive with regard to his characterization as an economist. In part this is because, in the main, his role as an economist has been overshadowed by his work in other fields, be it as the lead organizer of the Vienna Circle of philosophers or as the initiator of the visual language known as Isotype, and in part because his work in economics has been seen largely through the mirror placed by those who opposed him. Nonetheless, there is no question that Neurath's view of and approach to economics constituted a road not taken in economics in the twentieth century.

Neurath and Sraffa also had in common an association with Marxism and, in their economic thought, the construction of a serious challenge to the primacy accorded prices in mainstream economic thought, represented above all by the dominant neoclassical school of the first half of the twentieth century, but also given great weight by the Austrian school.

G.C. Harcourt's appreciation and assessment of Sraffa, contained within his 2003 review of Terenzio Cozzi and Roberto Marchionatti's (2001) set of essays on the occasion of Sraffa's centenary, makes clear that Sraffa saw the need for a conceptual critique of economic theory (see also Harcourt 2012). What is also evident in Sraffa's work is the central place accorded the "standard commodity", which Sraffa devised in order to establish an "invariant measure of value" separate from and independent of the need for a defining system of prices (Bellino 2004: 121). Instead, the "standard commodity" was rooted in physical measures of sustenance to allow for the input of labor, and hence also distinguished from standardized units of labor.

Neurath entered into a critique of economic concepts in his early writings on economic theory, published in 1910 and 1911. For example, one can trace his linkage of observed fact to concept formation in the 1910 article on the "Theory of the Social Sciences", in which he contrasts Wilhelm Wundt's reliance upon "a few examples", noted as the common practice among economists, with Duhem's and Poincaré's plumbing the depth of concepts to "the initial observation of facts" (Neurath [1910] 2004: 269). And it was Neurath who emphasized at every turn that what mattered in economics was establishing a theory of value (Wertlehre in German), where such value was recognized as more qualitative than quantitative. For Neurath the immersion in price theory represented a misdirection, even a false pathway in economics.

Biographical parallels

One can observe certain striking similarities between the two in the tensions between their political activism and perspective, on the one hand, and the trajectory of their academic careers and work, on the other.

Both of them reflected, at various moments in their own thought and careers, the influence of Marxian ideas and approaches, however much they may have limited and shaped those ideas and approaches on their own terms. Even when Neurath singled out Marxian thought as the best route to the establishment and elaboration of a scientific sociology, at least in part because of its roots in a materialist philosophy, his "unorthodox" take on Marxism remained apparent, and was evident in his advocacy of in-kind calculation over money and his enthusiasm for what he called 'scientific utopianism'.

Sraffa, as Bertram Schefold noted, famously told Palmiero Togliatti, the head of the Italian Communist Party, in 1964 that with regard to economics, "Marx had stayed put in the nineteenth century" (Schefold 2005: 550). In particular, this meant steering clear of the Marxian labor theory of value.

Moreover, beyond any association they had with left-wing schools of thought, both engaged in political activity in the heady days after the end of World War I that placed them in serious jeopardy and shaped the arc of their subsequent careers and lives.

Neurath, who had taught for a time at the University of Heidelberg as a junior colleague of Max Weber, plunged into a strenuous effort to promote the 'total socialization' of the economy of Saxony and Bavaria. He accepted the position to head the central planning office of Bavaria at the invitation of its then president, Kurt Eisner, and stayed on in that post through the tumultuous period after Eisner's assassination, the creation of a Bavarian soviet republic, and its overturning by the right-wing Freikorps. Subsequently placed on trial for treason, Neurath was able to gain safe passage to Austria through an agreement reached with Austria's then socialist foreign minister, Otto Bauer.

This proved to be the first of three forced exiles Neurath would experience. The next one came in 1934, when the Austrian prime minister, Engelbert Dollfuss, seized power and was then assassinated in an attempted coup d'état. Consequently, Neurath had to leave Austria. The third occurred in 1940, when Neurath, then living in the Netherlands, had to flee to Great Britain, when the Nazi invasion of Holland took place. It should be noted that after losing his position at Heidelberg, Neurath never again held a similar academic post, working instead through more popular educational forums, like the Social and Economic Museum in Vienna (P. Neurath 1994).

For his part, Sraffa's life and career were altered by the rise of fascism in Italy in the early 1920s. He had found himself in the crosshairs of Mussolini's forces when he wrote a critical piece about Mussolini's monetary policy shortly after his ascension to power, which Mussolini's supporters had attempted – unsuccessfully – to get Sraffa to retract.

Nerio Naldi has described Sraffa's early career in politics in Italy, which would precede his turning to academics and an academic life in economics in England:

> Upon his re-entry in Italy in June 1922, Piero Sraffa, known as a communist to the Italian police, most likely attracted the attention of fascist

> groups. In fact, he had been appointed direttore of Milan Province's Labour Office, a post that included aspects of a more explicitly political-organizing nature. Sraffa resigned from that post on 2 December 1922, just after the collapse of the socialist administration of the Province of Milan (led by his friend Nino Levi).
>
> (Naldi 2005: 382)

In the end, Sraffa went into exile in England, but was able to secure a place in Cambridge University, thanks largely to the auspices of John Maynard Keynes. Unlike Neurath, Sraffa subsequently devoted himself much more to the insular life of an academic, with halting efforts at lecturing replaced by a decades-long project of editing the works of David Ricardo and ultimately producing his own classic volume, *Production of Commodities by Means of Commodities* (Sraffa 1960).

Nonetheless, Sraffa's political connections remained central to him, as he notably served as a lifeline to the Marxist theorist and Italian Communist leader Antonio Gramsci, who had been imprisoned by the Italian fascist government. It was Sraffa who provided a crucial conduit for Gramsci's communication with the outside world, ultimately published as his influential *Letters from Prison.*

All of this has led to the curious situation in which it is possible to view Sraffa in a multi-faceted role. First of all, later economic thinkers, among them Amartya Sen, have explored the extent to which Sraffa might have served as well as a conduit for ideas shaped by Gramsci and other Italian Marxists that then influenced the philosophical framework and ideas of Ludwig Wittgenstein (Sen 2003). Second, in his own time he could assume the role of ideological sparring partner within the academic debates that roiled economic thought in the 1930s, perhaps most notably when Keynes asked Sraffa to take on and, if possible, eviscerate Friedrich von Hayek's theory of capital (Sraffa 1932; Kurz 2015). But third, and most germane to this discussion of the treatment of prices by both Neurath and Sraffa, was the work Sraffa did in examining closely the writings of the classical economists, especially Ricardo, and reformulating what classical theory entailed.

The Neurath construct

Neurath's construct is generally thought of in terms of his advocacy of 'in-kind' calculation, which he saw as laying the basis for a 'natural economy', in which the role conventionally accorded money had been superseded. As such an economy required conscious coordination among all economic agents, hence it would be 'administered'. Were this administrative economy to be guided by egalitarian principles, it would take the form of a socialist economy.

'In-kind' calculation was posed in opposition to money calculation. From Neurath's perspective turning away from money calculation meant diminishing the role of prices, as valuations in monetary terms led naturally to thinking in terms of prices, the most direct and obvious expression of a monetary measure. Moreover, the conventional resort to money and prices had resulted from the ease with which they would provide a quantitative measure, but also from an ideological bent: their permeation and seeming ubiquity in a capitalist economic order (Neurath [1925] 2004).

A contemporary note would highlight the circular process Neurath sought to reveal. The single number used to account for gross domestic product (GDP) is produced, before being tweaked statistically, by multiplying the prices of all goods (and services) times the quantities associated with their corresponding quantities. In sum, a price vector is multiplied by a quantity or output vector. Although money might have been initially taken to be simply a medium of exchange, the monetary value attached to GDP then comes to be accepted as a foundational figure for the entire economy.

Neurath's championing of 'in-kind' calculation appears to place his case for diminishing the role of prices squarely within the debates that arose about the efficacy of 'socialist calculation', which occupied the attention not only of economists deeply opposed to socialism, like Ludwig von Mises and Hayek, but also of socialist economists as well (Bauer 1923).

However, Neurath's 'problem with prices' was founded upon an array of other sources, of which three ought to be highlighted:

1 As a graduate student in economics in Berlin at the turn of the twentieth century, Neurath focused upon economic history, writing his dissertation on the economy of classical antiquity under the direction of Eduard Meyer, and influenced unquestionably by the demonstrable emphasis upon economic history in the work of his father, Wilhelm Neurath. The younger Neurath early on latched on to the notion that the ancient Egyptian dynasties had proven that a large-scale and long-lasting administered economy, relying upon 'in-kind' operations for production and exchange, could be successful. From Meyer he took up the idea that money arose not as a result of the complexity of exchange in all but the most primitive economies, but rather only as a requirement for overseas exchanges.
2 Not unlike many other central European economists at and shortly after the turn of the twentieth century, Neurath engaged in discussions about the boundary between economics and psychology. In opposition to the marginalists, who touted the centrality and importance of price theory, Neurath joined those, like Lujo Brentano, who saw price theory, or at least the resort to theory of marginal utility within it, as essentially steeped in psychology.
3 Instead, Neurath pointed to a serious disjuncture between price theory and Wertlehre, or theory of value, which he regarded as the proper subject of political economy, and had a long history encompassing both mercantilist or cameralist thought and that of the early classical school. There was a corollary to this: valuations of economic activity necessarily involved complexes or constellations of goods and services to be produced and consumed. Under the circumstances the information provided by any one price was insufficient – and might even be deceptive or illusory – in establishing the economic value of such complexes.

Sraffa's classical reformulation

Sraffa's major tome, noted just above, takes for its subtitle a "prelude to a critique of economic theory". Schefold captures Sraffa's embrace of classical thought, as well as his way of limning such a critique, in describing "the rhetoric of Sraffa's book":

> Parsimonious in extent, rich in content are first of all the references to the literature, which just suffice to indicate that the theory to be presented is rooted in classical economic thought, that it adopts the physiocratic idea of production as a circular process, as opposed to the neoclassical image of a one-way avenue from factors of production to consumption. The appropriate classical concepts for prices are named. It is mentioned that the term 'capital' is avoided in order to provide a critique of the (neoclassical) concept, and one detects on closer examination that there are some important references to specific classical ideas rediscovered by Sraffa such as the maximum rate of profit.
>
> (Schefold 2005: 525–526)

As Enrico Bellino encapsulated Sraffa's construct: "Sraffa suggested using a bundle of commodities, that he called 'Standard commodity', ... claiming that it was a standard of value invariant with respect to changes in the distribution of value" (Bellino 2004: 121). Much like Walras' numeraire, but with this exception, the standard commodity is effectively independent of prices, so that "the vector of prices disappears from the wage-profit relationship" (Bellino 2004: 121).

The abstracted model of the economy that Sraffa created draws heavily from Francois Quesnay and Ricardo. His is a much more formal approach to comprehending the proper role of prices in the economy than Neurath's, even as he also found a way to treat prices as a secondary phenomenon. Sraffa was able to configure first a two-sector, then a multi-sector model of the economy, so as to show that for any given ratio of wages to profits there was a standard commodity produced and exchanged from which – and around which – the composition of all other goods produced and exchanged could be derived. Hence, physical quantities replaced prices as the central mechanism that established the composition of consumption.

Observables, the labor theory of value, and prices

Amartya Sen's characterization of Sraffa's model as based upon observables rather than counterfactuals, presented as an insight into the philosophical influences shaping Sraffa's economics, is a reasonable entry point into the philosophical foundations of both Neurath's and Sraffa's conceptual framework for economics.

Neurath's construction of the economy, like Sraffa's, is built upon physical quantities, identifying thereby what goes into production on the basis of comprehending productive capacity, rather than the generic abstractions of land, labor, and capital. This approach bears some kinship with the 'ingredients' – actually physical quantities – informing Wassily Leontief's input-output analysis. In Leontief's case those 'ingredients' stand in the service of a 'recipe', a term that Leontief himself had employed, constituting an economic model with a Walrasian structure. Intriguingly, Neurath had also used the term 'recipe' to characterize economic constructs (Neurath [1910] 2004: 272), though a Walrasian general equilibrium seems quite distant from Neurath.

In that regard it would be worthwhile taking into account both Neurath's and Sraffa's treatment of Quesnay's ([1758] 2005) *Tableau économique*. Neurath provided the first translation of parts of Quesnay's work into German in the economics reader he and his first wife produced in 1910. In his later writings, most notably *Empirical Sociology*, which appeared in 1931, he sketched out Quesnay's model of the circular flow of exchanges between the major strata of economic classes, accepting it as a framework but challenging it because of its failure to account for imbalances, like overproduction, that would result in crises and unemployment, citing the criticism voiced first by Sismondi and then more expansively by Marx (Neurath [1931] 1973: 340–345).

Could Quesnay's notion of the economy as a system, complete with abstracted elements, have staying power, even if different elements were used in its construction and different implications might be drawn from it? This is to some degree the conundrum in economic thought posed by the contention that as a system-builder, Quesnay, a Physiocrat, might serve as the precursor to other system-builders, including Marx, their vastly different understandings of and outlook upon political economy notwithstanding.

This proves to be pertinent here on at least two counts. Unlike Neurath, Sraffa was very much a system-builder. His model of a two-sector economy, while Ricardian in inspiration and hence informed by the perspective of the classical school, can be seen as drawn ultimately from Quesnay's 'tableau'. Quesnay's construct was built around the relation of different economic classes, and the levels of production and consumption that would follow from their relations. Sraffa's construct sought to depict the levels of production and consumption for different ratios of wages to profits, a Ricardian approach, providing what Sen referred to as an 'analytical determination' (Sen 2003: 1247–1248), but in a format and framework that harkens back to Quesnay.

Moreover, as the Leontief model of inputs and outputs suggest, the Walrasian framework exists at least as counterpoint, with physical quantities occupying a central role in it despite its resolution through the grand equilibration of prices.

These physical quantities are taken to be eminently observable; not abstracted nor hypothetical. But there are complications and nuances that accompany the primacy of observables. Both Sraffa and Neurath distanced themselves from the labor theory of value, which occupied a central place in Marx's *Capital,* and, in various forms, had been a foundational element of the economic thought of the classical school.

Consequently, both Neurath and Sraffa would have to contend with their discarding of the labor theory of value as framed by Marx. In Sraffa's case the relation of his ideas to those of Marx has been the subject of decades-long controversy, as has the extent to which he should be seen as 'heterodox' (Aspromourgos 2013), and it should be noted that there have been recent efforts to see the possibility of "an implicit endorsement of a labour theory of value" in Sraffa's work (Preti 2014).

Neurath's trumpeting of the virtues of in-kind calculation in an administrative economy, which predated his embrace of socialism and Marxism, proved to be quite contentious among Austromarxists of the 1920s, playing out on the pages of leading Austrian socialist journals like *Der Kampf.* More generally, Neurath's enthusiasm for a scientific utopianism cast him among nineteenth century figures like Fourier and Cabet whom Marx and Engels had lambasted in *The Communist Manifesto.* Accordingly, Neurath's philosophical assertion that no one measure could serve as a standard in gauging economic activity, including labor, drew less attention in the criticism of his unorthodox ideas, yet may be one of the most important strands in his economic thought.

Taking the long view, one might see the labor theory of value, as espoused in general terms by and through the classical school, as a critical response to what members of the school regarded as one of the crucial foundational failings of the mercantilists. The latter had identified bullion, in the form of gold or silver, as the source of wealth, and its acquisition thus the central economic task of the nation-state. Bullion had an important advantage in that regard: it was visible and easily measurable. Wars and skirmishes over its collection were also easy to visualize, with engagements between privateers from one state and the galleons and galleasses of another filling the narratives of European military and political history between the sixteenth and the eighteenth centuries.

For the former, the classical school, a more sophisticated – and complex – analysis was required. A homogeneous unit of labor, essentially universalized, would stand instead as the foundational measure of value. Adam Smith's famous, if somewhat bizarre, example of the exchange value of deer and beaver in a primitive economy, that of North American Amerindians, as derived from the labor (and labor time) required for their trapping set the standard (Turk 2010: 537–539). This standard, though, was an abstraction, as the unit measure was meant to capture not the toil of an individual laborer but a homogeneous representation of it, rendering possible comparisons within one economy and across several. As value then inhered within production itself, and was present in economic activity, it was invisible as such.

The significance of its abstract nature and its invisibility should not be overlooked. When the marginalist counter-revolution in economic thought occurred in the last third of the nineteenth century, the labor theory of value in all its various forms was cast aside, at least in part in opposition to Marx's central weighting of one version of it, with anti-Marxists rallying around the critique authored by Eugen von Böhm-Bawerk. What replaced it? The marginalists shifted dramatically the locus in economic thought from supply – and production – to demand, so that prices now emerged as the signal indicator of economic value. And prices, as one might see as producer or consumer, were visible; to borrow Sen's expression, they are 'observable'.

Their usefulness as a measure of value, though, depends upon the framework in which they are set: what exactly are these prices telling us? From Neurath's philosophical perspective the significance of prices, effectively their meaning in an economic context or system, would require the introduction of an auxiliary hypothesis (see Neurath [1913] (1983) on the ubiquity of this requirement). Beyond justifying the resolution of partial equilibria via one price, in the course of the second half of the twentieth century, a version of that auxiliary hypothesis would also take shape as the theory or thesis of 'efficient markets'. Prices could simply be assumed to present and embody accurately the economic value of things.

Curiously, Neurath does not appear to have explicitly made the case for the necessity of introducing such an auxiliary hypothesis to create a coherent theory of prices, if nonetheless a wrongheaded one. Instead, his contention about its limitations and distortions, from early on, that is, as delineated in his 1910 and 1911 papers on the theory of the social sciences and political economy, centered about its being rooted in psychology and its supplanting of the study of wealth and value (Wertlehre), the proper domain of inquiry of political economy. In the 1910 article Neurath went on to say that the adoption of price theory as the core of economic theory and theorizing had further consequences, especially with regard to the need to incorporate opaquely formed terminology into it (Neurath [1910] 2004: 268–269).

Instead, Neurath championed the use of comparative measures like scales or rankings, typically thought of as ordinal measures that were necessarily qualitative rather than quantitative (Neurath 1911), as the only means by which the totality of economic experience could be gauged. For Neurath planning entailed comprehending totalities that could not be disaggregated into constituent elements, with the concomitant that there could not be one standard unit of measurement of economic activity. In one fell swoop this placed Neurath squarely in opposition to any reliance upon the classical school's notion of a labor theory of value, on the one hand, or upon the marginalist and neoclassical schools' notion of a system of prices calculated in terms of money. As Neurath put it succinctly: "neither units of money nor hours of work" would suffice.

Transcendance of the physical, as measure or otherwise

In Pierangelo Garegnani's 2005 paper situating a critical – perhaps even the critical – turning point in Piero Sraffa's thinking about the nature of cost and prices, he noted the emergence of the notion of "physical real cost", which he described as: "intended to refer to the subsistence required by the labour necessary for the direct and indirect production of the commodity in question, and not to labour itself along Ricardian or Marxian lines" (Garegnani 2005: 464).

Garegnani saw Sraffa's introduction and acceptance of this notion as foundational, serving as the linchpin upon which the "standard necessary commodity", the centerpiece of Sraffa's reconstruction of an abstracted economy, is tethered. *The Production of Commodities by Means of Commodities*, the work in which this model appeared, represented the culmination of Sraffa's rethinking of what constitutes a valid model of the economy, and appeared in print decades after this turning point had taken place.

One can find a certain kinship between Sraffa and Neurath on this matter of economic fundamentals, as well as, or even in spite of significant differences between them. To begin with, one of the consequences of Neurath's abiding anti-foundationalism was his rejection of any standard measure that would serve as a base upon and from which economic value might be determined. As noted above, Neurath explicitly abjured either the use of money or labor as the standard measure of value. As Bertram Schefold noted of Sraffa: "Sraffa's prices are based neither on utility, nor on labour, but on the structure of production" (Schefold 2005: 529).

Needless to say, the anti-foundationalism of Neurath's approach and outlook, in conjunction with his notion that value could be assessed only as a totality, drawn from combinations or constellations of different goods found in differing 'life situations' and 'economic orders', sets a stark contrast with Sraffa's foundational 'standard necessary commodity', as the physical version or counterpart of the marginalist numeraire. The 'standard necessary commodity' would, by serving as a base, presume a certain universality that Neurath believed was, from his theory of knowledge, unattainable.

However, there is another intriguing overlap here between these two economic thinkers. Sraffa's turn to "physical real cost" was predicated on gauging the requirements of 'subsistence' for labor to produce "the commodity in question". On one level, one might treat this as ultimately an 'in-kind' measure, with subsistence thought of in physical terms. In his notes Sraffa spoke of tracing

> The genealogy of production (and stopping along each branch so soon as we have resolved it into our necessary commodity) [so that] we might find exactly the total amount of corn (if this were the ideal necessary commodity [...]) that has actually entered into ... production ...
>
> (cited by Garegnani 2005: 465)

But it is also the case that the requirements of subsistence figure heavily in Neurath's modern-day and modern-age administrative economy, drawn largely from wartime experience. In this regard Neurath was strongly influenced by the utopian designs of Josef Popper-Lynkeus, who in 1912 had drawn up tables outlining the requirements of production and consumption to meet subsistence in a contemporary national economy. Neurath's approach entailed a great deal of generalizing but clearly was not an abstracted one. Instead, it relied substantially on statistics, upon which Neurath would later contend a 'scientific sociology' was dependent.

For Neurath the upshot of the figures drawn from Popper-Lynkeus is a gauge of the labor time required to attain and obtain the requisite level of subsistence. Hence, while Sraffa was employing a physical measure of a pertinent commodity to underlie and determine the level of production, Neurath used subsistence-level measures of production to establish the pertinent labor associated with them.

As an aside, there is a serious complication in this that brings forth critical tensions in Neurath's economic thought. On the one hand, Neurath accepted Popper-Lynkeus' figures as the basis of what we might regard as a minimum standard of living, the physical equivalent of a guaranteed minimum annual income, leaving aside, for the moment, Neurath's rejection of a money-based standard, as income might still be comprehended in in-kind terms. Yet this stands in sharp contrast, perhaps even in opposition, to Neurath's embrace of complexes or clots for which no simple standard, including one that is set for a reasonable or necessary modicum of goods, can obtain.

A broader problem emerges here. Implicit within the tension besetting Neurath's approach to establishing a measurable standard of living is what one might take to be the macroeconomic conundrum: are countrywide standards or measures inevitable if one is to describe or plan aspects of a national economy? For Neurath, then, do statistical constructs, which he favored on both 'scientific' and political grounds, run afoul of Neurath's epistemology of changing complexes and necessary incompleteness?

Whither prices?

Whither prices in either of these constructs? One would be hard pressed to find references to a supply function in Neurath's writings over the course of his career. Instead, prices are associated with quantities at specific, discrete, and fundamentally 'isolated' points. Something similar appears to arise in Sraffa's work, especially upon entering Garegnani's 'turning point' in 1927–1928. For Sraffa, though, this constituted an engagement with – and a rethinking of – the notion of supply among the classical economists, putting in view, even heralding, a reinterpretation of the classical school itself, elevating cost as the basis for value.

In "denying the existence of a supply function in the Classics" (Garegnani 2005: 481), Sraffa moved toward the following assessment of the Classical School's comprehension and treatment of prices:

> In effect, if the Classical economists ignore the inter-dependence of prices and outputs, while at the same time not assuming constant returns, their procedure can only have consisted of determining prices for the quantities produced in the situation under consideration, i.e., of taking outputs as given when determining prices.
>
> (Garegnani 2005: 481)

Returns to scale represented a matter at the heart of Sraffa's earlier critique of Marshall, challenging the latter's notion of 'free competition' while set within the general framework of a Marshallian microeconomic construct (Sraffa 1926). However, returns to scale enter into Neurath's considerations in only the most general of terms. Neurath raised objections to the restrictive and limiting evocation of purely competitive relations by early twentieth-century marginalist and neoclassical economists like Pareto (Neurath [1910] 2004: 277–278), while pointing to the differences in production and consumption that would arise as monopoly and structures of similar ilk increasingly prevailed. This is captured by varying combinatorial outcomes, rather than through a challenge to, or the lifting of, an economic assumption, like 'constant returns to scale', in any model constructed. Again one sees at work in this regard the 'generalizing' approach of Neurath pitted against the 'abstracted' approach of Sraffa.

Nonetheless, there is other common ground between Neurath and Sraffa. Both identified a distributional principle as the key to determining the composition of goods produced and consumed. Sraffa, relying upon his reexamination of the thinking of the Classical School, turned to the balance between or ratio of wages and profits, fundamentally the distribution of income by factor of production, to effect a specific outcome in production and consumption. For his part, Neurath noted that those participating in the decision-making about the economic plans would have to settle upon a set of principles regarding matters of distribution. While Neurath made clear that an administered economy need not be a socialist one – and the example upon which he drew more than any other, the administrative state and structure of Ancient Egypt, offers a clear case in point – he did not specify what the principles for distribution in a socialist economy would be, other than to highlight its more egalitarian than hierarchical approach and an emphasis upon meeting human needs (Neurath [1919] 1973: 136–137).

The Wittgenstein connection

Amartya Sen contends that from a philosophical point of view, Sraffa shaped his economic model, and the assumptions that underlay it, on observables rather than counterfactuals. This does appear to be a recognition of the fact that the neoclassical construction of supply and demand curves, building upon Marshall's work, is essentially a series of hypothetical and counterfactual 'ifs, thens'. Sen employs a variant of this way of conceiving economic relations, focusing upon how one might account for marginal changes, but frames it in the same terms.

One cannot help being struck by the resemblance this bears to Neurath's philosophical case, most strenuously advanced in the early 1930s, that all meaningful statements, hence those thought of as scientific, are observations; the rest are revealed to be metaphysical. Neurath identified the philosophical outlook associated with this understanding of what informs a 'scientific conception of the world' as physicalism. It is certainly consistent with the view that physical measures constitute the starting point for comprehending and analyzing economic activity.

Curiously, the term 'physicalism' appears in an oppositional pairing limned by Mathieu Marion about Ludwig Wittgenstein. Wittgenstein's two seemingly disparate treatments of the nature of language and its relation to the 'facts of the world', found in the *Tractatus Logico-Philosophicus* and the *Philosophical Investigations*, are characterized as forms of, respectively, 'physicalism' and 'constructivism', where the former conceives of language and the world as atomistic, while the latter takes shape contextually, more a maze of interconnections (Marion 2006).

Within the evolving discussions and debates within the Vienna Circle in the late 1920s and early 1930s, it is difficult to see how these terms might be applied in that way. Neurath had advocated vigorously for adopting the notion of 'physicalism', challenging the 'phenomenalistic' framework that had inspired Rudolf Carnap, most notably in *Der Logische Aufbau der Welt*. However, his thought in general, but especially in political economy, emphasized the primacy of complexes and totalities against the possibilities of atomism, casting any pairing of physicalism and atomism in doubt.

This assumes greater importance when that same oppositional pairing (that is, of atomism and contextual shaping), is taken up by Alessandro Roncaglia (1978) as setting the terms of the distinction drawn between marginalists and their evocation of price theory, on the one hand, and Sraffa's reformulation of classical economics, on the other. Indeed, various writers exploring Sraffa's ideas and influences have attempted to trace in his work what in Wittgensteinian terms might be thought of as a 'social epistemology' associated with the *Philosophical Investigations* back to Antonio Gramsci.

One need look no farther than Neurath's early writings, though, to see a case for contextual comprehension and a concomitant critique of marginalism and its reduction of political economy to price theory grounded in a version of 'social epistemology'. Again, what stands out here is that this critique predates Neurath's association with Marxism, but does fit within the mode of inquiry laid down by Wilhelm Roscher, the dean of the German Historical School, of examining different 'systems' of economic order.

In some sense Neurath and Sraffa share ties to Wittgenstein that differ from any other economists, in that their connection involves essentially an engagement in philosophy rather than political economy. Hence, John Maynard Keynes, who otherwise ought to be included in this short list, could not be seen in the same light.

For Sraffa this is apparent in Wittgenstein's rare – one might say exceedingly rare – attribution of Sraffa's serving as a major influence upon him. In particular, it was through Sraffa that Wittgenstein saw the basis for the rejection of his earlier pictorial theory of language and his construction of a new theory grounded in context. This is sometimes telescoped into the apocryphal story of Sraffa's challenging Wittgenstein's pictorial theory aligning statements with 'facts of the world' with a Neapolitan gesture, though it is also the case that the two engaged in conversation on a regular basis at Cambridge University for a decade-and-a-half, until Sraffa broke them off in 1946.

By contrast, Neurath had no such conversations with Wittgenstein. However, as a member of the Vienna Circle, Neurath had to participate in extended sessions where fellow members read and absorbed Wittgenstein's *Tractatus* as a seminal, even semi-mystical text, though Neurath proved to be the most skeptical among them (see, for example, Heinrich Neider's account in Neider 1973). Nonetheless, in the Vienna Circle manifesto, as well as in his own writings, Neurath would invoke Wittgenstein's name as one of the major figures in philosophy supporting the 'scientific conception of the world'. At the same time, Neurath was careful to distinguish and distance himself from what he deemed the metaphysical in Wittgenstein, including Wittgenstein's notion of an 'anticipatory' ladder whereby the knowledge required to ascend could and should be discarded once one has achieved a higher understanding.

Yet even in his *Empirical Sociology*, in which his affinity with a materialist outlook and a Marxist inflection stand out, Neurath found a way to include Wittgenstein among the figures providing an "analysis of the pursuit of science …[that] can also be applied to the sociological field" (Neurath [1931] 1973: 413).

For Neurath those figures played an important role by emphasizing the way that the careful examination of language would elucidate "which concepts and statements can be considered as part of genuine science", what we might term a methodological consideration as to how one goes about doing something (here an intellectual inquiry), rather than presenting any of the pertinent statements that ought to be found in, say, sociology or political economy. As Neurath put it: "Here it is not the length of possible deductions or the subtlety of analysis that are essential" (Neurath [1931] 1973: 413).

Hence the question arises: how solid is the notion of a connection with significant economic or philosophical content linking Wittgenstein and the economists, among whom Sraffa and Neurath would appear to be the most likely candidates?

Much has been written about possible cross-influences between Sraffa and Wittgenstein, where the more problematic relation is that which concerns Wittgenstein's effect upon Sraffa's economic thought. See, for example, Richard Arena's recent reflection on the community of interests in a social epistemology found in 'forms of life and snapshots' (Arena 2013).

By contrast, far less has been said about possible cross-influences between Neurath and Wittgenstein. This may on some level be attributed to the fact that Neurath's work and ideas in economics have garnered little attention in general, with the exception of Neurath's embrace of in-kind calculation and economic planning. Still, for all that one might see a certain similarity between Wittgenstein's later social epistemology and Neurath's resort to framing economic matters by reference to history or historical conditions and thus as fundamentally contextual, the intellectual – and personal – lineage of Neurath's economic thought can and should be traced without any reference to Wittgenstein.

Moreover, the evolution of Wittgenstein's later thought was such that it began to take shape in the 1930s, gaining its fullest expression in his *Philosophical Investigations*, produced and published only in the 1940s. Neurath's economic ideas had been well formed long before, evident in his first major articles, published before the outbreak of World War I.

As for Sraffa, if Garegnani is correct, the crucial turning point in his economic thought took place in 1927–1928, predating his encounter with Wittgenstein at Cambridge University. Moreover, Sraffa's rethinking and reformulation of the tenets of the classical school could reasonably be understood within the frame of reference of the history of economic thought as well. The radical step of effectively rediscovering and remaking in a certain sense Petty, Quesnay, Smith, and Ricardo, that is, a reversion back to the roots of classical economic theory, would in and of itself constitute a major intellectual journey. It would be fair to ask what philosophical dispositions or predispositions Sraffa brought to this inquiry, but what of Wittgenstein would actually be found in it?

Both Neurath and Wittgenstein held out special significance for the role and place of language in all matters of inquiry. It was the focus upon the relation between statements and facts of the world that drew the Vienna Circle to Wittgenstein's *Tractatus*, and Neurath's concerns about how language might mask rather than elucidate economic content were longstanding.

Is it possible in Sraffa to find a similar, heightened interest in the ways that matters of language would affect significantly the formation or use of economic concepts or even the nature and construction of economic models? Therein lies the place where a philosophical connection between Wittgenstein and Sraffa's economic thought ought to be sought, a possibility alluded to by Sen (2003: 1245). In that regard one might consider the extent to which Sraffa's inquiry, subtitled, "Prelude to a Critique of Economic Theory", entailed an examination of language elucidating "which concepts and statements can be considered as part of genuine science" (Neurath [1931] 1973: 413).

The language of capital

One other area of congruence between Neurath and Sraffa pertained to the classification of inputs as generic factors of production, especially capital. Throughout his career Neurath scored the use of the term, famously challenging statements attributed to him during his trial for treason in Munich in 1920 when he asserted that the speeches in question contained the word 'capital'. Neurath averred that he had never used that word (Marie Neurath 1973: 7). In a more scholarly context Neurath wrote at length in his 1935 paper on what constitutes rational economic theory that generic factors of production masked an illusion in economic thought, in the case of 'capital' papering over a term that was meaningless. Instead, 'capital' needed to be comprehended as different specific items or goods that he then proceeded to enumerate by example. Effectively, it was necessary to disaggregate the term to render it meaningful in any scientific inquiry (Neurath 1935: 41–45).

Sraffa's challenge to the notion of capital as a factor of production advanced along similar lines. As Sen described Sraffa's perspective:

> Aggregative neoclassical models with capital as a factor of production are irreparably damaged. But neoclassical economic theory need not be expounded in an aggregative form. It is possible to see production in terms of distinct capital goods and leave it at that.
>
> (Sen 2003: 1246)

A critical difference between the two remains: Sraffa was working to refurbish and reformulate the approach and understandings of the classical school, if with a Marxian inflection; Neurath, by contrast, engaged in a rethinking of economic ideas and approaches far more within a framework, broadly conceived, of central European economics and philosophy, even if also with a Marxian inflection of his own.

Note Neurath's theoretical framework, as presented in his 1910 article exploring the 'theory of the social sciences':

> Now the question can be raised: What conditions allow a certain way of transfer of goods at a certain time, by what laws or what customs can one succeed in establishing certain ways of transfer of goods? All these questions are of decisive scientific significance. They become amenable to successful treatment once the theory of price formation stops its continuous interference.
>
> (Neurath [1910] 2004: 278)

The reference to 'laws and customs' is hardly coincidental, as Neurath makes explicit his effort to incorporate ideas and approaches from the German Historical School (Neurath [1910] 2004: 278).

Conclusion: the variation in economic value

A disjuncture between economic theorizing built around value rather than price lies at the heart of what I have called Neurath's and Sraffa's 'problem with prices'. In this both are joined in their criticism of marginalism's elevation of price theory to an effective congruence with what would come to be termed 'microeconomics'. Moreover, both set this elevation within a historical context: the dominance of the capitalist system. Thereby they made price theory at least as much an affair of ideology as a matter of intellectual inquiry. For Sraffa that sufficed to cover the place of the historical in economic analysis. For Neurath, though, the history of price movements and the like was an essential feature of economic analysis.

One might then be drawn to the conclusion that both Neurath's and Sraffa's critiques should be placed within the framework of the continuing debate that has roiled Marxian economics since the publication posthumously of Volume

Three of *Capital*. For more than a century, Marxian economists have explored, tried to resolve, modified, or on occasion simply shunted aside the 'transformation problem', the linkage sought between value based upon labor and prices. From the outset, that is, beginning in the late nineteenth century, this debate took on greater significance and intensity with the challenge posed to it by the Austrian and anti-Marxist Eugen von Böhm-Bawerk, who claimed that no such transformation could be effected.

Moreover, in the long view one might characterize the embrace of price theory by the marginalists as the means whereby the problematic aspects of the labor theory of value, which had informed the thinking of the classical school, with all its variations acknowledged, might be resolved by rendering the question of determining any sort of inherent value moot. That is, borrowing from a Kantian dictum, the 'counter-revolution' wrought by marginalism was brought about in part by 'turning problems into postulates'. Inherent value, like the labor that went into production, no longer mattered. Instead, prices, visible to presumably all who entered into markets, would be taken as the points of departure, for an economic analysis of exchanges.

On one level the marginalists would be in the position of claiming that prices, an observable phenomenon, were a superior measure to imputed abstractions like a homogeneous unit of labor, with which Smith and Ricardo began. Thus it is noteworthy that both Neurath and Sraffa would overturn this contention, in part by focusing upon physical measures of quantity and in part by casting the marginalist and neoclassical construct of a price equilibration of supply and demand functions as itself grounded in counterfactuals, in Sraffa's case, or built upon a questionable and ideological 'auxiliary hypothesis', in Neurath's case, and hence for both 'nonobservable' elements. For neither did the Marshallian supply and demand functions accord with sound economic analysis.

Yet there is a divergence between Neurath and Sraffa that is also noteworthy in the same context. Since the appearance of *The Production of Commodities by Means of Commodities* in 1960 there has been an abundance of critical discussion about the implications of Sraffa's theory of value for matters of the distribution of income, largely from a Marxian perspective or, at the least, from the standpoint of challenging some of the conventions associated with Marxian economics. In the mid-1970s, for example, John Eatwell wrote an article entitled, "Mr. Sraffa's Standard Commodity and the Rate of Exploitation" in *The Quarterly Journal of Economics* (Eatwell 1975: 543–555), in which he laid out the following version of Sraffa's impact:

> Piero Sraffa's work on problems of the theory of value, which has provided the analytical framework for the recent debate on distribution theory, encompasses two distinct, though interrelated themes. The first, a critique of the marginalist theory of distribution, culminated in his demonstration of the generality of the 'reswitching phenomenon'.
>
> (Eatwell 1975: 543)

Then he goes on to describe the theme that will serve as the main avenue into his consideration of the rate of exploitation: "The second involves an analysis of the relationship between wages, profits, and the rate of profit by means of a 'physical' analogue freed from the complications introduced by the interdependence of prices and the distribution of income" (Eatwell 1975: 543).

More recent works may have sought to reevaluate the relation between Sraffa's 'standard commodity' and various strands of Marxian thought, but the fundamental framework remains the same: interpretations based upon resolving or at least rethinking that relation. And so a new set of essays published in 2014 under the title *Towards a New Understanding of Sraffa* (edited by Riccardo Bellofiore and Scott Carter) includes a chapter by Scott Carter entitled, "Sraffa and the Standard Commodity" (Carter 2014: 47–78), downplaying efforts to extract a rate of exploitation from Sraffa's text.

By contrast, Neurath's take on the disjuncture between price theory and theory of value, for all that it might be fitted into and made to conform to a Marxian perspective, has little to do with the 'transformation problem' as it has been posed. This may prove to be obvious on grounds of his personal chronology alone: the disjuncture occupied a central place in Neurath's thought well before his embrace of Marxism, nor did said embrace change in any significant way his thinking about the importance of Wertlehre in economics and the wide gap between it and price theory in constructing economics and assaying its purpose.

It might be best to set Neurath into a largely central European milieu, with questions of philosophy appearing to be inseparable from those regarding the nature of economics. One might also see the looming presence of the German Historical School, even if Neurath might not be viewed as fully adhering to its tenets and philosophy at any stage of his career. Nonetheless, a greater concern for history within economics and a heightened interest in gathering and making use of statistics certainly mark Neurath's economic thought.

Instead, Neurath's emphasis upon a theory of value as the core of economics rested upon a longstanding, indeed lifelong, attachment to an Epicurean philosophy embodied in achieving 'social happiness'. In this term Neurath appears to be outlining the possibilities for and the outlook of latter-day ecological economists, seeking to gauge the worth of economic activity through some version of a 'happiness index'. Neurath gave great weight – effectively primacy – to qualitative judgments about achieving 'social happiness' that nonetheless were capable of comparison on an ordinal or topological basis. Such calculations had to take into account 'complexes' of experience, weakening the role of and information provided by individual prices. Hence, for all the overlaps identified between Neurath and Sraffa, one might well describe the theories of value associated with each as framed conceptually in different or alternative worlds, perhaps set on parallel tracks.

Consequently, for Neurath it would be reasonable to posit a theory of value distinct and separate from marginalist or neoclassical price theory rooted more in a central European intellectual or philosophical milieu than a Marxist one.

Neurath figures at best as an idiosyncratic and unorthodox representative of the German Historical School, even for those times that he appeared most closely aligned with it. On a broader scale, though, recognition of a 'third' understanding and construction of a theory of value in the early decades of the twentieth century has a certain resonance with the positioning asserted by the school in the second half of the nineteenth century. Then its leading figures spoke of themselves as constituting a 'third force' or 'third way' in political economy, rejecting crucial elements of what they termed 'Manchester liberalism', effectively the classical school of Adam Smith and his followers, as well as its later avatars, but at the same time rejecting as well crucial elements of Marxian socialism, including its belief in overturning by radical means the existing economic order.

However, the reflection that a 'third' approach or way with regard to a theory of value might have existed in the first decades of the twentieth century, set broadly in the context of a central European intellectual milieu and shaped at least to some degree by the thinking and outlook of the German Historical School, suggests that some of the intellectual ferment affecting and influencing economic thought in that period has been obscured, perhaps even lost.

The stakes here are not insignificant; on the contrary, they are quite high. Just as one might posit the notion of central planning as brought to fruition in a central European context, shaped at the least by concerns within the German Historical School as much as by Marxism, so in the case of ecological economics, built upon an alternative theory of value, one might discern the larger influence of the same central European milieu. And what is most noteworthy is that it is Otto Neurath who plays a central role in laying out the basis for economic planning, in establishing the broad terms for the construction of an ecological economics, and in promoting an alternative theory of value in the process.

References

Arena, Richard (2013) "Sraffa's and Wittgenstein's Reciprocal Influences: Forms of Life and Snapshots". In Enrico Sergio Levrero, Antonella Palumbo, and Antonella Stirati, eds., *Sraffa and the Reconstruction of Economic Theory: Volume Three. Sraffa's Legacy: Interpretation and Historical Perspectives*. Basingstoke: Palgrave Macmillan, pp. 84–105.

Aspromourgos, Tony (2013) "Sraffa's System in Relation to Some Main Currents in Unorthodox Economics". In Enrico Sergio Levrero, Antonella Palumbo, and Antonella Stirati, eds., *Sraffa and the Reconstruction of Economic Theory: Volume Three. Sraffa's Legacy: Interpretation and Historical Perspectives*. Basingstoke: Palgrave Macmillan, pp. 15–33.

Bauer, Helene (1923) "Geld, Sozialismus und Otto Neurath". *Der Kampf* 16.

Bellino, Enrico (2004) "On Sraffa's Standard Commodity". *Cambridge Journal of Economics* 28(1): 121–132.

Carter, Scott (2014) "Sraffa and the Standard Commodity". In Riccardo Bellofiore and Scott Carter, eds., *Towards a New Understanding of Sraffa*. Basingstoke: Palgrave Macmillan, pp. 47–78.

Cozzi, T., and Marchionatti, R. (eds.) (2001) *Piero Sraffa's Political Economy. A Centenary Estimate*. London: Routledge.
Eatwell, John (1975) "Mr. Sraffa's Standard Commodity and the Rate of Exploitation". *The Quarterly Journal of Economics* 89(4): 543–555.
Fourastié, Jean (1958) *Documents pour l'histoire et la theorie des prix* ...Paris: A. Colin.
Garegnani, Pierangelo (2005) "Sraffa's 'Turning Point'". *European Journal of the History of Economic Thought* 12(3).
Harcourt, Geoffrey C. (2003) "Review of Terenzio Cozzi and Roberto Marchionatti's essays on Sraffa". *History of Political Economy* 35(3): 582–586.
Harcourt, Geoffrey C. (2012) "Piero Sraffa: A Tribute". *Cambridge Journal of Economics*, 36(6): 1263–1266.
Kurz, Heinz D. (2015) "Capital Theory, Crises, and Business Cycles: The Triangular Debate between Hayek, Keynes, and Sraffa". *Journal of Reviews on Global Economics* 4: 186–191.
Kuznets, Simon (1941) *National Income and Its Composition, 1919–1938*, vol. 1. New York: NBER.
Marion, Mathieu (2006) "Sraffa and Wittgenstein: Physicalism and constructivism". *Review of Political Economy* 17(3): 381–406.
Neider, Heinrich (1973) "Recollection". In Marie Neurath and Robert S. Cohen, eds., *Empiricism and Sociology*. Trans. Paul Foulkes and Marie Neurath. Dordrecht: Reidel, pp. 45–49.
Neurath, Anna Schapire, and Neurath, Otto [1910] (1913) *Lesebuch der Volkswirtschaftslehre*. 2nd edn. Leipzig: G.A. Gloeckner.
Neurath, Marie (1973) "Neurath's Trial". In Marie Neurath and Robert S. Cohen, eds., *Empiricism and Sociology*. Trans. Paul Foulkes and Marie Neurath. Dordrecht: Reidel, p. 7.
Neurath, Otto [1910] (2004) "Theory of the Social Sciences". In Robert S. Cohen and Thomas E. Uebel, eds., *Economic Writings/Selections 1904–45*. [Multiple translators]. Dordrecht: Kluwer Academic Publishers, pp. 265–291.
Neurath, Otto (1911) "Nationalokonomie und Werlehre: eine systematische Untersuchung". *Zeitschrift für Volkswirtschaft, Sozialpolitik und Verwaltung* 20: 52–114.
Neurath, Otto [1913] (1983) "The Lost Wanderers of Descartes and the Auxiliary Motive". In Robert S. Cohen and Marie Neurath, eds. and trans., *Philosophical Papers 1913–1946*. Dordrecht/Boston: D. Reidel Publishing Company, pp. 1–12.
Neurath, Otto [1919] (1973) "Through War Economy to Economy in Kind". In Marie Neurath and Robert S. Cohen, eds., *Empiricism and Sociology*. Trans. Paul Foulkes and Marie Neurath. Dordrecht: Reidel, pp. 123–157.
Neurath, Otto [1925] (2004) "Economic Plan and Calculation in Kind". In Robert S. Cohen and Thomas E. Uebel, eds., *Otto Neurath: Economic Writings/Selections, 1904–1945*. [Multiple translators]. Dordrecht: Kluwer Academic Publishers, pp. 405–465.
Neurath, Otto [1931] (1973) *Empirical Sociology*. In Marie Neurath and Robert S. Cohen, eds., *Empiricism and Sociology*. Trans. Paul Foulkes and Marie Neurath. Dordrecht: Reidel, pp. 319–421.
Neurath, Otto (1931) "Physicalism: The Philosophy of the Vienna Circle". *The Monist* 41(4): 618–623.
Neurath, Otto [1931] (2004) "On Global Productive Capacity". In Robert S. Cohen and Thomas E. Uebel, eds., *Otto Neurath: Economic Writings/Selections 1904–1945*. [Multiple translators]. Dordrecht: Kluwer Academic Publishers, pp. 475–505.
Neurath, Otto (1935) *Was bedeutet rationale Wirtschaftsbetrachtung?* Wien: Verlag Gerold & Co.

Neurath, Paul (1994) "Introduction and Biography". In Paul Neurath and Elisabeth Nemeth, eds., *Otto Neurath oder Die Einheit von Wissenschaft und Gesellschaft*. Wien: Bohlau Verlag.

Preti, Dario (2014) "On the Neoricardian Criticism of Irrelevance". In Riccardo Bellofiore and Scott Carter, eds., *Towards a New Understanding of Sraffa*. Basingstoke: Palgrave Macmillan, pp. 25–46.

Quesnay, Francois. [1758] (2005) *Tableau économique*. In Christine There, Loic Charles, and Jean-Claude Perrot, eds., *Oeuvres Economiques completes et autres textes*. Paris: INED.

Roncaglia, Alessandro (1978) *Sraffa and the Theory of Price*. Trans. J.A. Kregel. London: Wiley.

Schefold, Bertram (2005) "Joint Production: Triumph of Economic over Mathematical Logic?" *European Journal of the History of Economic Thought* 12(3): 525–552.

Sen, Amartya (2003) "Sraffa, Wittgenstein, and Gramsci". *Journal of Economic Literature* 41(4): 1240–1255.

Smith, Adam [1776] (1976) *An Inquiry into the Nature and Causes of the Wealth of Nations*. Ed. Edwin Cannon. Chicago: University of Chicago Press.

Sraffa, Piero (1926) "The Laws of Return under Competitive Conditions". *Economic Journal* 36(144): 535–550.

Sraffa, Piero (1932) "Dr. Hayek on Money and Capital". *The Economic Journal* 42(165): 42–53.

Sraffa, Piero (1960) *Production of Commodities by Means of Commodities*. Cambridge: Cambridge University Press.

Turk, Michael (2010) "Economics as Plausible Conjecture". *History of Political Economy* 42(3): 521–546.

7 Otto Neurath and the linguistic turn in economics

Otto Neurath's place in the history of economic thought remains somewhat elusive. He has served largely as a foil for his advocacy of in-kind calculation and economic planning. In 1920 Ludwig von Mises cited Neurath's ideas about the virtues of in-kind or natural calculation superseding monetary calculation in effectuating a planned economy as one of the bases against which he made his case that socialist calculation, and hence a planned economy, was not possible (L. Mises 1920: 102, 119). In 1935 Friedrich von Hayek followed suit, identifying Neurath and Otto Bauer, a well-regarded Marxist economist and leading figure among the Austrian Socialists, as the "most interesting" or "most representative" exponents of socialization (see, for example, Bauer 1919), a form of collectivist economic activity to which Hayek was unalterably opposed (Hayek 1935: 30–31). Neurath served as an intellectual foil for Hayek on a second count: late in life Hayek recounted that it had been the stridency of Neurath's position on the unity of all sciences that had propelled Hayek to comprehend an insuperable methodological divide between economics and the physical sciences (Hayek 1994: 50).

Neurath, a polymath in the central European tradition, is best known for his intellectual and organizational efforts spearheading the development of the Vienna Circle of philosophers. However, Neurath's educational background and academic career centered about the field of economics. He prepared his dissertation on trade and industry in classical antiquity at the University of Berlin, defended it before Eduard Meyer and Gustav Schmoller, then taught for a time at the Vienna Handelsakademie and later at the University of Heidelberg.

Moreover, Neurath wrote extensively about economic matters and ideas over the course of his lifetime. A volume of his major economic writings appeared in 2004, edited by Robert S. Cohen, with a lengthy overview of his ideas provided by Thomas Uebel. In examining his economic writings leading Neurath scholars like Elisabeth Nemeth have described Neurath's ideas about economics as having crystallized in the period prior to the establishment of a new consensus about economic theory in the 1920s and 1930s, characterized by George Shackle as a defining "age of high theory" (Nemeth 2008: 5). They tend to situate Neurath's contribution to economic thought in his call for qualitative standards, beyond the now current quantitative measures, to gauge economic well-being, anticipating in certain respects the outlook of Amartya Sen. In addition, they cite his innovative use of graphic art to represent the 'totality' of economic experience (Leonard 1999). Beyond this, John O'Neill has sought to highlight what he sees as an early or inchoate version of 'ecological economics' in Neurath's work (O'Neill 1999, 2004).

I would contend that there is yet another strand to Neurath's legacy in the history of economic thought: that underlying Neurath's rethinking of the traditional cul-de-sacs found in the philosophy of science was a critique of the nature and use of language in any and all scientific disciplines, characterized as a 'linguistic turn', and that this critique held with special force for economics.

Here Neurath's central place in the workings of the Vienna Circle of philosophers is pertinent. If one looks at the salient aspects of the Vienna Circle's work and program as it emerged in the late 1920s, one finds a heightened, even defining role for language in establishing the bases upon which any field or discipline might be understood as scientific. As the circle's manifesto indicated, an unambiguous language, free of all metaphysical accretions and distortions, underlay the possibility of attaining a unity of all science. In part, the circle's focus upon such a role for language grew out of intense discussions of the relation between statements and propositions, on the one hand, and the facts of the world, on the other, initially raised by Ludwig Wittgenstein's *Tractatus*. It was also evident in the continuing discussion within the circle in the 1930s about the use of 'protocol sentences' and the debate about the primacy of a phenomenalist or a physicalist language upon which all fields of science could be built.

For Neurath economics had to be subject to a strenuous critique of its language, as the failure to attend to the terms used to form essential concepts and establish thereby the bounds and significance of the field's content meant that the foundation upon which economics was built was fundamentally flawed.

As such, one might well argue that this kind of philosophical inquiry, with its sweeping methodological implications, paralleled the work of Neurath's arch-rival, Hayek, whereby a linguistic turn in economics might have opened the field to new possibilities, just as Hayek's emphasis upon the role of information in economics did. The difference here is that this linguistic turn did not occur until many decades later, without any apparent awareness of Neurath's presaging work. Oftentimes this turn was more at the level of rhetoric than in the substantive way that Neurath had emphasized, namely as the imprecise transfer of the language of customary or institutional practices to an intellectual discipline. This difference in impact may also be viewed as stemming from a broader recategorizing of the ideas and concerns raised by Neurath as 'sociology' rather than 'economics', the often overlooked default that followed from the failure to produce and sustain a robust historical economics, affecting Max Weber as well as Neurath.

As a preliminary matter it is important to note that much of the recent scholarship on Neurath's philosophical stance has taken shape through a nuanced inquiry into and rethinking of his perspective on the nature of philosophy and science, emphasizing his anti-foundationalism and naturalism, the notion that there is no philosophy separate from science. I do not see these elements of Neurath's thinking as necessarily inconsistent with his treatment of a linguistic turn in economics. The intersubjectivity of language, which he contended made science possible, informed Neurath's naturalism (Cartwright et al. 1996: 141), and required the elimination of terminology weighted down by any metaphysical baggage – in the case of economics, a wholesale enterprise. Moreover, Neurath's anti-foundationalism appears rooted in the conventionalism of, among others, Henri Poincaré and Pierre Duhem, discussed in greater detail below, however much he may have modified and deepened it.

Situating Neurath in economics

It is worth situating Neurath within the world of economic theorizing and thought, noting that his involvement with the discipline of economics changed markedly over the course of his variegated career. He was actively engaged in writing about 'theoretical economics' in the years leading up to World War I, and was clearly conversant in the prevailing economic discourse of the period. At the same time he produced an economics textbook and, in collaboration with his first wife, Anna Schapire Neurath, was preparing a reader in the history of economic thought.

In articles appearing in leading central European journals in 1910 and 1911, he challenged the construction of economics around markets and price theory, abetted, he contended, by the loose use of what were deemed to be fundamental concepts. In these essays Neurath referenced, cited, and critiqued major contemporaries, or near contemporaries, like Stanley Jevons, Alfred Marshall, Vilfredo Pareto, and Leon Walras, along with central Europeans like Carl Menger, Eugen von Böhm-Bawerk, Joseph Schumpeter, Ladislaus von Bortkiewicz, and Max Weber. He attended to a raft of German economic thinkers, from the mercantilist J.J. Becher, through Friedrich List and H.H. Gossen, to the 'state socialist' Rodbertus and the leading figures of the German Historical School, including Wilhelm Roscher, Karl Knies, Schmoller, and Lujo Brentano.

In the two-volume reader in the history of economic thought Neurath introduced texts and excerpts from, variously: Plato, Aristotle, Oresmus, Becher, Hume, Smith, and Ricardo (in Volume I); and Thunen, Roscher, Gossen, Marx, Mill, and Vogelsang (in Volume II). Notably, the Neuraths took pride in presenting selected texts from Oresmus, Quesnay, and Turgot that had been translated into German for the first time (Neurath [1910] 1913: I, VII).

With the end of World War I, and the full flowering of his political and social activism, combined with an embrace – characteristically unorthodox – of Marxist ideas, Neurath became less engaged in the economics profession, no doubt spurred on further in that direction with the loss of his academic post at Heidelberg. This was evident in his later theoretical work, as the economic thinkers to whom he refers in his 1944 monograph on the 'Foundations of the

Social Sciences" were little changed from those he cited three decades before. For example, in this later piece he faults the flaws in the use of language by Thomas Malthus and Marshall, and emphasizes more the ideas of classical economists rather than neoclassical ones.

Neurath's distance from the debates among economists that took center stage in the 1920s and especially the 1930s should not vitiate the significance of his insights about the problematic nature of the language used – and the concepts formed thereby – in economics. It may in fact have opened the way to seeing things differently, and brought out links, however partial, between the turn-of-the-century philosophical debates and conventionalism, and more contemporary ideas or perspectives, including postmodernism, focused upon the role of language and narrative.

On the trail of Poincaré and Duhem

As a longtime critic of capitalism, Neurath was steadfast in his opposition to limiting economics to price theory and the conventional treatment of markets. This was the case both in his early, formative days when one can detect some affinity to the German Historical School and manifested as well when he was most closely associated with Marxism. At the same time, what stands out forcefully in his critique of economics is his criticism of the use of language in economics. Here Neurath sees the words and phrases favored by economists as essentially a mask, concealing both the lack of clarity and solid empirical grounding for such terminology, as well as the institutional or customary framework that serves as the sole basis for making it appear meaningful.

As Neurath recounted:

> I started in my university days rather primitively by making a collection of 'dangerous terms'. Before I started making this collection (I sometimes called it in joke [sic] my 'Index Verborum Prohibitorum'). I tried to criticize books and articles. Particularly I was busy with reading Adam Smith's *The Wealth of Nations* along the lines of an analysis of language … I altered successively my own terms in all my articles and books in accordance with my increasing Index by eliminating 'emotional', 'concealing', and 'confusing terms'.
>
> (Neurath 1941:132)

Moreover, for Neurath economics as a field tended to parlay a grand illusion of scientific precision, whether through its use of empirical data or its incorporation of mathematical nomenclature and techniques. He invoked the advances made in theorizing about physics and its nature as a discipline, especially by the turn-of-the-century conventionalists like Henri Poincaré and Pierre Duhem, as well as Ernst Mach, as a rebuke to economists, who failed, he felt, to grasp their insights or approaches. Indeed, the notion of such scientific precision as a mask echoes the critique of scientific language by Poincaré in *Science and Hypothesis*, a work to which Neurath referred in his 1910 essay on the theory of the social sciences (Neurath [1910] 2004: 266). Notably, the preface to the German translation of Poincaré's work, which served as Neurath's source, gave particular emphasis to Poincaré's view of the axioms of geometry and the principles of mechanics as none other than "verkleidete Definitionen" (Poincaré 1906: IV–V).

According to Rudolf Haller, a survey of the indices of Neurath's methodological and philosophical writings over the course of his career reveals that, apart from his 'contemporaries' associated with the Vienna Circle and the logical empiricist movement, Mach, Poincaré, and Duhem were the most cited (Haller 1991b: 108).

Neurath scholars, among them Jordi Cat and Thomas Uebel, have traced Neurath's philosophical rejection of the construction of any science on a 'pyramidal' foundation back to the influences of these conventionalists. In fact, both Cat and Uebel see Neurath's view of the necessary lack of any foundation to the making or practice of science, captured metaphorically as 'Neurath's Boat', as more all-encompassing (Cartwright et al. 1996; also Uebel 1996: 106–107).

Of Poincaré and Duhem, Neurath most often referred to the two of them together for contemplating the necessary existence and problematic nature of 'systems of hypotheses', recognizing that multiple plausible ones can be produced in construing a given set of circumstances (Neurath [1946] 1983: 231).

This provides a remarkable counterpoint to the more general, if not universal tendency of economists to align their work with that of the supposed paradigm offered up by classical physics (Turk 2006). It held even when, as was the case for Walras, correspondence with Poincaré and other French mathematicians reveals serious cautions on their part about the path he was pursuing, among other considerations the assumption of unerring clairvoyance and rationality (Turk 2012). For Neurath such assumptions constituted a misguided form of Cartesianism or Laplacian 'absolutism' that he also categorized as 'pseudorationalism'.

The powerful influence of both Poincaré and Duhem on the thinking of Frank, Neurath, and Hahn, the core figures in the first Vienna Circle, was captured in Frank's retrospective account of its genesis and development. Speaking for the group, Frank downplayed the influence of Ernst Mach (Frank 1949: 7).[1] Instead, it was Poincaré who received special approbation for "bridg[ing] the gap" between the "vague and complex" nature of empirical observation and the generalizing concepts and statements forming the "principles of science" (Frank 1949: 8).

While Neurath's early, yet lasting embrace of critical aspects of the conventionalism of Henri Poincaré and the pluralism and holism of Pierre Duhem has been noted as an essential strand within his philosophy of science (Uebel 1996: 122–133), less attention has been given to the extent to which Poincaré and Duhem influenced Neurath's ideas about and critique of economic theory.

Poincaré's influence can be felt in at least two ways that can be regarded as formative for Neurath's treatment of economic theory. In his popular writings about science Poincaré scored what he saw as the lack of content of many of the terms commonly used by physicists, including 'mass'. He sought to root out impredicative definitions, in which supposedly scientific terms were defined in circular fashion, ultimately, in other words, in terms of themselves, and so were effectively devoid of any substantive meaning.

For Neurath economic concept formation suffered similarly from a fundamental weakness in the language in which such concepts were couched. In his early 1910 essay, built around a critique of the then highly influential work of Wilhelm Wundt,[2] he referred to the "unsorted terminology" employed by economic theorists. He drew a contrast between the looseness with which economic theorists put together their concepts and the rigor of the approach pursued by physicists, like Poincaré and Duhem, for whom "the origin of the concepts and of the problems are traced right from the initial observation of fact, if at all possible" (Neurath [1910] 2004: 268–269). Whereas, for economists, "[n]ot infrequently there is only very general talk of 'capital', 'price', 'value', etc." (Neurath [1910] 2004: 269)

Neurath also challenged the emergence of marginalism as dependent upon the faulty adoption of language. This proved to be the case for the most basic concepts used. For example, he pointed to the longstanding and continuing difficulty of defining the object of economic activity as "the economic good", a term embraced by the marginalists (Neurath [1910] 2004: 274).

This wobbly foundation engendered new problems. "It became necessary to create a simplified science of motivations; partly under this influence, marginal utility theory was developed, a purely psychological discipline" (Neurath [1910] 2004: 274). (This last characterization echoed the view of Brentano, whose blistering critique of Menger on this point prompted a strenuous counterattack by Weber.)

In *Science and Hypothesis* Poincaré also made a strong case for rethinking the notion of measure in science, advancing claims for a more qualitative mathematics in the process. Poincaré laid out the basis for treating 'non-measurable magnitudes' as measures worthy of science, emphasizing their role in ordering or arranging relations between pertinent scientific variables to achieve significant results (Poincaré 1906: 28). In making his case, Poincaré drew upon Gustav Fechner's 'psycho-physical' studies to demonstrate the disjuncture between the 'physical continuum' and a mathematically constructed one (Poincaré 1906: 22–28).

This might appear, on the surface at least, as a call for ordinal rather than cardinal measurement, which indeed did appear in Neurath's critiques of measurement in economics (Neurath 1944: 33). In fact, Uebel has suggested that in doing so, like Poincaré, "[Neurath] was influenced in part by considerations from [Fechner's] psycho-physics" (Uebel 2004: 37). Neurath's critique of the limitations of quantitative measurement in economics was evident early on in the 1910 essay: "Wundt emphasizes that political economy developed because measurable quantities were available. This indeed is the position of most political economists: only where there are measurable quantities can there exist a theory" (Neurath [1910] 2004: 274).

Neurath elaborated upon the virtues of qualitative or ordinal measures in his discussion of 'transfer conditions', through which term he meant to broaden the framework or bases for exchange beyond the exclusive reliance upon market prices. Here Neurath contended that a ranking system, what he referred to as "relations of order", was all that was required to provide the exactitude associated, mistakenly, with only "measurable quantities" (Neurath [1910] 2004: 276–277).

However, there are additional nuances to discern in highlighting the primacy of relations among variables. Neurath would establish tables, in symbolic form, to compare the value of different combinations of goods and, from that, life situations that would make possible the rational comprehension of the reallocation of resources to produce the most desirable outcome. At the same time, he stresses, time and again, the straitjacket imposed upon economics by the demand or requirement that any and all phenomena of significance be measurable as quantities. Neurath sees this as the means whereby economic theory is reduced to price theory, and monetary calculation comes to be understood not as one of the variety of means of exchange but rather as the standard measure for all economic calculation (also Neurath [1945] 2004: 547).

In his later work Neurath put forward a 'holistic' view of economic activity that was consistent in its initial outline with Pierre Duhem's treatment of the philosophy of science. Uebel in fact sees Neurath as "extend[ing] and radicali[zing] Duhem's result … to all sciences", but also incorporating into it "the historical conditioning of concept formation" (Uebel 1996: 131).

But Neurath's 'holism' in grappling with economic systems of organization also has a certain resonance with the approach taken by the German Historical School. The influence of Duhem is likely greater in one crucial respect, as Neurath took as one of the central tenets of his philosophy of science the need to introduce auxiliary hypotheses. This was Neurath's counterpart to Duhem's notion of 'underdetermination' in all scientific theorizing. As Neurath stated in his 1944 essay, "in the social sciences" even "relatively simple stories are full of hypotheses" (Neurath 1944: 14), requiring a choice to be made among various additional or 'auxiliary' hypotheses to determine the narrative ultimately put forward.

Neurath's critical program in economics

Neurath's critical program in economics was built around three essential elements that can be traced in the papers and monographs he wrote across the entire span of his career and lifetime, from a relatively early essay entitled "Zur Theorie der Sozialwissenschaften", dating from 1910, through a 1935 tract, "Was bedeutet rationale Wirtschaftsbetrachtung?", to a 1944 monograph titled "The Foundations of the Social Sciences".

First of all, according to Neurath, the nature and scope of economics tended to be conceived of too narrowly, as economics needed to be comprehended as the study of 'systems of organization' of economic life, rather than be limited to the activities and affairs of the 'market economy' (Neurath [1910] 2004: 272–273). While this may, with reason, be thought of as either a Marxist understanding of the nature of economics[3] or a framework initiated anew by Karl Polanyi,[4] the initial inspiration for this approach to economics cited by Neurath was List (Neurath [1910] 2004: 273). Thus, it grounds the notion of 'systems of organization' in the terrain of the German Historical School, which is in fact a concept that Neurath identified at the center of Roscher's work as the founder of that school (Neurath [1910] 1913, vol. I: 100). Even in somewhat later works in which Neurath had come to embrace Marxist ideas, he continued to cite List as one of his major influences, including in an article on "Total Socialisation", which appeared in 1920 (Neurath [1920] 2004: 374).[5]

Neurath's approach to economics was reinforced by his fondness for two economic visionaries who were both utopian and unorthodox in their outlook: Josef Popper-Lynkeus and Carl Ballod-Atlanticus. The latter's *Zukunftsstaat*, first published in 1898, laid out a statistically-based program for a transformative 'leisure-oriented socialism' infused with the virtues of mass production and the utopianism of Edward Bellamy. For all that, Ballod managed to run afoul of both "bourgeois" and socialist economists, as Neurath would later as well (Balabkins 1978: 5)[6] Late in his career, while in England, Neurath reflected upon the fact that thinkers like Popper-Lynkeus, who had also early on laid out the bases for some sort of economic plan, were not easy to pigeonhole as distinctly capitalist or socialist (Neurath 1943: 149).

For Neurath the focus upon economics as the study of various systems of organization (presumably economic and social, and perhaps, following the track taken by the historical school, cultural as well) placed him in opposition to Vilfredo Pareto, whose "mechanical analogy has contributed specifically to the advancement of the study of *homo oeconomicus*" (Neurath [1910] 2004: 273–274). Moreover, according to Neurath,

> Exact economics [for which Stanley Jevons and Pareto serve as exemplars] has neglected almost entirely the theory of the crises of overproduction, which is amenable to symbolic representation since it contains relations which concern the circulation, the transfer of goods, etc., and not just the level of prices.
>
> (Neurath [1910] 2004: 277)

Pareto's reliance upon 'measurable quantities' in constructing a system of level curves, which Neurath regarded as a crucial failing (Neurath 1911: 79), brought to light the second element in Neurath's program: the need to establish "a calculus of relations independent of measurable magnitudes" that would inform "all of political economy". Such a calculus would allow for the "exact treatment" of "comparable magnitudes" and take into account "combinatorial problems" as well (Neurath [1910] 2004: 278–279).

Hence, from Neurath's perspective, all sorts of 'non-measurable magnitudes', borrowing directly from the language of Henri Poincaré, needed to be incorporated into an economics that addressed a 'complex' of experiences that Neurath characterized as 'living situations'. This stood in contrast to any individual or disaggregated datum couched as a number. Poincaré's discussion of non-measurable magnitudes also emphasized the importance of capturing 'relations' among phenomena or variables, much as Neurath championed the role of relations between and among various economic phenomena.

Within the scope of comprehending measurement, Neurath also saw the virtue of using symbolic measures. Building upon his study of Ernst Schröder's algebraic logic, Neurath trumpeted the advances made in the fields of combinatorics and symbolic logic, and envisioned a logical calculus as facilitating the comprehension and calculation of relations among objects of nonmeasurable magnitude.

For all that, Neurath's subsequent work in economics tended to draw upon mathematical techniques, intuition, or models only to a rather limited degree. This, though, should not be treated as an intellectual pathway not pursued or as a consequence of Neurath's shift toward sociology. Instead, one might see Neurath's pedagogical experimentation in visual communication in the 1920s and afterward as constituting an outlet for his methodological inquiries in economics. As Keith Tribe has suggested, Neurath's introduction of *Bildstatistik* and the Isotype method was intended to provide a more adequate representation of economic data than numbers or indices could, through the creation of a visually-accessible totality that captured the complexity of 'living situations' (Tribe 1995: 163–167). This notion has been elaborated upon by Robert Leonard (Leonard 1999) and was the subject of an International Ludwig Wittgenstein Symposium devoted to an exploration of the range and implications of 'Otto Neurath's Visual Language' (Heinrich et al. 2011).

It was also a matter of language. As Neurath noted: "The rules of picture writing are different. Starting with 'icons' implies far reaching limitations of language, but these limitations sometimes eliminate much danger" (Neurath 1941: 133), thereby alluding to the 'dangerous terms' he had consistently sought to eliminate from the economics lexicon.[7]

All of this in turn led Neurath to the third element of his critique, which was to characterize economic experiences as 'clots' that could not be captured by the kind of law-making or rule-making that characterized the thought of classical economics or the newly emergent neoclassical economics. These 'clots' were formed from the "irregularities" and "indistinct" qualities of the world as observed, and are conveyed as such through "our daily speech". They stand in contrast to the notion that any scientific inquiry begins with "'simple basic assertions', 'atomic ideas', 'sense data', or their phraseological substitutes, i.e., something elementary, primitive, and poor" (Neurath 1944: 18).

Instead, such complexes comport with the 'incompleteness' Neurath, in line with his anti-foundationalist perspective, associated with the notion of scientific knowledge as an encyclopedia, which informed the scholarly project, the International Encyclopedia of the Unified Sciences, in the last decade of his life.

As Neurath expressed this notion in a 1941 presentation before the Aristotelian Society on 'Universal Jargon and Terminology', this was a matter that had to be comprehended through language, whether as speech, noted above, or as statements, below:

> Our initial observation statements in the sciences are not 'atomic', but are already imbedded [sic] in a body of statements derived from various sources, composed of indefinite terms such as 'microscope', 'looking through', 'inconsistent group of observed data'. Consequently no 'unique system of the world' remains, such as the 'rationalists' expected to find behind the screen, but bundles of bodies of statements which all more or less fit into our scientific pattern.
>
> (Neurath 1941: 129)

Accordingly, Neurath adopted a critical view of efforts to create scientific systems that proved more far-reaching than that taken by skeptical conventionalists, as such systems should be regarded as falling short of even becoming systems at all. Moreover, he noted, "it frequently happens that a certain theory useful in a determined field contradicts another theory useful in a different field. We have to compare bodies of statements which are not yet 'systems'" (Neurath 1941: 130).

Rational economics

Neurath's monograph on the theory of a rational economics dates from 1935, and forms part of a series devoted to the creation of a unity of sciences across disciplines. It carries forward many of the themes about the nature of economics that he had advanced from the earliest days of his economic pursuits. In the monograph Neurath retained and amplified the notion that the object of economics, and hence that which should accordingly be measured in economics, is what he called 'life situations'. From that Neurath contended that monetary calculation could not provide the full measure of economic value (Neurath 1935: 45–46), and against which he continued to set in contrast 'natural calculation', despite the opposition to this idea from both anti-socialists and socialists (Chaloupek 1990: 668–670). For Neurath, monetary calculation is identified as historically based, that is, as a customary practice and, like the terms 'cost', 'gain', and 'loss' is derived from commercial activity (Neurath 1935: 31–33). Neurath's enthusiasm for in-kind calculation was in fact rooted in his study of the economic organizations of the major states of classical antiquity, but especially that of ancient Egypt.

His focus upon the centrality of 'life situations' led him to see the need for applying an institutional framework to evaluate the virtues of different systems of economic organization, as the assessment of the 'correlation' of different 'life arrangements' with 'life situations' formed the basis for a 'rational economics' (Neurath 1935: 46).

The 1935 critique challenges, at least obliquely, any recourse to 'subjective value' in economics. Neurath's contemporaneous monograph on 'empirical sociology', whose treatment of the history of economic ideas drew heavily from the materials the Neuraths had presented in their 1910–1911 reader, was nonetheless more infused with a Marxist perspective. As such, in this work Neurath was at pains to point out that the introduction of valuations of the rightness or fairness of any economic action or development, which necessarily has a subjective quality to it, undermines the ability to establish an empirical test (Neurath 1931a). At this stage Neurath took the position that neither ethics nor volition produced changes in society; only the assertion of economic interests capable of forcing change could, and that was a measure of the class struggle.

Instead, such ethical or volitional valuations represented one form or another of metaphysical pseudo-rationalization, the nemesis of the 'scientific worldview' espoused by the Vienna Circle and articulated in its manifesto. In turn, Neurath emphasized the importance of analyzing 'behavior' in economics, as behavior could be subject to meaningful empirical testing. Curiously, though, one might posit, along with neoclassical, Austrian, or Keynesian theorists, that economic behavior sprang from psychological sources or motives, which would reintroduce subjective elements into economic analysis.

It is also set in tension with Neurath's view of the centrality of 'life situations', as these call for valuations that might be regarded as ethical, where 'happiness' trumps technical efficiency, evoking ironically at this moment the 'ethical standard' that Schmoller had touted. Here Neurath sought to transcend any seeming disjuncture between subjectivity and objectivity by claiming the possibility that all terminology and measures could be translated into an empirically based physicalist language (Neurath 1935: 9–11; also Neurath 1931b).

One of the most striking aspects of Neurath's 1935 critique of economics was his rejection of the conventional notion of capital, an exemplar of his case that a flawed linguistic foundation underlay broadly accepted economic concepts. Fundamentally, Neurath saw no basis for treating capital as homogeneous.

Geoffrey Hodgson contends that Thorstein Veblen's 1908 article challenging neoclassical capital theory constitutes one of the earliest signposts in this later critique of the nature and meaning of capital (Hodgson 1997: 101–102). Neurath's aversion to the term 'capital', though, was equally longstanding, dating back to his student days in Berlin in 1906, when it entered, and remained henceforth on, his index of dangerous terms (Marie Neurath 1973: 7).

Neurath took the matter a step further, linking it to an illusory practice of categorizing and quantifying (Neurath 1935: 41–45). He viewed the pricing of the cost of factors of production as essentially unnecessary or arbitrary, a form of naming that masks a lack of content. In this regard Neurath appears once more to be following elements of the conventionalism of Poincaré. Moreover, one might see in this challenge to the very notion of generic factor pricing a response and rebuke to neoclassical economic thought generally. See, for example, Neurath's critique of the use of factors of production in economic analysis as "insufficiently analyzed" and "mostly unnecessary" (Neurath 1911: 76).

In this instance it is directed at those like Ludwig von Mises who had contended that socialist, that is, natural or in-kind calculation had no mechanism to adequately price factors of production. After all, it was with regard to production itself, the generation of capital goods required, that von Mises had identified as the most glaring weakness in any 'socialist calculation'. The implication in Neurath's critique was that monetary calculation only appeared to establish 'logically satisfactory' factor pricing.

Neurath chose to demonstrate the heterogeneity of resources required through the example of the wherewithal required for a naval conflict. Hence, Neurath's example hewed to the model of a wartime or command economy, whereby the changes wrought by the exigencies of war are understood to have a lasting effect upon the operation and structure of the economy (Neurath 1935: 44–45). At the same time, to be consistent, this left open the question as to whether this critique of the use of the term 'capital' applied fully to all economic systems of organization.

1944 volume: a sharpened focus on language

The 1944 volume on "The Foundations of the Social Sciences", written in English, was one of a series of monographs intended to form an International Encyclopedia of the Unified Sciences. One of its most striking features is its sharpened focus on language, which as both text and footnotes bring out, reflects Neurath's involvement with the Vienna Circle and the panoply of activities related to it. It also serves as the source of the majority of economics terms deemed to be excluded on Neurath's 'Index' (see Reisch 1997b: 473–476). While the 1910 article takes the critique of the nature of scientific disciplines by Wilhelm Wundt as its point of departure, the 1944 work is replete with references to Rudolf Carnap, Hans Reichenbach, and Charles Morris, among others, all of whom were connected with the logical positivist, logical empiricist, or 'unity of science' movements that had been at the center of Neurath's life's work since the 1920s. This attention to language was intended to lay out the means of preventing the common pseudo-rationalizations that Neurath saw as the bane of genuine scientific inquiry; here, it would appear, to provide a more sure footing for an empirical sociology.

And yet in some ways there is an unmistakable subtext in this endeavor: while the text addresses primarily sociology, if in a manner embracing other disciplines, Neurath displays a strong need to highlight the failings, or at least the serious limitations, of economics as a scientific discipline. This should not come as surprising, since from the inception of the encyclopedia project in the mid-1930s Neurath had seen "economic theory" as having "its own place" in the project (Becchio 2013: 151).

If one compares the references in the 1910 and 1944 pieces, which serve as bookends to Neurath's effort to lay out the general terms of a theory of the social sciences, there is some overlap among the economic thinkers represented. Among those who do reappear are Jeremy Bentham, Pareto, Weber, Wilhelm

Neurath (Neurath's father, an economic historian), and Sismondi. Two figures of note from the interwar period surface only in the later piece: Henry Schultz and Lionel Robbins. Both appear at critical junctures in Neurath's critique, with Schultz viewed more favorably than Robbins. Neurath appeared to give some approbation to Schultz's attempt to bridge economic theorizing about consumer demand and the use of mathematical constructions, including econometric ones, with a mass of statistical evidence, an unspoken reconciliation of the conventionally posed sides in the "Methodenstreit". Nonetheless, Neurath also pressed on what he saw as Schultz's lack of full grounding of the correlations made, in essence calling into question the scientific basis for the use of econometrics. Robbins was viewed more critically. Neurath was derisive of Robbins' attempt to characterize macroeconomic measure like national income as "conventions", while treating them at the same time as standard measures in economics.

In the 1944 monograph Neurath challenged once more the presumption that economics was a science from the perspective of the philosophy of science, invoking again the lead provided by Mach, Duhem, and Poincaré in physics, but focusing upon the rhetoric and the complexities presented by the use of language in social interactions (Neurath 1944: 37–38).

Moreover, while framed as a critique of the 'Scientific Procedures in Sociology', Neurath's text attends largely to the flaws in economics as a discipline. Neurath saw economics as often taken – mistakenly – to be scientific, where "the empiricist character of statements" in the field is deemed sufficient to offer up "a comprehensive scientific analysis". By contrast, Neurath identified the bulk of what constitutes economics as rooted in tradition and history through the practice of "the systematized transfer of certain traditional institutions" (Neurath 1944: 38).

Neurath then clarifies what this distinction portends in limiting the scientific scope of the discipline, differentiating "a scientific investigation" from "a systematized, i.e., scientifically supported, transfer of traditions" (Neurath 1944: 38).

Moreover, this in turn becomes a more extended disquisition on the use of language and its implications for economics, where the expressions used represent "a kind of old folklore" or "speech customs" (Neurath 1944: 38–39). As an example he notes: "One speaks of the 'cost' of a production and goes on using this expression not only in our bookkeeping departments but also in social analysis" (Neurath 1944: 39).

Neurath then lays out the broader challenge by setting the "uneasiness" over economic "phraseology" in historical perspective, detailed in an extended note critiquing an array of economic thinkers:

> Very characteristic are the defects in the whole terminological approach made by Malthus, *The Principles of Political Economy* (2d ed., 1836), pp. 21, 47; in Richard Whately's *Elements of Logic* a great many of the 'ambiguous terms' in his appendix are economic ones, a topic on which the Archbishop also lectured. L. M. Fraser, in *Economic Thought and Language*

(London 1937), depicts the situation without suggesting a way out. Others criticize the terminological situation too (e.g., P. Sargent Florence, *Uplift in Economics* [London, 1929], and in other writings). Marshall and others try to justify what they call ' elasticity' in the use of terms (*Money Credit and Commerce*) [London, 1929], p. 13.

(Neurath 1944: 49)

Advancing to a late twentieth-century setting

One might look to aspects of Neurath's unorthodox or heretodox views about the nature of the social sciences, including economics, that prefigure critiques and countervailing approaches which came to the fore only decades later.

It is certainly the case that Neurath's longstanding concern that economics had to capture and measure 'life situations' rather than the prices and quantities of goods bought and sold, or, for that matter, a construction like 'national income', has a real resonance with the critique of traditional economic measures advanced by Amartya Sen (Lessmann 2008: 115–130) or advocates of an alternative index for gauging national economic well-being like Jean-Pierre Fitoussi and his collaborators.

There are other ways in which Neurath offers up a distinctive critique of economics, along with other social sciences, through his emphasis upon the need to "analyz[e] the science of language" (Neurath 1931b: 619). Moreover, his notion of the overriding role of hypotheses of varying sorts in arranging and explaining the 'facts' within any discipline represents an earlier version of what has come to be known as the 'metanarrative', which gained significant attention as part of a general 'linguistic turn' across various disciplines in the 1970s. Within economics the potential relativism associated with these ideas drew heavily from philosophers of science like David Bloor (Bloor 1976).

This continued in the 1980s with a heightened emphasis upon, variously, 'economic discourse', 'the rhetoric of economics', or 'the conversation among economists' in academic circles through the work of such figures as Deirdre McCloskey, Arjo Klamer, Warren Samuels, and Willie Henderson, among others. This 'linguistic turn' in economics drew upon a seemingly new awareness of the role that language, literary figurations like metaphor, and narratives played in shaping the nature of economic thought, and arose at the same time as a greater interest in and more formalized treatment of economic methodology emerged. As a late twentieth-century intellectual current, it was predicated on a distancing from, even an outright rejection of what was supposed to be the reigning philosophical outlook of the preceding period in the twentieth century: positivism. Oftentimes this new current was associated with its own version of relativism, as multiple narratives, each potentially valid in its own terms, were seen as superseding the singular, dominant 'narrative' of positivism.

Yet it was Neurath, one of the major figures in the logical positivist movement, who made the case for 'pluralism' decades before. In his 1944 essay, essentially a critical disquisition on the foundations of sociology and economics, he wrote that "[W]e should not overlook that even the simplest report [whether appearing in physics or the social sciences] is based on hypotheses and, therefore, pluralist" (Neurath 1944: 14).

In fact, early on Neurath had expressed the concern that theoretical advances – and here he focused upon a physical science like physics – depended upon the construction of different "systems of hypotheses", stating: "As we require theories in order to order facts, so we require theories in order to order theories" (Neurath 1914/1915: 101). The 'linguistic turn' in Neurath's approach is also tied to his anti-foundationalism. Throughout his career Neurath saw all "statement[s] about the world" as necessarily deriving their meaning from an unbounded network of statements in which they were embedded. So, in an early essay entitled, "The Lost Wanderers of Descartes", published in 1913, Neurath stated: "It is absolutely impossible to formulate a single statement about the world without making tacit use at the same time of countless others. Also we cannot express any statement without applying all of our preceding concept formation" (Neurath [1913] 1983: 3).

Then, in "The Orchestration of the Sciences by the Encyclopedism of Logical Empiricism", published posthumously in 1946, Neurath struck a similar chord: "We do not discuss 'isolated' items in chemistry, geology, or history, but every item is, as it were, an element of a 'cosmic aggregation'" (Neurath [1946] 1983: 232).

He then elaborated upon the implications of this 'aggregational attitude', contending that the limitations to prediction and predictability in science extended beyond "our incomplete knowledge of the situation", but rather inhered within the unbounded quality and connectivity of all statements and concepts (Neurath [1946] 1983: 232).

Here Neurath rebuffs any claims by scientists of the possibility of omniscience, ascribing that notion to the "absolutism of Laplace" (Neurath [1946] 1983: 232); rather, the unbounded quality and connectivity of all statements and concepts necessitates a continuing state of incompleteness, contradiction, and lack of full clairvoyance (see also Neurath 1938: 20–21).

Moreover, Neurath found greater stability in the terms found in everyday language than in scientific theories. But, as such terms are intended to capture essentially indeterminate concepts of everyday life, they do not lend themselves readily to prediction (Neurath [1936] 1983: 150).

Similarly, Neurath, following suit with Philipp Frank's conventionalist critique from the days of the First Vienna Circle (Frank 1949: 53–60; see also Uebel 2000: 68), challenged the false mold of causality formed by the language of 'cause-and-effect'. Again, this becomes a matter of language for Neurath, as he relates it to an 'asymmetry of expressions', rooted in the 'asymmetry of our speaking and writing', and sees it manifested in both scientific and 'everyday' 'terminological' contexts (Neurath 1944: 21).

Neurath extended his critique of the use of 'causation terminology' to "Marxist literature" for what he called its "strange" prioritizing of 'substructure' and 'superstructure' (Neurath 1941:142). In addition, he rejected as a form of "absolutism" the use of "terms which speak of certain 'standards'" (Neurath 1941: 142), singling out in particular Weber and the use of 'ideal type terms' (Neurath 1941: 142–143).

But it is also the case that Neurath retained the belief that such underdetermination and multiplicity of interpretations were not inconsistent with, indeed were essential to, establishing the unity of science (Reisch 1997a: 457), which effort fell within the purview of Neurath's lifelong campaign to advance an anti-metaphysical conception of the world. Moreover, unlike much of the discussion about the 'rhetoric of economics' that ensued in the 1980s and after, there was no tension in Neurath's conception between style and substance, evident, by contrast, in the criticisms leveled by Robert Solow (Solow 1988) and Robert Heilbroner (Heilbroner 1988).

Because Neurath did not conceive of this linguistic critique as riven by style and substance, the linguistic turn he set forth was in many ways more far-reaching and radical than that which emerged four decades later. After all, Neurath was calling into question the conceptual foundations of economic theory through it. As he stated in the 1944 monograph, what may appear to be, and is routinely presented as a science is lacking as such in fundamental ways, for it turns out to be in actuality a less-than-fully-systematized set of concepts couched in often ambiguous language grafted from 'customary practices', though not acknowledged as such. Thus, this was less the revelation that economics depended upon metaphors in its formation of concepts or constituted a discourse and more an examination of the flawed structure of economic ideas when built upon a precarious or even illusory linguistic foundation.

What might Neurath's critique of the language of economics portend for any reconsideration or reexamination of economic thought today? There are several strands that might be worth pursuing. For one, there is the continuing challenge of the fuzziness of economic concepts resulting from the incomplete 'sorting' of terminology that Neurath identified as far back as 1910. While Neurath gave primary attention to the ambiguity and haziness of terms like 'capital', one might readily extend such discussion to the difficulties attendant upon the use of 'saving' and 'investment', and, for that matter, 'national income' as well.

This in turn folds into a second line of inquiry. To what extent has the formation of concepts in economics occurred on an ad hoc basis, without sufficient effort to establish their connectivity, that is, their relation to one another, in a more systematic way (even allowing for the fact that none of them, in Neurath's view, can be comprehended as anchoring)?

Thirdly, that connectivity may depend upon "reasonable knowledge of [their] historical conditions", as Uebel has phrased it (Cartwright et al. 1996: 126). This would capture and account for the impact upon and the shaping of concepts Neurath deemed as drawn from 'bookkeeping' or accounting practices or from 'folklorist' tradition. At the least it would suggest the need for delving into the historical context in which the language of economic concepts is formed in order to achieve a greater measure of the 'scientificality' of economics, which Neurath found so elusive.

Epilogue: modernist or postmodernist?

How far does any such prefiguration go? A reassessment of Neurath's thought in recent decades has led to a greater emphasis upon his anti-foundationalism and 'naturalistic epistemology', reweighting his role as a positivist in far more ambivalent terms. Thomas Uebel cast this revised view of Neurath as 'overcoming logical positivism from within' (Uebel 1992).

To what extent does this break down the barriers between 'modernism' and 'postmodernism'?

In "The Genealogy of Postmodernism', published in 2001, Deirdre McCloskey advances the portrayal of Otto Neurath as the embodiment of modernism leading the charge for the imposition of a form of 'social engineering' in all matters of intellectual inquiry, referring to Neurath as one of the "bossy genius[es]" of modernism (McCloskey 2001: 108). McCloskey depicted Neurath scornfully as "subordinat[ing] everyone to his conveniently brief plan", "us[ing] a claim of transcendence to batter the opposition" (McCloskey 2001: 109).

One might point to Neurath's St.-Simonian evocation of the new age of the 'sociological organizer' replacing that of the 'priest' in his short piece on "Physicalism" in *The Monist* in support of McCloskey's claim of Neurath's modernism (Neurath 1931b: 622).

Yet it was also the case that in his own writings Neurath gave great weight to the role of 'pluralism' and anti-absolutism, including in this same article: "All [those following in the footsteps of Mach, Poincaré, and Peano] reject anything that smacks of the 'absolute' … " (Neurath 1931b: 619). He emphasized the 'underdetermination' of facts and the consequent requirement for multiple interpretations, based upon varying hypotheses. This might readily be translated into the multiple paradigms routinely associated with the ideas of Thomas Kuhn and the methodological critique of Paul Feyerabend[8] or the metanarratives of the linguistic turn itself. In fact, Kuhn's *The Structure of Scientific Revolutions*, was part of the same series of monographs as Otto Neurath's "Foundations of the Social Sciences", namely the International Encyclopedia of the Unified Sciences.

George Reisch argues strongly that Neurath's case was fundamentally modernist, in that all his challenges to the possibilities of prediction in science and his evocation of the rough edges of complexity found in 'aggregations' were all in the service of the 'unity of science', rather than the postmodernist 'disunity' adumbrated by John Dupré (Reisch 1997a).

Even so Reisch does note a certain resonance between Neurath's outlook and that of leading late twentieth-century thinkers often labeled as postmodern. For example, Reisch sees shades of Neurath's anti-Cartesianism in "Foucault['s] problematiz[ing of] the notion of an 'author'" (Reisch 1997b: 472). Also, one cannot overlook Neurath's emphasis upon "incompleteness" in conceiving of science as an encyclopedia, containing conflicting narratives.

There is a way to reconcile these seemingly contradictory pulls without grievously distorting the thrust of Neurath's work and ideas. Adapting an approach and understanding suggested by the *Annales* school of historians, especially Lucien Febvre, one might posit that the intellectual discourse of the early twentieth century would never have contemplated or contained the kind of disintegrative relativism, overturning any and all standards, associated with late twentieth-century postmodernism. But one can also posit the evolution of ideas, including in the history of economic thought, whereby older ways of thinking or tenets of schools of thought are carried forward, remixed, intertwined, or even revived in newer ways that may bear striking similarities and, as the frame of reference for intellectual discourse shifts, also hold differences with that which was espoused by an earlier generation.

Thus, while postmodernist ideas would have seemed anachronistic – out of time – in the first decades of the twentieth century, Neurath's conventionalism clearly presaged key elements of the postmodernism of the linguistic turn in economics in the late twentieth century. These include the necessity of treating economic subjects as a matter of narrative, the recognition of the multiplicity – and lack of congruence, even the "incompleteness" – of such narratives, and the centrality of an inquiry into the language of economics to establish its validity as a field, or critique its failings in that regard.

Notes

1 Elisabeth Nemeth has given great weight to a glowing letter which Neurath wrote to Mach in 1915, emphasizing its importance in shaping his 'holistic' perspective, yet Frank's account suggests at the least some tension between Mach's influence and that of Poincaré and Duhem, a point noted by Rudolf Haller (Haller 1991b: 99).

2 While primarily a psychologist, Wundt gained scholarly renown, especially in central Europe, for his *Logic of Science*, in which he sought to classify and differentiate among the physical sciences and the 'intellectual' or 'cultural' sciences. Like Neurath, Max Weber challenged Wundt's schema at the center of his 1906 methodological critique of Karl Knies.

3 One might see this presented along the lines, say, of Paul Sweezy's *Theory of Capitalist Development,* intended to serve as a counterpart and response to his mentor Joseph Schumpeter's *Theory of Economic Development.*

4 Giandomenica Becchio in fact sees something of the reverse, with Neurath's notions of 'administrative economy' and 'economy in-kind' serving as important influences upon Polanyi's emerging framework for economics (Becchio 2005: 16).

5 Eduard Meyer was also cited as a major influence in that article. Notably, Neurath made the case that in-kind economy gave way to a money economy not because of the exigencies of complex economic relations in the states of classical antiquity, but rather because of the perquisites of international trade.

6 Ballod (Ballod-Atlanticus was a pen name) had seen certain limitations to Marxism. In particular, "in Ballod's eyes, Marxism was only a theory of capitalist breakdown, not a theory of socialism" (Balabkins 1978: 218). This was a concern that Neurath, both as a writer about socialization and a socialist planning administrator, also had to contemplate.

7 In the last decade Neurath's interest in the use of visual symbols to serve as a universal language has also been explored in greater detail in relation to his work in urban and community planning and his association with architects like Le Corbusier and Laszlo Moholy-Nagy. (See, for example, Vossoughian 2008.)

8 Rudolf Haller made the following connection between Neurath and Feyerabend: "Neurath shares with Paul Feyerabend the view that basic elements of the scientific world-conception are already contained in magical practices; ... but Neurath already published these views nearly 50 years ago" (Haller 1991a: 35)

References

Balabkins, Nicholas W. (1978) "Der Zukunftsstaat: Carl Ballod's Vision of a Leisure-oriented Socialism". *History of Political Economy* 10(2): 213–232.

Bauer, Otto (1919) *Der Weg zum Sozialismus*. Wien: Ignaz Brand.

Becchio, Giandomenica (2005) "Two Heterodox Economists: Otto Neurath and Karl Polanyi". Centro di Studi sulla Storia e I Metodi dell'Economia Politica (CESMEP). Working paper No. 11.

Becchio, Giandomenica (2013) "Economics in the International Encyclopedia of Unified Science". *History of Economic Thought and Policy* 2: 145–156.

Bloor, David (1976) *Knowledge and Social Imagery*. London: Routledge and K. Paul.

Cartwright, Nancy, Cat, Jordi, Fleck, Lola, and Uebel, Thomas (1996) *Otto Neurath: Philosophy between Science and Politics*. Cambridge: Cambridge University Press.

Chaloupek, Gunther K. (1990) "The Austrian Debate on Economic Calculation in a Socialist Economy". *HOPE* 22(4): 659–675.

Frank, Philipp (1941) *Between Physics and Philosophy*. Cambridge, MA: Harvard University Press.

Frank, Philipp (1949) *Modern Science and Its Philosophy*. Cambridge: Harvard University Press.

Haller, Rudolf (1991a) "History and the System of Science in Otto Neurath". In Thomas Uebel, ed., *Rediscovering the Forgotten Vienna Circle*. New York: Springer, pp. 33–40.

Haller, Rudolf (1991b) "The First Vienna Circle". In Thomas Uebel, ed., *Rediscovering the Forgotten Vienna Circle*. Dordrecht: Springer, pp. 95–108.

Hayek, F.A. (1935) "The Nature and History of the Problem". In F.A. Hayek, ed., *Collectivist Economic Planning*. London: G. Routledge, pp. 1–40.

Hayek, F.A. (1994) *Hayek on Hayek: An Autobiographical Dialogue*. Eds. Stephen Kresge and Leif Wenar. London: Routledge.

Heilbroner, Robert (1988) "Rhetoric and ideology". In Arjo Klamer, Donald N. McCloskey, and Robert M. Solow, eds., *The Consequences of Economic Rhetoric*. Cambridge: Cambridge University Press, pp. 38–43.

Heinrich, Richard, Nemeth, Elisabeth, Pichler, Wolfram, and Wagner, David, eds. (2011) *Image and Imaging in Philosophy, Science and the Arts*. Volume 2. New Brunswick, NJ: Ontos verlag.

Hodgson, Geoffrey (1997) "The Fate of the Cambridge Capital Controversy". In Philip Arestis, Gabriel Palma, and Malcolm Sawyer, eds., *Capital Controversy, Post-Keynesian Economics*. London: Routledge, pp. 95–110.

Leonard, Robert J. (1999) "'Seeing is Believing'. Otto Neurath, Graphic Art, and Social Order". *History of Political Economy* 31(4): 452–478.

Lessmann, Ortrud (2008) "A Similar Line of Thought in Neurath and Sen: Interpersonal Comparability". In E. Nemeth*et al.*, eds., *Otto Neurath's Economics in Context*. Dordrecht: Springer, pp. 115–130.

McCloskey, Deirdre M. (2001) "The Genealogy of Postmodernism: An Economist's Guide". In Stephen Cullenberg, Jack Amariglio, and David F. Ruccio, eds., *Postmodernism, Economics and Knowledge*. London: Routledge, pp. 102–128.

Mises, Ludwig (1920) "Die Wirtschaftsrechnung in sozialistischen Gemeinwesen". *Archiv für Sozialwissenschaften und Sozialpolitik* 47(1): 86–121.

Nemeth, Elisabeth (2008) "'Freeing up One's Point of View': Neurath's Machian Heritage Compared with Schumpeter's". In *Otto Neurath's Economics in Context*. Dordrecht: Springer, pp. 13–36.

Nemeth, Elisabeth, Schmutz, Stefan W., and Uebel, Thomas E., eds. (2008) *Otto Neurath's Economics in Context*. Dordrecht: Springer.

Neurath, A. and Neurath, O. [1910] (1913) *Lesebuch der Volkswirtschaftslehre*. 2 vols. 2nd ed., Leipzig: G.A. Gloeckner.

Neurath, Marie (1973) "University Days in Berlin". In Marie Neurath and Robert S. Cohen, eds., *Empiricism and Sociology*. Trans. Paul Foulkes and Marie Neurath. Dordrecht: Reidel.

Neurath, Otto [1910] (2004) "On the Theory of Social Science". In Thomas E. Uebel and Robert S. Cohen, eds., *Otto Neurath: Economic Writings/Selections 1904–1945*. [Multiple translators.] Dordrecht: Kluwer Academic Publishers, pp. 265–291.

Neurath, Otto (1911) "Nationalokonomie und Wertlehre, eine systematische Untersuchung". *Zeitschrift für Volkswirtschaft, Sozialpolitik under Verwaltung* 20: 52–115.

Neurath, Otto [1913] (1983) "The Lost Wanderers of Descartes and the Auxiliary Motive". In Robert S. Cohen and Marie Neurath, eds. and trans., *Philosophical Papers 1913–1946*. Dordrecht: D. Reidel Publishing Company, pp. 1–12.

Neurath, Otto [1914/1915] (1981) "Zur Klassifikation von Hypothesen systemen". In Rudolf Haller and Heiner Rutte, eds., *Gesammelte philosophische und methodologische Schriften*. Volume 1. Wien: Holder-Pichler-Tempsky, pp. 85–101.

Neurath, Otto [1920] (2004) "Total Socialisation". In Thomas E. Uebel and Robert S. Cohen, eds., *Otto Neurath: Economic Writings: Selections 1904–1945*. [Multiple translators.] Dordrecht: Kluwer Academic Publishers, pp. 371–404.

Neurath, Otto (1931a) *Empirische soziologie*. Wien: J. Springer.

Neurath, Otto (1931b) "Physicalism: The Philosophy of the Vienna Circle". *The Monist* 41(4): 618–623.

Neurath, Otto (1935) *Was bedeutet rationale Wirtschaftsbetrachtung?* Wien: Verlag Gerold & Co.

Neurath, Otto [1936] (1983) "Encyclopedia as 'Model'". In Robert S. Cohen and Marie Neurath, eds. and trans., *Philosophical Papers 1913–1946*. Dordrecht: D. Reidel Publishing Company, pp. 145–158.

Neurath, Otto (1938) "Unified Science as Encyclopedic Integration". In Otto Neurath, Rudolf Carnap, and Charles Morris, eds., *International Encyclopedia of Unified Science*. Vol. 1, numbers 1–5. Chicago: University of Chicago Press, pp. 1–27.

Neurath, Otto (1941) "Universal Jargon and Terminology". *Proceedings of the Aristotelian Society* 41 (New Series): 127–148.

Neurath, Otto (1943) "Planning or Managerial Revolution?" *New Commonwealth Quarterly*: 148–154.

Neurath, Otto (1944) *Foundations of the Social Sciences*. Chicago: University of Chicago Press.

Neurath, Otto [1945] (2004) "Alternatives to Market Competition". In Thomas E. Uebel and Robert S. Cohen, eds., *Otto Neurath: Economic Writings/Selections 1904–1945*. [Multiple translators.] Dordrecht: Kluwer Academic Publishers, pp. 546–548.

Neurath, Otto [1946] (1983) "The Orchestration of the Sciences by the Encyclopedism of Logical Empiricism". In Robert S. Cohen and Marie Neurath, eds. and trans., *Philosophical Papers 1913–1946*. Dordrecht: D. Reidel Publishing Company, pp. 230–242.

O'Neill, John (1999) "Ecology, Socialism and Austrian Economics". In E. Nemeth and R. Heinrich, eds., *Otto Neurath: Rationalität, Planning, Vielfalt*. Vienna: Weiner Reihe, pp. 123–145.

O'Neill, John (2004) "Ecological Economics and the Politics of Knowledge: The Debate between Hayek and Neurath". *Cambridge Journal of Economics* 28: 431–447.

Poincaré, Henri (1906) *Wissenschaft und Hypothese*. Authorized German edition with explanatory noes by F. & L. Lindemann. 2nd improved edition. Leipzig: B.G. Teubner.

Reisch, George (1997a) "How Postmodern was Neurath's Ideas of Unity of Science?" *Studies in History and Philosophy of Science Part A* 28(3): 439–451.

Reisch, George A. (1997b) "Economist, Epistemologist ... and Censor? On Otto Neurath's Index Verborum Prohibitorum". *Perspectives on Science* 5: 452–480.

Solow, Robert (1988) "Comments from inside economics". In Arjo Klamer, Donald N. McCloskey, and Robert M. Solow, eds., *The Consequences of Economic Rhetoric*. Cambridge: Cambridge University Press, pp. 31–37.

Tribe, Keith (1995) *Strategies of Economic Order: German Economic Discourse, 1750–1950*. Cambridge: Cambridge University Press.

Turk, Michael (2006) "The Fault Line of Axiomatization". *European Journal of the History of Economic Thought* 13(2): 195–212.

Turk, Michael (2012) "The Mathematical Turn in Economics: Walras, The French Mathematicians, and the Road Not Taken". *Journal of the History of Economic Thought* 34(2): 149–167.

Uebel, Thomas E. (1992) *Overcoming Logical Positivism from Within*. Amsterdam: Rodopi.

Uebel, Thomas E. (1996) "Normativity and Convention". In E. Nemeth and F. Stadler, eds., *Encyclopedia and Utopia: The Life and Work of Otto Neurath*. Amsterdam: Kluwer, pp. 97–112.

Uebel, Thomas (2000) *Vernunftkritik und Wissenschaft: Otto Neurath und der erste Wiener Kreis*. Wien: Springer-Verlag.

Uebel, Thomas (2004) "Introduction". In *Otto Neurath: Economic Writings Selections 1904–1945*. Dordrecht: Kluwer Academic Publishers, pp. 1–108.

Vossoughian, Nader (2008) *Otto Neurath: The Language of the Global Polis*. Rotterdam: NAi Publishers.

8 Socialist calculation in an age of information

Economic debates often prove to be proxies for political debates. Perhaps nowhere is this more apparent than in the debate over socialist calculation, in which the clash of economic ideas serves as an intellectual forum through which the possibilities for socialism are weighed against those for capitalism; hence, as much as one might find in any crossfire of economic ideas, the debate is made to turn on predicting outcomes: 'who won' and 'who lost'.

If accepted in this form, one is left to consider whether economics should be regarded primarily as an instrument, casting aside any pretense of being a science. But one also faces the possibility that economic theory ought to arise from 'rational' inquiry independent of any school of economic thought or political perspective. This was the position taken by Otto Neurath, despite the fact that as an advocate for socialization he himself was a central figure in the debate over socialist calculation, even if typically treated as a foil within it.

All of this sets the stage for an exploration of such a crossfire of ideas between Neurath and the leading Austrian economists of the day that marked this debate. To this, though, must be added two elements about how to think about economic life that have emerged in recent decades. Both may have a profound impact upon the terms of the debate, as they center upon matters central to the critiques of socialist calculation regarding the scope of information and the place and nature of measurement in economics. First, what are the implications of the surfeit of information now available with the advent of an 'age of information'? Second, to what extent do ecological considerations in economics reopen questions about the nature of economic value and measurement?

Historical setting: an Austrian affair

The debate over socialization in central Europe took place in the wake of the economic and political collapse accompanying the defeat of the Central Powers in World War I. One of its most important crucibles was the pre-war seminar in economics held in Vienna under the auspices of Eugen von Böhm-Bawerk.

Böhm-Bawerk resumed his economics seminar at the University of Vienna in 1905/1906, after he left his post for the last time as finance minister in the administration of the (k.k.) Austro-Hungarian Empire.[1] For his own work on the theory of capital and his critique of Marx's theory of capital in the posthumously published third volume of *Capital,* Böhm-Bawerk was identified as one of the leading figures in the emergent Austrian school of economics, often acknowledged in his time as the second most foremost economist, after Alfred Marshall.

His seminar was noteworthy for its inclusiveness. The often imperious Ludwig von Mises remembered with approbation, even a touch of amazement, the dueling debate over the nature of value in economics between Böhm-Bawerk and Otto Bauer, then a leading young Marxist, that provided the cynosure for discussion for an entire semester (Mises 1978: 39–40).

Equally remarkable, though, was the fact that the participants in this seminar would go on to form the near-universe of economists most directly engaged in the claims and debate over socialization in central Europe after World War I. Two of the Marxists (or neo-Marxists) attending the seminar, Rudolf Hilferding and Emil Lederer, were joined by a non-Marxist attendee, Joseph Schumpeter, to constitute the German Socialization Committee that explored the possibilities of socializing the German economy in 1919 and 1920, a moment of seemingly peak fluidity before the postwar economic and political mold defined as the Weimar era had formed.

Meanwhile, it fell to Otto Bauer to head up the socialization committee in the newly formed republic of Austria, whose subsequent collection of writings in that capacity was titled *Der Weg zum Sozialismus* (Bauer 1919). Though less noted as a presence in the seminar, Otto Neurath was also an attendee, much to the dismay of von Mises (Mises 1978: 40). It was Neurath who advanced most fully the idea that a form of in-kind or natural calculation should supersede monetary calculation, which, modeled on wartime economies or ancient ones (or both), would serve as the hallmark of a new socialized economy.

Neurath wrote extensively about the subject, but, alone among all these figures, was at least briefly able to serve as a practitioner as well, in the short-lived radical republics formed in Saxony and Bavaria. For his part, Ludwig von Mises wrote the first substantive attack on the notion that 'socialist calculation' was possible, citing Neurath's work in particular (Mises 1920: 102, 119). Finally, while Friedrich von Hayek belonged to a later generation and was too young to attend the seminar, the title of his 1944 work challenging all manner of collective activity and planning, *The Road to Serfdom* (Hayek 1944), seems clearly intended to present a response to Bauer's (1919) *Der Weg zum Sozialismus,* as one might imagine a parallel verbal construction to that employed by Alfred Hitchcock as a movie title, "[It takes a thief] to catch a thief".

Moreover, it was no doubt a major achievement in plumbing the depths of the foundations of economics when, in 1937, Hayek advanced the notion that economic affairs were predicated upon the exchange of information, signals of intent or purpose, encoded in some fashion, from which economic decisions were made and economic activity entered into and effected (Hayek [1937] 1948). This thesis about economics and information would inform Hayek's critique of claims made in support of socialization and central economic planning.

Yet Hayek's exploration of a theory of knowledge which underlay economics can also be situated in the intellectual and political ferment pervading Vienna that both preceded and followed World War I. Hayek himself alluded to the stimulation he received in reacting to and opposing the philosophical claims set forth by Neurath within the Vienna Circle and subsequent logical empiricist movement in promoting the unity of science (Hayek 1994: 50).

One especially keen insight into the atmosphere of the period and the commonality of concerns for properly grounding all forms of intellectual inquiry, despite – and across – ideological differences, can be found in the appreciation provided by Karl Popper, a longstanding friend of Hayek's from their days of acquaintance in London in the late 1930s, of Otto Neurath after his death:

> Neurath and I had disagreed deeply on many and important matters, historical, political, and philosophical; in fact on almost all matters which interested us both except one – the view that theory of knowledge was important for an understanding of history and of political problems
>
> (Popper 1973: 56)

Neurath and 'In-kind' calculation

Neurath put forward the case for what was termed 'in-kind' calculation, which was intended to supersede monetary calculation and serve as the vehicle for transforming economies, like those of the various German states, into a 'natural economy'. Neurath produced a remarkable number of papers, both published and unpublished, on this subject, most evident in the period beginning in the midst of World War I but extending well into the 1930s. At the same time Neurath showed great interest in the formation of an economy based upon communitarian principles, captured early on in a letter from Max Weber to a colleague in 1917, in which Weber mused about Neurath's engagement with the notion of "Gemeinwirtschaft", referring to it as a metaphorical "herring salad" (Weber 2008, letter of 1 September 1917: 760).

However, the genesis of this idea, and the role that in-kind calculation might play in it, can be traced to an array of different notions and influences that had surfaced well before World War I. In the years just prior to its outbreak Neurath had produced a detailed study for the Carnegie Commission of the operation of the economies in the Balkans during the First and Second Balkan Wars, highlighting the distinctiveness of the command economy engendered by the exigencies of wartime conditions.

This dovetailed with, and elaborated upon, three other elements underlying the possibility of introducing alternatives to the existing economic order, that is, the current state of capitalism in central Europe at the turn of the twentieth century. These included the following:

1 Neurath's study of the economies of classical antiquity, especially that of dynastic Egypt, which appears as a constant refrain in his own writings – and speeches, including in addresses to workers councils at the height of the campaign for socialization.
2 A response, not altogether unlike that of Rudolf Hilferding (1910) in his more well-known contemporaneous work, *Das Finanzkapital,* to the omnipresence of cartelization and the rise of finance capitalism, with the concomitant increasing centralization of major economic enterprises. Here Neurath reflected the influence of his father, Wilhelm Neurath, who had written and lectured about the economic crises wrought by increasing cartelization, overproduction, and large-scale unemployment.
3 Neurath's own attraction to and enthusiasm for utopian schemes, most notably those proposed and sketched out by Carl Ballod-Atlanticus (1898) and Josef Popper-Lynkeus (1912). It is not insignificant that the former was viewed as idiosyncratic from more conventional socialist perspectives, while the latter was in fact if anything an anti-Marxist. Even at the end of Neurath's career he continued to note that these utopian proposals were quite ambiguous in drawing any bright line between capitalism and socialism (Neurath 1943: 149).

These elements were striking to Neurath's contemporaries. In his autobiography Lujo Brentano, whom Neurath himself had once described, with a touch of irony, as Germany's greatest living economist (Neurath 1973: 18), castigated Neurath both for his romance with ancient Egypt and his utopianism in pursuing the 'total socialization' of the Bavarian economy in 1919:

> The central administration has called upon, among others from Austria, the 'utopia-talking' Dr. Neurath, who advocates for 'total socialization'. I once had to participate in a meeting in which he laid out his economic plans for the future. They corresponded in foundational principle with an economic organization, as might have existed in ancient Egypt, when everyone lived directly or indirectly under kings.
>
> (Brentano 1931: 364)

For all this, though, what stands out about the idea behind 'in-kind' calculation is that it is drawn from two sources in Neurath's thinking about economics, neither of which, on the surface, is necessarily associated with a socialist perspective or the advancement of the cause of socialism. In fact, Keith Tribe has gone so far, with reason, to declare that "Neurath was not a Marxist economist; he did not derive his proposals for socialist economic administration from any specific political doctrine" (Tribe 1995: 143).

First of all, from Neurath's 1906 doctoral dissertation, that is, his Habilitationsschrift, he cast an economic model drawn from the experience of classical antiquity, with the influence of Eduard Meyer, an economic historian from the German Historical School, most evident, asserting that the requirement for conducting transactions in money grew out of international trade and exchange rather than economic complexity per se. Hence, a coordinating entity that could oversee the organization and acquisition of resources and goods and identify the requisite system of credits to render it operational was essential. In the context of dynastic Egypt this was a Girobank; in the world of newly socialized economies in postwar Europe this would take the form of a central planning office.

Second, and of equal, or perhaps even greater, importance were the limitations Neurath had observed and descried in the marginalist and neoclassical constructions of economic satisfaction and value, a result, he thought, owing to their mistaken reliance upon monetary calculation. This challenge stood at the center of Neurath's critique of the economic orthodoxy of the first decades of the twentieth century in his journal articles published in 1910 and 1911, which appear more reflective of an outlook shaped by the German Historical School than any Marxist ideals. Fundamentally, Neurath felt from early on in his career that monetary calculation mistook what was of value in economic life.

Tribe went on to characterize Neurath's case for the natural economy in the following way:

> [Neurath's] arguments for natural economy and the administration of economic life with respect to defined social ends derived from his belief in the essential rationality of 'modern man' and his ability purposefully to order the world in a socially optimal fashion.
>
> (Tribe 1995: 143)

The 'defined social ends' though, are not too clearly defined. In fact, one might contend that they are subsumed by the notion of "order[ing] the world in a socially optimal fashion". As the 'end goal' stated by Neurath was the maximization of 'social happiness', the embodiment of a "specific", if not in all respects "political doctrine", namely social epicureanism. Neurath, it should be noted, was able to make himself a Marxist in part by inverting the terms by which one would discern and distinguish political perspectives, as he then referred to Marxism as fundamentally a doctrine of "social epicureanism" (Neurath [1928] 1973: 282–290).

Neurath did strive to place economics on a rational footing (see his 1935 tract, for example), and did associate the rationality of the Enlightenment and the scientific inquiry that would conform to it with the 'modern world", as was the case in the 1939 volume on *Modern Man in the Making*. Nonetheless, he did not explicitly link 'rationality' and 'modernity' as the keys to attaining a 'natural economy'.

The critique in short form

John O'Neill (1999) has rightly pointed out that there were two strands in the critique by Austrian-school economists of Neurath's case for 'natural calculation' and central planning in a socialist economy. The first of these came from Ludwig von Mises, who derided the possibility of a socialist economy, pointed to the need for prices to emerge out of markets in order for economic activity to succeed. For Mises the difficulty was a matter of measurement. The lack of commensurability in valuing resources and goods would undo the possibility of making rational and efficient economic decisions. In Mises' mind such commensurability could be attained only through the instrument of money and a system of prices set in monetary units. Moreover, as Don Lavoie (1985) pointed out, Mises saw the creation and operation of such markets as contingent upon the existence of private property relations.

Meanwhile, Hayek's critique of Neurath's notion of the virtues of in-kind over monetary calculation and the possibilities afforded by central planning centered upon the relation between economics and the information necessary for its effectuation. It appeared in an essay published in 1935 as part of a larger collection of pieces amassed as a rejoinder to calls for collectivist economic organization of any sort. It was rooted fundamentally in an epistemological conceit, upon which Hayek elaborated in his 1937 paper on 'economics and knowledge'.

Hayek saw the translation of economic decision-making into a matter of exchanging information as the basis for the necessity of decentralized markets to effectuate economic activity and thus the death knell for any central economic planning. O'Neill cast this in terms of the capacity to gauge accurately the "dispersal of local knowledge" (O'Neill 1999: 133). Hayek reasoned that the number of exchanges required in even the simplest of economic decisions was so large as to defeat the efforts of any conscious calculator attempting to grasp and control the situation (Hayek [1935] 1948: 154–156). Moreover, Hayek saw as pertinent knowledge what he called "technique of thought", embodied in thoughts, actions, and skills, that would not be explicitly expressed (Hayek [1935] 1948: 155). In Hayek's view, socialist calculation was an impossibility.

In Hayek's critique prices became the necessary "bits of information" (Hayek [1937] 1948: 50–51) underlying all exchange; it was price signaling that encoded such information, which might include "unarticulated" elements, and such signaling could only take place in decentralized structures, namely markets (Hayek [1945] 1948: 85–86). Signaling in such a manner was necessary because the information encoded would include elements of belief or perception that could not be 'articulated' as distinct and discrete quantities, subject to physical measurement. Price signaling, markets, and bits of information all formed part of one philosophical package. Hence, both philosophical and economic assumptions, as well as implications, must be taken into account in measuring the state of Hayek's case today.

On language and information: a philosophical tug-of-war

In the contest between Neurath and Hayek, the intellectual groundwork is largely epistemological, with information and communication at the center.

Through this philosophical tug-of-war one can see the wellspring for new ideas about the role of language and information in economics to emerge. Several themes surface within that framework: (1) the centrality of epistemological inquiry in political economy; (2) the comprehension of the possibilities afforded by understandings drawn from other scientific fields; and (3) the interplay of 'modern' and 'postmodern' elements. In short, it would be worthwhile introducing and engaging with other aspects of both figures' thought in looking anew at the matter of socialist calculation.

One could posit that Neurath was as engaged in matters of information as Hayek, with a similar interest in the philosophical foundations underlying its value and purpose, if not necessarily comprehended primarily in terms of the exchange of information, Hayek's price signals. Neurath emphasized the importance of statistics and the requirement of relying upon observables. The need for coordination and planning meant at least implicitly that the communication of such information held great weight as well; hence the design of a central office for gathering statistics.

For all that such information might be represented visually, a major pursuit in Neurath's life's work, though, it would be difficult to cast these visual depictions and their symbolic notations as 'postmodern', in contrast to Hayek, at least as portrayed as such by Deirdre McCloskey (2001: 111). This is so because Hayek translated economic information into the exchange of bits of information, encoded as price signals. Neurath's observables, taken to be communicable as 'observable statements', were linked to the representation and analysis of behavior, with differing degrees of pleasure serving as crucial measures of the satisfaction associated with such behavior.

Yet it is Neurath who presaged a 'linguistic turn' in economics, while Hayek's turn to encoding and decoding information, for all its 'postmodern' sensibility, must be understood as conforming to an abstracted and ultimately more traditionally understood structure of language. Hence, an unlikely cross-current exists with regard to matters of information and language between the two figures. Moreover, their views on the limitations of knowledge provide yet another, taken up below in considering the paradox regarding the possibility of omniscience.

One essential difference stands out in this focus upon language and information. Neurath's distance from Wittgenstein notwithstanding, his concerns about information can and should be comprehended as the relation between facts and statements, that is, set in the context of the Wittgensteinian 'facts of the world' as put forward in the *Tractatus Logico-Philosophicus*.

Hayek's version of information is subsumed by a theory of communication (whether Claude Shannon, a contemporaneous pioneer in this field, is acknowledged in this discussion or not) involving the transmission of bits of information. In general Hayek was far less inclined to draw from the physical sciences than Neurath; that, after all, according to Hayek's own reflections, was one of the decisive elements in his thought consciously set against the views of Neurath. But it was also the case that Hayek delved into matters of sensory perception to undergird his thesis about price signaling (Hayek 1952), while Neurath often, if not consistently, resorted to a depiction of economic behavior based upon gauging stimuli and responses (Neurath [1931] 1973: 362–364).

The road to 'an age of information'

The vastly increased ability to gather and sort information through technological developments in recent decades has presented a new challenge to Hayek's epistemic critique. Have these technological advances created a critical pathway toward planning? In certain respects, the model for this transformation can be found in the system used by U.S. airlines that led to the broader reservation systems underlying contemporary transportation networks, affecting thereby the planning for such systems. Once again, a crucial role in examining these economic and philosophical contentions must be accorded historical context.

In the early 1950s, amidst the deepening of the Cold War, the U.S. Department of Defense nurtured the development of a system to facilitate the flow of messages for the U.S. airforce by using computers, then the province of the U.S. military, under the aegis of the Defense Department, and selected universities. In 1957 the leading U.S. firm in the business of constructing electronic machinery, International Business Machines (IBM), devised a civilian application of this technology for the U.S. airline industry, specifically the carrier American Airlines, known as SABRE (Semi-Automated Business Research Environment). It is noteworthy that this occurred at a moment when the airline industry was itself undergoing a major transformation that had been fueled by two other wartime technological advances: the introduction of the jet engine and the widespread use of improved systems of radar detection.

The broadening and systematizing of this approach to coordinating and managing reservations into a smooth network then became the prototype for both business and government to gain mastery over what had heretofore been seen as overwhelming pieces of information. As reported in the archives of IBM, "By the mid-1960s, Sabre became the largest private, real-time data processing system, second in size only to the US government's system". Moreover, as this model gained more widespread use, it fundamentally altered the capacity to absorb and order bits of information across wide swaths of economic activity and life in the last decades of the twentieth century. As the IBM archive described it, "[Sabre served as] the precursor for the entire universe of electronic commerce that exploded in the mid-1990s".[2]

Revisiting the critique

Thus, the first matter to take up in revisiting this critique of socialist calculation is the impact of 'an age of information' upon the possibility of calculation. Hayek argued that the number of pieces of information required for any single market exchange would simply overwhelm the calculators at the central planning office, adducing figures (or estimates) seemingly beyond comprehension. At best, then, central planners would be compelled to rely upon a tiny fraction of the information underlying the operation of any single industry; those planners would act in ignorance of the vast sea of knowledge within the industry and produce thereby only the crudest estimate of needed or desired output or the requisite resources to be marshaled in order to reach that goal.

Curiously, this critique raises as a secondary concern a subject routinely discussed in microeconomics, even at the rudimentary level: the meaning of perfect information. It is understood as a point of little contention that markets characterized as pure or perfect, that is, markets taken as the norm or starting point in standard, neoclassical economics, require all economic agents to possess "perfect information". This, though, does not translate into all such agents knowing everything about the market; rather, it demands only that all economic agents have sufficient information to act rationally, as an "economic person" might do. So, one may ask, should the requisite omniscience of the calculating central planner be, in effect, similarly downgraded to the level of sufficiency, enough information, in short, to make a rational set of decisions?

As a corollary, might one find a statistical version of this sufficiency via the central limit theorem, so that a rational organization of information through correct sampling would relieve the calculating planner of the impossible task Hayek foresaw? This, of course, would make the matter of correct sampling crucial. For example, would observed outcomes, in which it is presumed that intentions and expectations, the 'inarticulated' pieces of information, would be subsumed, be equal to the task? Or, would this prove to be difficult, or even insurmountable? How readily could it take into account "techniques of thought"?

Paradoxically, it is the central limit theorem to which some theorists have turned to buttress the case for the tendency of markets, on their own, to be efficient, linking it mathematically, for example, to the notion of the random walk. The caution raised by skeptics as to whether economic phenomena and experience comport readily with the critical assumption of randomness is too easily overlooked. Neurath, for one, would hardly have accepted this case, in that from his long-held philosophical perspective this entire operation would require the positing of an auxiliary hypothesis about the efficiency of markets, thus effectively embedding the conclusion in the underlying assumptions of the model.

The notion that the planner might find salvation from the mathematical nightmare suggested by Hayek and other similarly minded critics holds a further irony. Firms commonly derive working demand curves for their products in this way; the growth of marketing as a field within business administration, now a century old, is both predicated upon this, and follows from it. Moreover, the capacity to produce such projected patterns of consumer behavior has been enhanced dramatically through the development of electronic commerce, 'e-commerce', in the last two decades. Firms now have the ability to use as information for marketing purposes the interests and preferences of innumerable consumers, both potential and actual, through the signals they provide on their own computers. The sophisticated nature of these firms' probes suggests that 'unarticulated' elements might well have been absorbed into their calculus of consumer behavior. Firms are able to track patterns of "hits" in what is often trumpeted as part of the triumph of capitalism, even though libertarians of right and left, among others, would likely deplore the invasion of privacy associated with these new practices.

In a certain sense this greatly enhanced capacity to sort through a massive surfeit of information may constitute a parallel to the phenomenon of cartelization witnessed at the turn of the twentieth century, which strongly influenced both Hilferding and Neurath, but also affected Schumpeter's thinking as well: that is, the trends in economic life themselves militate toward a societal transformation, where the question becomes one of deciding under whose auspices the newly established forms of economic activity and life ought to be guided – private or public?

All of this leads to the more general point about the impact and implications of the new age of information, centered about the computer: the calculations which Hayek discussed as past any human capacity can now be made. How planners might structure the organization of resources to obtain the necessary information, as noted above, remains to be addressed. This is a matter of no small concern, but it needs to be taken up directly, as the initial threshold or barrier constructed by Hayek no longer exists.

One might see this as falling more under the purview of Mises' challenge, highlighting the problem he viewed as entailed by the need for commensurability. It should be noted that Mises conceded that patterns of consumption might be amenable to some version of distributional planning (Mises [1920] 1935: 102). He focused instead upon the necessity of monetary calculation to effectuate rational decisions regarding investment, the application of capital, and the acquisition of resources. He chose the following example: "Picture the building of a new railroad. Should it be built at all, and if so, which out of a number of conceivable roads should be built?"

The answer, he claimed, required the use of "monetary calculation" (Mises [1920] 1935: 108).

On commensurability and capital

Thus, Neurath's critique of the use of the term 'capital' is of special significance in his disputation with Ludwig von Mises. In part he saw its use as possible only because of the mistaken introduction of monetary calculation, rendering the heterogeneity of the physical and constructed resources that went into production as somehow homogeneous, a matter Joan Robinson would later take up as well. In part Neurath challenged the use of the term for the false precision that characterized much of economic thought: transform a murky and imprecise subject into a seeming 'term of art', presumed thereby to be scientific, by naming it, without the full-scale thought and empirical inquiry it required. This contention was drawn from both his 1910 article on the theory of the social sciences and the 1935 essay on the basis for a rational theory of economics, in which Mises' acceptance of a generic notion of capital was specifically taken to task (Neurath 1935: 41–45). Here Neurath was following closely in the footsteps of Poincaré in attempting to 'unmask' the faulty language of economics.

There is another arrow in Neurath's quiver. He was at pains to show that the individual components of any piece of machinery – the example he used was that of the steam engine – could not be aggregated into the machine serving effectively as 'capital'. This was a distinction between quantity and quality that surfaces throughout Neurath's writings. The steam engine is not simply more than the sum of its parts; it is qualitatively different from them, making it impossible to 'value' the steam engine through any sort of correspondence with its parts (Neurath [1917] 2004: 335–336). Hence, the first step toward valuing the machine accurately is to recognize that it cannot be rendered as 'commensurate' with its parts, and a monetary reckoning is consequently simply wrongheaded. In intellectual terms, but certainly not in the political terms that clearly underlie the conflict between the two, this constitutes the main battleground between Neurath and von Mises on the matter of 'socialist calculation'.

When Mises raised the problem posed by the lack of commensurability in assuring the proper and efficient allocation of resources, he pointed to the limitations presented by a reliance upon scale and rankings, an ordinal system of measurement, in the absence of establishing 'cardinal prices', that is, market prices. In this he cited the work of Franz Čuhel, who had written a volume in 1907 delineating the relation and boundaries between economics and psychology (Čuhel 1907). For his part, Neurath effectively championed the role of ordinal forms of measurement as far more conducive to capturing essential qualities of economic life (Neurath [1910] 2004: 276–277). This may be most apparent and striking in the need he saw for the accounting of ecological elements within the framework of standard, quotidian economic decisions.

Is this a dispute over the nature of measurement itself, more mathematical and philosophical than economic? Are their economic concerns fundamentally at cross-purposes, concentrated in different theaters of activity (building a railroad or balancing a host of societal needs, including projections into the future), or is Neurath's construction simply broader in scope, since building a railroad would come within the purview of societal needs? On the other hand, to what extent is this a political disputation with economic theory the chosen vehicle?

These differences about the nature and import of economic measurement extend back into the period before World War I for both Mises and Neurath. As noted above, Mises drew upon the work of Čuhel, whom Jack High and Howard Bloch identified among a series of turn-of-the-century Austrian economists as "apparently the first to show that ordinal preference can result in market prices" (High and Bloch 1989: 359). But for the Austrians the acceptance of some form of ordinal measurement came with an important caveat:

> Čuhel ... also concluded that, because utility is immeasurable, economists cannot make interpersonal utility comparisons. Since it is not possible to assign a cardinal number to the utility received by an individual from a

good, it is clearly impossible to measure the ratio of the utilities received by two or more people.

(High and Bloch 1989: 354)

Moreover, and this was crucial to Mises' case against Neurath's 'natural calculation', Čuhel had laid out what the Austrians saw as a limitation to a reliance upon ordinality: "[J]udgments of value do not measure; they merely establish grades and scales" (Mises [1920] 1935: 96–97).

What both Čuhel's and Mises' paradigmatic examples of the linkage between ordinal preferences and cardinal prices have in common is their reliance upon a schematic with two goods, from which the possibility of determining a price at which exchange might occur.

Neurath had a counter of his own to this. One of the most salient aspects of Neurath's critique of the theory of the social sciences in his 1910 and 1911 articles was his effort to eviscerate the foundation upon which that schematic stood. Through the use of combinatorics he showed that the range of possibilities far exceeded the strictures provided by the merely hypothetical and abstracted examples such as those employed by Čuhel and Mises. Infusing a qualitative assessment of the economic value of all such choices was crucial.

Neurath had taken up the question of the scope of commensurability directly in the 1911 article, challenging the terms of the price theory Gustav Cassel had laid out in his *Grundriss,* published in 1899: "A common measure of value is not a necessary assumption for a comparison" (Neurath 1911: 55).

Moreover, Neurath regarded the focus upon realizing some sort of exchange as also quite limiting, ignoring other reasons and bases why goods – and resources – might be transferred or shifted, an approach pursued by the German Historical School. Instead, the emphasis upon exchange was intended to diminish and devolve political economy into price theory. In short, then, the disputation over measurement can also be seen within the context of the challenge raised by Neurath to the ascendancy of an economic model and construct forged by the marginalists and the emerging neoclassical school, for all that the Austrians would also separate themselves from the latter.

Omniscience or necessarily incomplete knowledge?

A central paradox in the debate over the possibility or efficacy of 'socialist calculation' is that ostensibly a leading charge made against Neurath involved his supposed presumption of an unattainable – and undesirable – omniscience in ordering and organizing economic affairs. This was clearly linked to Neurath's fondness for invoking the term 'social engineering' as the consummate expression, according to his critics, of the positivist overreach underlying the advocacy for 'socialist calculation'.

Why does this constitute a paradox? On at least two counts. First of all, Neurath's references to 'social engineering' need to be read more as a call for innovation in technique, essentially imaginative quests to make society work better, a strong strain of utopianism, to be sure, but not a mechanically devised master plan. The model upon which Neurath drew is that of Leonardo da Vinci and his prescient sketches of flying machines, realized only centuries later. (See Chapter 9 on modernism vs. postmodernism for a further elaboration of this topic.)

One might consider the linkage Neurath made between socialization and social engineering in the following essay:

> These powerful forces can only become creative if socialization, the conscious realization of the new order of life is based on an intellectual analysis and if utopianism becomes effective as science, as social engineering. This essay seeks to delineate the possible directions of this development. It starts from the uncontroversial premise that in addition to other factors, one also has to take into account one's own will as an influence on the 'historically necessary development'.
>
> How we think about historical events – this is itself conditioned historically – significantly affects these events, whereas astronomy cannot significantly affect the course of the stars.
>
> (Neurath [1920/21] 2004: 346)

This was written in the heady days shortly after the end of World War I, when serious discussions were underway about the possibilities of 'socializing' the state of Germany, the main topic of Neurath's essay (see also Neurath [1920] 2004). Yet the perspective and the framework that Neurath brings to the analysis presented and case to be made may prove revealing about his way of thinking more generally about political economy. His reference to the role that utopianism might play as 'social engineering' is one of many that have surfaced in his various writings across his career. It is a part of his notion about the centrality of imagined possibilities of what might be, rendering utopianism as scientific, whereas Marx and Engels effectively created a dichotomy between utopian socialism and scientific socialism, and castigated the former as reactionary and unworkable.

Moreover, the attention that Neurath gives to the role of consciousness is quite noteworthy, even striking. Socialization itself is a matter of consciousness, and Neurath points out accordingly that historical agency will affect the actual path taken in historical development. One might see this as an outgrowth of Neurath's recognition of the inexorability of an 'auxiliary motive' in human affairs, so that as an intellectual turn in Neurath's thinking Pierre Duhem meets Marx.

Second, and this goes to the heart of the matter raised in the critique of socialist calculation, throughout his career Neurath challenged and rejected the notion of any kind of omniscience. From his perspective the idea that one might potentially know everything, even if that were not the case today, constituted what he referred to as the 'absolutism of Laplace', a falsely accepted determinism (Neurath [1946] 1983: 232). It was in this context that Neurath spoke of the need to conceive of knowledge as a continuing work in progress, always incomplete, and hence better understood as an encyclopedia rather than a system. While Neurath's allusions to the encyclopedia appear with greater frequency in his writings from the mid-1930s on, it is nonetheless the case that his comprehension of the limitations of knowledge and insight is fully in evidence in his early 1913 paper on "The Lost Wanderers of Descartes", presented to the Philosophical Society of Vienna. In it Neurath characterizes the belief in fully grasping any state of affairs as a form of 'pseudo-rationalization', for in the end, some additional choice or decision, what Neurath would call an 'auxiliary hypothesis', was required (Neurath [1913] 1983: 10).

Hence, on the basis of the above, one might see Neurath as making the most compelling philosophical argument against the notion that this contemporary age of information, with its overwhelming surfeit of data, had overcome the barriers to a centralized planning operation that Hayek had raised as his chief argument against the possibility of effective economic planning (see O'Neill 2004 on their shared 'epistemological skepticism'). However, this did not preclude other bases upon which, from Neurath's standpoint, central planning was not only possible, but necessary.

The complication here is that Neurath's model for economic planning did not hinge upon omniscience; rather it was a matter of establishing effective coordination across different sectors of the economy and different economic agents within it. Hayek's decentralization, for example, might well be associated with isolated or insular activity that would weaken or even undermine the overall condition of the economy, and the goals sought for it.

In laying out the case for socialization in "The System of Socialisation", Neurath emphasized the need for coordination across the economy; the danger he saw was a fractionalization of economic aims or goals if individual industries or sectors operated in isolation, promoting, for example, wage increases to offset cost increases that, in the end, would produce a general inflation of prices and thereby thwarting the initial effort. In Neurath's view, this meant that the 'right hand did not know what the left was doing': in effect a recipe for disaster. Organization, the gathering of statistics, and publicity for the broad dissemination of information were thus crucial for achieving a positive economic state.

To a significant degree, this view of planning carried its own theory of knowledge: both coordination and publicity were understood as means whereby information would be exchanged, effectively establishing lines and modes of communication. At the same time, the gathering of statistics, clearly an abiding passion of Neurath's, manifested in the Economic and Social Museum he spearheaded in Vienna and in his development of "Isotype" for the visual display of information, was intended to deepen the content of the information transmitted. Overall, then, the openness and depth of knowledge available about the economy would hold the key to its amelioration and success.

How such coordination might work in practice is another matter. In the period after World War I Neurath suggested that in a socialized economy strikes would not be permitted, as they would tend to produce the adverse general result outlined above (Neurath [1920/21] 2004: 361). But how exactly might that be achieved? One might well conceive of a high level of participation at the workers councils, attempting to settle upon the best overall plan. Nonetheless, what if certain groups within these councils cannot or will not reconcile themselves to such a plan, at least as it affects them. Then what follows? If a strike is called, would it be suppressed, or would the plan in consequence be altered? This is the piece missing from Neurath's writings in this period. While Neurath characterized with a touch of irony those opposed to socialization as seeing it as 'coercive', just as he characterized the defenders of laissez-faire economics as allowing 'chaos' to prevail, was he able to rule it out as a possibility (Neurath [1925] 2004: 428)?

Neurath emphasized the importance of adhering to the economic plan, once it was agreed to. What rendered the plan 'consensual' rather than 'coercive' was the broad level of participation in its construction, and the requirement that the widest array of constituencies be represented in the process, including both workers and owners (see, for example, Neurath [1920/21] 2004: 364–367). On a global scale he set himself against the 'intolerant' – and 'violent'– tack taken by the Bolsheviks (Neurath [1920/21] 2004, p. 352); on a local scale he sought to advance 'grassroots' activity. Yet once the plan was set in motion, what would happen if a group of workers, for example, remained dissatisfied and prepared to strike?

One might cast this in the context of the command economy that had emerged in wartime, a notion to which Neurath adhered, seeing it as transformative. His 1935 tract is consistent with Neurath's earlier work on 'socialization' in that regard, with the wartime economy taken as paradigmatic, even after the war's end (Neurath 1935: 44–45).

There may be a useful historical aside here whose distance from this debate might help capture what is at issue. In the United States, during the height of the Korean War, President Truman threatened to nationalize the steel industry in order to prevent a strike from occurring, in light of wartime exigencies. However, he was thwarted when the U.S. Supreme Court in a pivotal decision ruled such action unconstitutional, exceeding the powers of the executive. Would Neurath have envisioned a participatory form of governance that would have allowed for a similar mechanism that would entertain challenges to the plan once constituted? As a juridical mechanism this should be understood as a matter separate and distinct from the operation of the bureaucracy itself, a central focus of Weber's critique of Neurath's plan for socialization (Weber 2012: 798–800; Weber 1947: 207–215).

O'Neill (1999) has noted what he deemed a decisive shift in Neurath's thinking about the capacity to challenge in this regard, opening the way in later years to a more decentralized approach. In the period after World War I Neurath favored "technocratic planning", in which the experts, having drawn together all pertinent information, do have the final say (Neurath [1919] 1973: 139–147). By the early 1940s Neurath emphasized the importance of "'overlapping' authorities", recalling the multiple sources of legitimacy and power in the world of medieval Europe (Neurath [1942] 1973: 433; O'Neill 1999: 143–145), or "overlapping institutions" (Neurath 1944: 31).

Economics as instrument

It is safe to say that the debate over socialist calculation has been taken as both symbol and matter of prediction in one of the most consequential developments of the twentieth century, namely the place of central planning in the comparison made between capitalism and socialism in providing for economic well-being. If it reveals a disjuncture between economic theorizing and political perspective or ideology, then what is one to make of economic theorizing apparently subordinated to, or placed in the service of, political outlook or ideology?

This is certainly not a new question, but if economics plays the role of instrument, does that also reveal profound limitations in its claims to be a science? A century ago Thorstein Veblen challenged the capacity of economics to assume the perquisites and predicates of an 'evolutionary science', relying instead upon an established 'classical canon' of thought; hence, it was more an orthodoxy than a science. Here the actual content of the economic thinking advanced seems somehow shunted aside or obscured in favor of the political argument, challenging in its wake the independence of economic theorizing itself.

Does this mean that fundamental questions in economics are never really answered? For example, how ought one measure economic value? One gauge of the differences associated with different schools of economic thought is the treatment accorded this question. Yet it is a trope in economics to say that only that which is quantifiable is measurable and accordingly has value in economics. That hardly seems sustainable from virtually any perspective, so how can it stand? Shoe-horning all sorts of experience and interactions into a quantifiable system evokes comparisons with other efforts in the realm of the sciences to provide what appears to be a consistent explanation, perhaps like a Ptolemaic system in astronomy or the introduction of the ether in physics. Here Neurath's point of departure about the importance of qualitative valuation in economics seems right on the mark.

In further pursuit of this disjuncture: what if one were to separate Neurath's contentions about 'in-kind' calculation from the vortex of socialist calculation? As Nancy Cartwright and Jordi Cat have emphasized (Cartwright et al. 1996), Neurath saw a melding of the scientific and the political; nonetheless, it is worth asking if there are the economic 'substrata' of issues in contention over the debate about 'socialist calculation' that might be treated as distinct from the political stances and perspectives that were central to it.

There are four elements that, taken together, might offer a pathway by which a reframed economic analysis about the nature of calculation, ostensibly without being grounded in doctrine or ideology, could be pursued. These include: (1) the proper role of money and prices; (2) the degree of interdependence between prices and output in various economic settings, including, but not limited, to conventionally conceived markets; (3) the forms of coordination possible across the economy and the terms under which it might take place; and (4) the types of evidence that might be adduced to support conflicting claims and assertions about the resulting outcome.

One might begin with the notion that money arises as a medium of exchange owing to the complexity inescapable in meeting the 'coincidence of wants'. From his study of the economic history of classical antiquity Neurath argued that a successful system coordinating the availability of resources and goods had been attained by a centralized administration in dynastic Egypt, without the need to facilitate the acquisition and distribution of resources and goods through the intermediary of monetary exchange. It did require a 'Girobank' through which presumably 'in-kind' credits could be managed across the economy.

Both Mises' and Hayek's critiques would obtain here, as the matter of commensurability in sorting out credits to properly meet needs could certainly be raised, as could the question as to whether sufficient information existed to effectuate acquisition and distribution reasonably. That is, on a theoretical basis both critiques might be assessed as to their validity in the case of dynastic Egypt. The socialist overlay, a matter of pressing importance to all three, need not be a part of the economic analysis nonetheless. Neurath would contend that empirical – in effect historical – evidence supports his claim. But does this apply to an economy that is essentially closed, and if so, at what point, or level of activity, does international trade affect the terms of the case that has been made?

In many ways, though, it is the second element that may be the most intriguing, as it goes to a set of concerns that arose well before the outbreak of World War I and do not appear, at least initially, to be drawn from a socialist construct. From Neurath's perspective: what if the construction of combinations of resources and goods, which in the neoclassical construct form isoquants and indifference curves, is fundamentally flawed, making the choices among resources and goods far too simple and arbitrary, and in the process challenging the Marshallian construct of market resolution as a partial equilibrium? The Austrians exhibit a fair degree of ambivalence here. On the one hand, they do not accept in full the neoclassical construction. On the other, they found a way to make the case for the existence and efficacy of market arrangements in which a unitary, 'market-clearing' price can be established. Mises saw the existence of markets as absolutely necessary to the functioning of any economy. What happens, though, if the notion of 'market' is understood to be at least as much a social construct as an economic one, as might accord, say, with Karl Polanyi's treatment of economic life?

The institutional nexus

Following from this is the third element, which considers the implications associated with attaining the requisite coordination within and across the economy. It involves an institutional nexus and a more contemporary historical context, giving rise to the possibilities that might be accorded a 'social economics', versions of which may differ.

In the wake of World War I and the collapse of both the Austro-Hungarian and German Empires, Neurath envisioned a historical moment in which a socialist transformation of society could – and should – take place. His anti-capitalist outlook, long grounded in his skepticism toward what the German Historical School referred to as 'Manchester liberalism', now merged with what might be deemed his 'socialist utopianism', but which he saw as a form of 'scientific utopianism'.

For their part, both Mises and Hayek sought to dampen or reverse the direction outright of this seemingly transformative moment in the twentieth century, holding to a nineteenth-century liberal view largely but not entirely supportive of a laissez-faire capitalism. Mises' initial assault on the notion of socialist calculation came in 1920, at a time when plans for socialization of the Austrian and German economies were under discussion, generally through the formation of governmental commissions. By the 1930s, when Hayek fully entered the fray, such plans for central Europe had long since faded, although very much in evidence in the Soviet Union. Taken in concert with the rise of fascism across much of Europe, Hayek framed the debate much more about a fundamental conflict between collectivism and individualism (Hayek 1994: 102), with the latter embodying in both economic and political terms the revivified spirit of nineteenth-century liberalism, though updated after World War I through the Mont Pelerin Society (Mirowski and Plehwe 2015).

Into this stage set Keith Tribe has rightly cast Mises and Hayek's critique of Neurath's 'in-kind' or 'natural calculation' and advocacy of central planning as a rearguard action, calling forth in essence a 'golden age' reaction in invoking the terms of nineteenth-century liberalism (Tribe 1995: 143), so that one might see the debate between the two as a matter of contrasting utopias. Instead, Tribe places Max Weber's critique of Neurath's ideas about socialization front and center as the more serious vantage point from which Neurath's claims ought to be assessed, in that in the twentieth century the role played by bureaucracy would assume far greater significance, consistent with the dominance of large-scale institutions, whether public or private, in quotidian economic and social life (Tribe 1995: 142–143). And it certainly is the case that Neurath's flow charts depicting the coordination of information, data (largely as statistics), and decision-making under a schema of central planning do not address, directly or indirectly, the kinds of issues and problems entailed by the existence of the bureaucracy so constructed thereby.

Hayek's approach appears to go more to the notion that a surfeit of information, in and of itself, would severely overwhelm a central planning office, while Weber, perhaps not surprisingly, proceeds to consider first and give greater weight to the role of institutions. Hayek's positive case for a thoroughly decentralized coordination of economic activity drew from psychology rather than sociology or 'social economics', as the spontaneous ordering of economic markets is likened to the formation of patterns from seemingly random events that inspired Gestalt psychology (Hayek 1952: 76–78).

It is noteworthy that for all of Neurath's early attention to 'law and custom' in shaping economic life (see the 1910 article as a prime example), there is little to no exploration in his writings of the place and impact of institutions in shaping economic life, beyond the somewhat perfunctory references to large-scale economic entities, as one might take note of as manifest in cartelization. For all that, Neurath's analysis of such large-scale entities has real significance, as it forms the basis for his case for price differentiation, decoupling the interdependence of price and quantity and challenging the resolution of partial equilibria.

Nonetheless, rather than laying out a theoretical case for his own version of 'social economics', Neurath tended to advance ideas about 'Gemeinwirtschaft' at a practical level, in developing projects involving community gardens, cooperative housing, and popularly based civic museums. All of these can surely be regarded as institutions, with attendant consequences for social living. These projects are more likely to have an impact – and perhaps not an insignificant one – on the margin, nor, crucially, do they offer insights of a more theoretical nature. How, in general, do societies create such institutions? What is the relation between particular changes and the general movement or transformation of society?

Whither history in economics?

And what significance may be found in the lack of inclusion of history as affording the possibility of explanation in economics, in effect setting the stage for it? Neurath himself had noted early on that "historical experience" had informed, indeed had established the initial foundation for economic theorizing (Neurath [1910] 2004: 285).

In the instant subject one might consider the matter of the disposition of capital resources and the development of railway systems, which played a central role in Mises' case. The French railway system may provide a pertinent illustration. Moreover, with more than half of France's gross domestic product now generated by and through the public sector, as measured by the level of government spending, France fits the mold that Hayek limned whereby social democratic states were seen as tilting toward collectivism.

Its formative elements need to be addressed here.

To invoke the formative is to give place, perhaps even primary place, to the historical in economics. Any such anchoring is missing from Mises' case about the centrality of a price mechanism to govern rational choices about the provision of capital (or capital stocks). Neurath certainly refers to the importance of the historical, but does not marshal historical evidence to frame an explanation for economic phenomena or transformation, as that would rely upon a historically grounded notion of causality.

Since Mises identified the provision of railway systems and networks as a critical – paradigmatic – example, and, in light of its significance in the transformation of the economic life of the newly industrialized states, it should be regarded as a reasonable, if not surprising choice.

However, the history associated with the development of various national railway systems will not only offer up a useful ancillary narrative to the economic factors, forces, and analysis weighed, but also serve as an essential part of that analysis, reframing those factors and forces cited in new ways. Moreover, the formative aspects of such development will in the process be accorded their proper due.

In the case of the French railway system, for example, one can trace a trajectory from its origins to the present day that is fundamentally coherent. In the 1830s and 1840s the initiative of the St.-Simonians, the 'social engineering' advocates that were the bane of Mises and Hayek, promoted the growth of a national railway as a transformative event that would usher in a new era of unity, prosperity, and peace. Such utopianism was espoused by the then St.-Simonian Michel Chevalier, who later became, in the era of Napoleon III, the leading advocate of 'free trade' in France. But this utopian vision was married to the practicality of St.-Simonians who, like the Pereire brothers, became the venture capitalists of their day, in organizing the financing and planning entailed by the construction of a national railway system. This in turn met the serious limitations facing the launch of such an ambitious project in France: lack of sufficient private funds.

Unlike Great Britain, whose industrial enterprises, trade, and colonial empire netted the requisite private funding to build the first major national system, nor as would be the case in the United States, where a massive infusion of British capital and local subscription campaigns would serve as a major source of funding, France would from the outset require – and also envision – a larger public role in funding the nascent railway plans. At the same time, the greater reliance upon public funding comported with the St.-Simonian view of a conscious, state-driven approach to economic transformation and social change. It should also be noted that this comported as well with a longstanding 'dirigiste' form of statecraft in France.

If one is then to come full circle, and take note of the emergence of a state-run national railway system especially after World War II, which then becomes a leading – and symbolic – project in France's economic development in the last decades of the twentieth century, it might still be regarded as a later instantiation of the initial St.-Simonian vision. In fact, starting in the early 1980s, the French railway system underwent a major overhaul and modernization. A state-run affair, the French national railway system depends upon an even more extensive network of information about schedules, seating availability, and reservations coordinated so as to operate efficiently, indeed as one of the most envied transportation systems in the world, than did the U.S. airline industry. Subsidized by the state, hence the subject of planned allocation of resources, the French railway system has been at the forefront of technological innovation in the field of transportation, dissolving the notion that state-run enterprises falter or fail in developing or incorporating new technology. These were all elements that Mises posited were outside the ken and capacity of central planners.

At the same time, through its permutations as a nationalized entity the French National Railway System (or SNCF) has clearly relied upon a monetary pricing system, thus far removed from Neurath's vision of a 'natural economy'. It is also the case, though, that the SNCF has proceeded to operate as a 'public service' monopoly with a pricing mechanism based upon 'tariff setting' rather than a "'natural' matching of supply and demand" (Finez 2014: 4); hence, in line to some degree with Neurath's notion of price differentiation.

In light of all this, is it possible to limit or restrict the decisions made about funding and the acquisition of resources under all circumstances to resolutions brought about within a system of prices? Does not the historical experience inform those decisions, and may reasonably be seen as affecting the path pursued? All of this would occur in a setting in which the actions of individual economic agents would be seen as largely interdependent. And so, paradoxically, the interdependence of economic agents, owing to historical circumstances, would be contrasted with the decoupling of prices and output in the construction of microeconomic markets. To some degree – and the extent to which this is the case will be important to ascertain – the interdependence wrought by historical circumstance negated the interdependence of the primary economic variables in the Marshallian microeconomic construct.

While it is true that Neurath asserted that the abstracted construct of neoclassical microeconomics did not hold, it is by no means clear that his allusions to the place of history in economics led him to assert that notion outright. 'Social epicureanism' engendered the need for collective measures of economic value; it did not, however, introduce a historical framework in which any such valuations would necessarily occur. Neurath's sociology thus is intended to meld history and political economy, but offers few specifics how real-world experiences would be comprehended in light of their merger, save for general references to the class struggle. For all its insightful use of statistics to produce country 'silhouettes' (Neurath 1939: 61), *Modern Man in the Making* does not afford a probing analysis linking historical circumstances with economic analysis. Neurath made that point explicit in the 'Foreword' to the text: "The aim is to trace the origin of 'modern man' and depict their behavior and achievements, without presenting any social or economic theory" (Neurath 1939: 7).

An addendum on the age of information

The transformative power of e-commerce's capacity to capture data about individual consumer preferences goes well beyond its passive collection. Instead, it forms the basis for a new version of 'hidden persuasion', as advertisements for products conforming to such data bombard the consumers so tracked. This of course raises the matter of dependence, with producers effectively exerting a form of producer sovereignty. It is notable and perhaps not altogether coincidental that in the parlance of twentieth-century mainstream economics (allowing for the mid-century 'neoclassical synthesis' to define the pertinent field) producer sovereignty is associated with non-competitive or less-than-fully-competitive market structures, the kind with which Neurath was concerned. He scored the general lack of attention to them by marginalist and neoclassical economists of the turn-of-the-century, and saw the cameralists and mercantilists offering up noteworthy insights about such structures.

However, there is yet a further caveat here: the ability of producers to create 'needs' that would otherwise not exist. Nowhere is this more apparent in the current moment than with the advent of high-tech consumer products. Steve Jobs is said to have claimed that people had needs of which they were unaware, until a new product, like the smartphone, appeared on the scene, and propelled Apple into becoming the largest private corporation by stock value in the world.

What would this mean for the debate over socialist calculation and/or central planning? The degree to which dependence and producer sovereignty are operative vitiates any notion of greater efficiency in decentralized markets, as Hayek would be wont to see it. Private large-scale entities would be in control.

The difficulty posed for Neurath is of a different sort. What happens if 'need' itself becomes much more fluid? In the country silhouettes of the more advanced industrial states of the 1930s, as depicted in *Modern Man in the Making,* Neurath noted significant differences, for example, in the number of automobiles or telephones in use. Should one infer a common standard regarding need for either automobiles or telephones (Neurath 1939: 50, 59–62), which in retrospect represent central and likely essential appurtenances of everyday life in the 'modern' world of the twentieth century? Neurath was wary of invoking any common or universal standard of measurement, but here it would seem the alternative to that would require some significant measure of subjectivity, or an embrace of cultural differences as a surrogate standard. This latter approach is reminiscent of the tack taken by the German Historical School.

Neurath did give great weight to Popper-Lynkeus' figures for basic human needs in an industrial society, but to adhere too strictly to this would entail accepting a universal standard, for one, and would fail to address the possible impact of a fluidity of needs, whether spurred on by technological innovations or other sources.

The contemporary twist here is that the technological changes underlying the current transformation of need are directly associated with the coming of the age of information itself. But it is also the case that the rather dramatic changes in the cost of producing computers, following a succession of technological advances involving transistors and microprocessors, subordinate price formation to costs of production per se and thus ultimately to a version of changing productivity. If so, then, it brings to the fore a case that comports well with the approach taken by the French economist Jean Fourastié.

Notes

1 "k.k." was a formal designation of the Austro-Hungarian Empire. It stands for: 'kaiserliche, königliche', the former referring to imperial Austria, the latter to the Kingdom of Hungary.

2 "Sabre: The First Online Reservation System". IBM Archives, www-03ibm.com/ibm/history

References

Ballod, Carl [1898] (1927). *Der Zukunftsstaat.* 4th reworked edition. Berlin: E. Laub.

Bauer, Otto (1919). *Der Weg zum Sozialismus.* Wien: Ignaz Brand.

Brentano, Lujo (1931). *Mein Leben im Kampf um die soziale Entwicklung Deutschlands.* Jena: E. Diederichs.

Čuhel, Franz (1907). *Zur Lehre von den Bedurfnissen: theoretische Untersuchung uber das Grenzgebiet der Okonomik und der Psychologie.* Innsbruck: Wager Universitates-Buchhandlung.

Finez, Jean (2014). "Ticket Pricing by the French National Railway Company (SNCF), a Historical Sociology of Tariff Setting". *Revue Francaise de Sociologie (English Edition)* 55(1): 1–32.

Hayek, Friedrich A. [1937] (1948). "Economics and Knowledge". In F.A. Hayek, *Individualism and Economic Order.* Chicago: University of Chicago Press, pp. 33–56.

Hayek, Friedrich A. (1944). *The Road to Serfdom.* Chicago: University of Chicago Press.

Hayek, Friedrich A. [1945] (1948). "The Use of Knowledge in Society". In F.A. Hayek, *Individualism and Economic Order.* Chicago: University of Chicago Press, pp. 77–91.

Hayek, Friedrich A. [1935] (1948). "Socialist Calculation II: The State of the Debate". In F.A. Hayek, *Individualism and Economic Order.* Chicago: University of Chicago Press, pp. 148–180.

Hayek, Friedrich A. (1952). *The Sensory Order.* Chicago: University of Chicago Press.

Hayek, Friedrich A. (1994). *Hayek on Hayek: An Autobiographical Dialogue.* Eds. Stephen Kresge and Leif Wenar. London: Routledge.

High, Jack, and Bloch, Howard (1989). "On the History of Ordinal Utility Theory". *History of Political Economy* 21(2): 351–365.

Hilferding, Rudolf (1910). *Finanzkapital.* Wien: Marx-Studien.

Lavoie, Don (1985). *Rivalry and Central Planning.* New York: Cambridge University Press.

McCloskey, Deirdre M. (2001). "The Genealogy of Postmodernism: An Economist's Guide". In Stephen Cullenberg, Jack Amariglio, and David F. Ruccio, eds., *Postmodernism, Economics and Knowledge.* London: Routledge, pp. 102–128.

Mirowski, Philip, and Plehwe, Dieter, eds. (2015). *The Road from Mont Pelerin.* Cambridge, MA: Harvard University Press.

Mises, Ludwigvon (1920). "Die Wirtschaftsrechnung in sozialistischen Gemeinwesen". *Archiv für Sozialwissenschaft und Sozialpolitik* 47(1): 86–121. Also in F.A. Hayek, ed. (1935) *Collectivist Economic Planning.* London: George Routledge & Sons, Ltd.

Mises, Ludwigvon (1978). *Notes and Recollections.* Trans. Hans F. Sennholz. South Holland, Ill: Libertarian Press.

Neurath, Otto (1906). *Zur Anschauung der Antike uber Handel, Gewerbe und Landwirtschaft.* Jena: G. Fischer.

Neurath, Otto [1910] (2004). "Theory of the Social Sciences". In Robert S. Cohen and Thomas E. Uebel, eds., *Otto Neurath: Economic Writings/Selections, 1904–1945.* [Multiple translators]. Dordrecht: Kluwer Academic Publishers, pp. 265–291.

Neurath, Otto (1911). "Nationalokonomie und Wertlehre, eine systematische Untersuchung". *Zeitschrift für Volkswirtschaft, Sozialpolitik und Verwaltung* 20: 52–114.

Neurath, Otto [1913] (1983). "The Lost Wanderers of Descartes and the Auxiliary Motive". In Robert S. Cohen and Marie Neurath, eds. and trans., *Philosophical Papers.* Dordrecht/Boston: D. Reidel Publishing Company, pp. 1–12.

Neurath, Otto [1917] (2004). "The Structure of the Conceptual Foundation of Economic Theory". In Robert S. Cohen and Thomas E. Uebel, eds., *Otto Neurath: Economic Writings/Selections, 1904–1945*. [Multiple translators]. Dordrecht: Kluwer Academic Publishers, pp. 312–341.

Neurath, Otto [1919] (1973). "From War Economy to Natural Economy". In Marie Neurath and Robert S. Cohen, eds., *Empiricism and Sociology*. Trans. Paul Foulkes and Marie Neurath. Dordrecht: Reidel, pp. 123–157.

Neurath, Otto [1920/21] (2004). "A System of Socialisation". In Robert S. Cohen and Thomas E. Uebel, eds., *Otto Neurath: Economic Writings/Selections, 1904–1945*. [Multiple translators]. Dordrecht: Kluwer Academic Publishers, pp. 345–370.

Neurath, Otto [1920] (2004). "Total Socialisation". In Robert S. Cohen and Thomas E. Uebel, eds., *Otto Neurath: Economic Writings/Selections, 1904–1945*. Dordrecht: Kluwer Academic Publishers, pp. 371–404.

Neurath, Otto [1925] (2004). "Economic Plan and Calculation In Kind". In Robert S. Cohen and Thomas E. Uebel, eds., *Otto Neurath: Economic Writings/Selections, 1904–1945*. [Multiple translators]. Dordrecht: Kluwer Academic Publishers, pp. 405–465.

Neurath, Otto [1928] (1973). "Personal Life and Class Struggle". In Marie Neurath and Robert S. Cohen, eds., *Empiricism and Sociology*. Trans. Paul Foulkes and Marie Neurath. Dordrecht: Reidel, pp. 249–298.

Neurath, Otto [1931] (1973). *Empirical Sociology*. In Marie Neurath and Robert S. Cohen, eds., *Empiricism and Sociology*. Trans. Paul Foulkes and Marie Neurath. Dordrecht: Reidel, pp. 319–421.

Neurath, Otto (1935). *Was bedeutet rationale Wirtschaftsbetrachtung?*Wien: Gerold & Co.

Neurath, Otto (1939). *Modern Man in the Making*. New York & London: A.A. Knopf.

Neurath, Otto [1942] (1973). "International Planning for Freedom". In Marie Neurath and Robert S. Cohen, eds., *Empiricism and Sociology*. Trans. Paul Foulkes and Marie Neurath. Dordrecht: Reidel, pp. 422–440.

Neurath, Otto (1943). "Planning or Managerial Revolution?" *New Commonwealth Quarterly*: 148–154.

Neurath, Otto (1944) *The Foundations of the Social Sciences*. Chicago: University of Chicago Press.

Neurath, Otto [1946] (1983). "The Orchestration of the Sciences by the Encyclopedism of Logical Empiricism". In Robert S. Cohen and Marie Neurath, eds. and trans., *Philosophical Papers 1913–1946*. Dordrecht/Boston: D. Reidel Publishing Company, pp. 230–242.

Neurath, Otto (1973). "Autobiographical Excerpts from Otto Neurath". In Marie Neurath and Robert S. Cohen, eds., *Empiricism and Sociology*. Trans. Paul Foulkes and Marie Neurath. Dordrecht: Reidel, pp. 18–28.

O'Neill, John (1999). "Ecology, Socialism and Austrian Economics". In E. Nemeth and R. Heinrich, eds., *Otto Neurath: Rationalität, Plannng, Vielfalt*. Vienna: Weiner Reihe, pp. 123–145.

O'Neill, John (2004). "Ecological Economics and the Politics of Knowledge: The Debate between Hayek and Neurath". *Cambridge Journal of Economics* 28: 431–447.

Popper, Karl (1973). "Appreciation of Otto Neurath". In Marie Neurath and Robert S. Cohen, eds., *Empiricism and Sociology*. Trans. Paul Foulkes and Marie Neurath. Dordrecht: Reidel, pp. 51–56.

Popper-Lynkeus, Josef (1912). *Die allgemeine Nahrpflicht als Lösung der soziale Frage*. Dresden: C. Reissner.

Tribe, Keith (1995). *Strategies of Economic Order: German Economic Discourse, 1750–1950.* Cambridge: Cambridge University Press.

Weber, Max (2008). *Briefe: 1915–1917.* Eds. Gerd Krumeich and M. Rainer Lepsius. Tubingen: J.C.B. Mohr. Letter of 1 September 1917, p. 760.

Weber, Max (2012). *Briefe: 1918–1920.* Eds.Gerd Krumeich and M. Rainer Lepsius. Tubingen: J.C.B. Mohr (Paul Siebeck). Letter to Otto Neurath, 4 October 1919, pp. 798–800.

Weber, Max (1947). *The Theory of Social and Economic Organization.* Trans. A.M. Henderson and Talcott Parsons (1964). New York: Macmillan/The Free Press.

9 Modernism and postmodernism revisited

Otto Neurath's philosophical inclinations, extending to the realm of political economy, underlie his thinking about the nature and scope of scientific inquiry, even as he saw a melding of the scientific with the political, as Neurath scholars like Nancy Cartwright, Jordi Cat, and Thomas Uebel, among others, have noted (Cartwright, Cat, Fleck, and Uebel 1996). Such inclinations are sufficiently broad as to raise a curious paradox. Setting his probing of the epistemology of science as a necessarily incomplete venture against his call for attaining a unity of science across all subject matter accorded scientific weight raises the question as to whether his thought and overall perspective make him the consummate representative of mid-twentieth century modernism or one of the precursors of late-twentieth century postmodernism.

At first blush, in light of the conscious gap understood to exist between modernism and postmodernism, it seems highly improbable that both categories might be applicable to the same thinker. In Neurath's case, though, there is a basis for such consideration. Critics of Neurath like Deirdre McCloskey have pointed to his championing of social engineering and the virtues of a planned society as evidence of a 'modernist' hubris imagining that all of society's arrangements could best be resolved by those with the knowledge to do so (McCloskey 2001: 108–109).

On the other hand, Neurath scholars like Rudolf Haller have noted that Neurath's critique of conventional scientific methodology anticipated by many decades the more well-known challenges to what would be taken to be a 'modernist' methodology from Paul Feyerabend, with his *Anti-Method* (Haller 1991: 35), as well as from those who would draw a postmodern framework of 'paradigmatic shifts' from Thomas Kuhn's *The Structure of Scientific Revolutions* (O'Neill 1999: 130).

An additional wrinkle to this seeming conflict in categorization came through the insight of another Neurath scholar, Thomas Uebel, who framed an inquiry into Neurath's philosophical perspective as "The Overcoming of Logical Positivism from Within" (Uebel 1992). Here Uebel opened up the possibility that the championing of logical positivism as central to the "scientific conception of the world" could co-exist with a historically conditioned, anti-foundationalist approach to and understanding of scientific inquiry that left such inquiry necessarily incomplete. Might Neurath be 'modernist' and 'post' or 'anti-modernist' at the same time?

I would like to elaborate upon this question in a number of ways. First of all, there is the matter of discourse; or, more precisely, one ought to conduct a discourse about discourse. At any given historical moment or period, are there bounds or limits as to what can and will be said, circumscribing the world of intellectual discourse, and affecting even those who might otherwise appear to offer up contrary or countervailing views?

Second, especially in light of Neurath's own focus on the role of words to illuminate or mask, I would like to explore the contemporaneous use and meaning of the following pertinent terms or phrases: 'modern', 'social engineering', and 'utopianism'. Third, as Neurath himself challenged the validity of intellectual dichotomies, it is necessary to examine more closely the notion of 'opposition' or 'oppositional pairings' as it applies to intellectual discourse and intellectual movements.

In light of all this I would like to grapple with the implications of the confluences and tensions between modernism and postmodernism as they might afford an insight into the philosophical foundations of economics, where Neurath offers an intriguing entry point.

The limits of discourse: casting Neurath in modernist times

As to the 'discourse on discourse': this assumes a relation between language and thought that should be made explicit. Words and phrases that are in use both reflect ways of thinking (about the nature of things), and also influence lines of thinking. It was the insight of the French *Annales* school of historians, especially through the work of Lucien Febvre, to recognize the limits of intellectual discourse as historically based and shaped. In Febvre's case it was the matter of 'belief' in Europe in the sixteenth century: whatever differences or divergences might exist with regard to the nature of Christian belief, there was no challenge to the idea of belief itself, nor even the notion that such a challenge might exist.

So, in turning to the matter of modernism and postmodernism, one might similarly contend that well into the twentieth century the notion of a fragmentation of objective reality sufficient to call into question the possibility of objectivity itself fell outside the bounds of intellectual discourse. This did not preclude vast differences and serious contentions within the then prevailing discourse, but it did set limits, including for those whose views, like Neurath, might have generally been taken as 'unorthodox'.

For Neurath this would mean that labeling him a 'postmodern' would be anachronistic, even if one might discern aspects of his work and thought that resonate with elements of postmodernism. Instead, one might regard those aspects as inchoate strains of new ways of thinking about scientific inquiry, so that if sustained, those strains would make Neurath a precursor. In his case this would largely fall to the role of silent precursor, more on the order of a figure like Herman Heinrich Gossen whose work languished in obscurity for decades.

The grand exception to this can be found in Willard van Orman Quine's identification of Neurath's anti-foundationalism, expressed in general terms, as the inspirational motto for his collection of essays and papers, *Word and Object* (Quine 1960)

At the same time, if Neurath was active across a wide swath of fields during an age that saw itself as 'modern', it would hardly be possible for him not to be, in some fundamental sense, 'modern', no matter the extent to which he went against the grain, offered up 'unorthodox' views or approaches, or even, in the case of economics, took the road not taken. It is a reflection of the idea that one lives 'in time' and cannot stand fully 'out of time'.

To a remarkable degree art styles and fashions, in their own time or retrospectively, have come to define distinct historical periods, and the bounds of discourse might be seen as the counterpart to these reigning art styles and fashions. European artistic styles like Gothic and Baroque, introduced as less-than-favorable descriptives, became at a later date the decisive terms encapsulating and encompassing entire eras in European history. The term 'modern' has special significance, in that, rather than being an appellation of opprobrium reversed and then elevated, it was instead adopted by its advocates and artistic representatives consciously as a positive breakaway from older traditions and patterns. Thus, in Neurath's own time, the early twentieth century, it was manifested in modern exhibitions, whether at the New York Armory in 1913 or the Paris 'Art Deco' exhibition in 1925, as well as through the publication of artistic manifestoes heralding a new age or a revolutionary departure from the accepted or traditional. Erwin Dekker has argued that the Vienna Circle's manifesto, issuing the call for and championing the 'wissenschaftliche Weltauffassung' in 1929 – and largely written by Neurath – was following a pattern laid out initially by the Italian Futurists in 1911 (Dekker 2014).

Arnold Hauser's (1958) multi-volume *A Social History of Art,* the seeds for which germinated in the interwar period in central Europe, made the case for a materialist accounting for the shifts that occurred in artistic styles, grounding their development and transformation in economic conditions and social change (Scherke 2005: 478), a view with which Neurath, an ardent materialist in his approach to scientific inquiry, would likely have been in accord.

At least as significant in Neurath's case, though, was his association with artists and architects who identified themselves as modern. His collaboration with Gerd Arntz and avant-garde Dutch graphic artists in the 1930s in developing the visual language known as Isotype constitutes a striking case in point. Neurath also worked with a number of the leading architects of the 1930s who played instrumental roles in advancing the notion of modernism in architecture and identified themselves as the Modernist school through the Congrès International d'Architecture Moderne (CIAM).

Peter Galison made the confluence of self-consciously innovative trends in politics, philosophy, and architecture in central Europe after World War I central to an understanding of Neurath as a 'modernist'. Citing the ubiquity of the term 'Aufbau' in each of those areas of life and thought noted above,

Galison situated Neurath at the heart of a European modernist project of the 1920s (Galison 1996: 17–44).

It is thus noteworthy as well that Nader Vossoughian has elevated Neurath to a central role in the development of modernist ideas and approaches in urban planning and architecture, writing in *Otto Neurath: Language of the Global Polis*:

> [This] book offers a revisionist account of the history of modernism, one that focuses on the role that sociology, economics, information design, visual communication and knowledge management played in early twentieth-century debates about architecture, politics and the city. At the same time, it uses Neurath as a vehicle through which to examine informal planning in the early twentieth century.
>
> (Vossoughian 2008: 11)

He goes on to state: "The global polis ... represented an ideal of public assemblage that was premised on the synthesis of community and modernity" (Vossoughian 2008: 11), a synthesis, he contends, that Neurath saw as essential, though it may prove to be a more complex matter.

There is a bit of a contradiction here. In both the sociology and the literature of central Europe in the first decades of the twentieth century Ferdinand Tönnies' dichotomy of 'community' and 'society' was typically translated into an alignment of 'society' with the 'modern', often accompanied by a critique in which this new society was viewed as urban, anonymous, and alienating. Rainer Maria Rilke's novel, *Malte Laurids Brigge,* captured well the anomie of the 'modern' world. Yet, following Vossoughian, Neurath's 'modernism' involved incorporating 'community' into economic thought and action. This was Neurath's 'Gemeinwirtschaft', which had amused and perplexed Max Weber and served as the focal point for the critique Ludwig von Mises launched against 'socialist calculation'.

One could well translate the notion of the 'modern', as indicated above, as both a break with the past, a sundering of more traditional approaches and ideas, and an advancement from that past. In doing so it is possible to detect that same notion of the 'modern' in Neurath's *Modern Man in the Making* (Neurath 1939: 45–62), consistent, it would appear, with the *Annales* school's notion of the legitimacy of the prevailing discourse circumscribed by the historical moment. On the one hand, Neurath emphasizes the development, largely in economic and social terms, that has taken place over the course of several centuries, especially in Europe. On the other, he seeks to distinguish the modern, as much in thought as in economic and social conditions, from the traditional, complete with a recognition of the vestigial presence of the pre-modern amidst the most emblematic of modern manifestations, even seeing the 'magical' as the precursor to the 'scientific'. And so he produces a graphical representation of a skyscraper lacking a floor numbered thirteen, with a question mark to highlight the continuing substratum of superstition (Neurath 1939: 131).

Utopianism and modernism

Deirdre McCloskey's criticism of Neurath's modernism links it to both his enthusiasm for social engineering and his embrace of utopianism. Taken altogether, these elements form a package that in McCloskey's view effectively melds planning with authoritarianism. Those who think they know best make the decisions that determine society's actions and rule the lives of individuals. Planning intervenes and imposes, aligning McCloskey with Ludwig von Mises, who, as Neurath put it, with a touch of irony, would see it as 'coercive' (Neurath [1925] 2004: 428).

Let us unpack this package. 'Social engineering' is addressed elsewhere, so the focus here is upon the meaning of utopianism and its implications for the relation between utopianism and modernism. The notion that the modern age represents a major advancement over previous periods and holds the seeds of a better future is unmistakable in Neurath's text, *Modern Man in the Making*. He holds out the possibility that through more comprehensive planning it would be possible to achieve what Neurath regarded as greater economic efficiency, which in his view meant greater collective human happiness. This would include an end to economic swings in which resources and goods that could be produced are not, or, worse, are actually destroyed in order to preserve or increase profits. Moreover, higher levels of production could be attained without increasing work hours, thereby raising living standards and potentially extending leisure time. One certainly could characterize those aspirations as socialist or ecological, or perhaps as befits Neurath, a combination of the two. But is improvement synonymous with utopianism?

In Neurath's case the line between the two may be blurred. Yet all of this begs the question at hand: would such utopianism (if that is what it seems to be) be tied to a modernist approach or outlook? Neurath's own treatment of the subject may provide an answer. He was clear in his call for a 'scientific utopianism', which set him directly at odds with Marx and Engels. Neurath was aware of this, and essentially chided them for not taking up the matter of social engineering (Neurath 1944: 31–32, also 49f44). Translated in other terms, Neurath's criticism was directed at their failure to extend a systematic critique of capitalism into a projection of what a future socialist society might look like.

Neurath did turn to near contemporaries to support his case for such planning, especially those set forth by Carl Ballod Atlanticus (1898) and Josef Popper-Lynkeus (1912). In the case of the former, the criticism launched at Ballod by both those who opposed and favored socialism foreshadowed the countervailing currents Neurath would encounter (Balabkins 1978). In the case of the latter, Neurath acknowledged him to be an 'anti-Marxist', whose work nonetheless would provide an essential roadmap to planning a socialist economy (Neurath [1925] 2004: 442).

But in some ways more striking, especially from the perspective of the history of economic thought, was the extent to which Neurath drew upon older expressions of utopianism, whether found in the projections of Charles Fourier or the adventures of Etienne Cabet. Perhaps most notable were Neurath's continuing references to Thomas More, whose work on utopia – More's own coinage – was excerpted in Neurath's economic thought reader from 1910–1911. Neurath also identified the possibilities of planning in the economic thought of Nicholas Oresmus and Francois Quesnay, both of whose work also appeared in the Neurath reader. Oresmus, More, and Quesnay all received significant treatment in Neurath's quick sketch of the history of political economic thought in *Empirical Sociology,* published in 1931.

Altogether this meant that Neurath's utopianism was rooted in the past, rather than in a modernist movement, which, remarkably, corresponds to the criticism leveled against utopianism by Marx and Engels. The latest literary expression of utopianism in which Neurath found inspiration was Edward Bellamy's *Looking Backward,* published in 1887. Moreover, influential utopian writings emphasizing new economic arrangements, like Theodor Hertzka's 'competitive utopia', to which Neurath referred in passing (Neurath [1917] 2004: 243), belonged to the Victorian era. In economic terms, Hertzka (1891), an Austro-Hungarian economist, offered up another 'third way', eschewing both communism and the exploitation accompanying unbridled 'free competition', and whose views on the economic role of private property and the land have been likened to those of Henry George (see Rosner 2006).

Thus none of the utopian writings upon which Neurath drew came as part of, or informed the modernist movement of the early twentieth century. The revolutionary moment that followed in the wake of the upheavals surrounding the end of World War I as the European dynastic empires, be they Russian, German, Habsburg, or Ottoman, dissolved, was another matter altogether.

Neurath's own views on the relation between utopianism and social engineering can be gleaned from a paper, more a tract than anything else, that he wrote in 1919, entitled "Utopia as a Social Engineer's Construction". The piece, though, was not published until 1973, as part of the collection known as *Empiricism and Sociology.*

In it Neurath states: "Utopias could thus be set alongside the construction of engineers, and one might with full justice call them constructions of social engineers." But he then goes on to analogize social engineering to mechanical engineering: "Mechanical engineering, too, began in the same fantastic way as social engineering" (Neurath [1919] 1973: 151).

This leads in turn to an accounting by Neurath of the translation of such utopian inclinations into a reality over the passage of time:

> Social engineering, to use the expression, likewise begins with fairy tale accounts of the golden age, of the distant island of Atlantis, and then turns to conscious creations of the kind given us by More, Cabet, Bellamy, and in fairly advanced form Rathenau; while in the end it called forth systematic constructions as well, as sketched by Ballod-Atlanticus and Popper-Lynkeus.
> (Neurath [1919] 1973: 151)

This view of the nature of 'scientific utopianism' and 'social engineering' was recapitulated along the same lines in Neurath's later treatise on the "foundations of the social sciences" (Neurath 1944: 30–32).

The consequences, and from Neurath's perspective the possibilities in the present day, follow, specifically in the realm of economic life, referring to 'orders of life' as broadly understood in the manner of the German Historical School:

> What yesterday was dreamers' work, today already appears as scientific work preparing the shaping of the future. We have attained the conviction that a huge part of our order of life can be shaped in a goal-directed manner, and in particular that consumption and production in quantities, can be determined and regulated.
>
> (Neurath [1919] 1973: 151)

Social engineering in the historical moment

In light of the frequent and favorable references that Neurath made to social engineering, it may be instructive to compare its use by Neurath with other contemporaneous appearances of the term or similar wording, as a way of discerning more clearly what it was meant to connote. Below I will take note of the importance attached to it in the 1920s and 1930s by Charles Houston, the pioneering African-American lawyer, who saw it as defining the mission for training lawyers, especially African-Americans, to engage in social action through litigation promoting civil rights, and indeed, the work that followed from it proved to be at the center of the legal campaign to end segregation in the United States.

Here I would like to take up the notion of 'engineer', or more specifically 'production engineer', as it appeared in the work of Thorstein Veblen, especially in the compilation of pieces that were published in *The Dial* shortly after the end of World War I under the title, *The Price System and the Engineers*. This in turn leads directly to a broader comparison of the similarities and links between Neurath's and Veblen's thought in the post-World War I period.

Both Neurath and Veblen were responding to the upheaval wrought by the war. While Neurath embarked upon making the case for and laying out the planning of the socialization of the economy, with particular attention to Saxony and Bavaria, Veblen sought to tamp down fears of a Bolshevik overturning of the established order in the United States (Veblen 1921: 83–104). Yet Veblen, ever the caustic critic, nonetheless presented his own case for remaking the way that business was conducted in the United States. In doing so Veblen raised concerns and questions, similar to those of Neurath, about the state and direction of the economy, and pointed to the virtues of introducing 'production engineers', effectively social engineers, to guide the economy to greater efficiency and, presumably, greater welfare.

Veblen, like Neurath, faulted the price system, with the profit motive held out as the foremost objective, as the source of significant inefficiency, set against a tendency toward overproduction. In Veblen's unique turn-of-phrase, it was 'sabotage', slowing down the wheels of production, that was an essential characteristic of production under the price system. Such sabotage was not confined to workers attempting to gain more control over the production process, the traditional view of it; rather, it constituted standard practice for the 'captains of industry' who sought to maintain higher prices (Veblen 1921: 1–26). Veblen had sketched out, in short, a version of the dangers of the paradox of plenty under the price system.

Veblen, like Neurath, was wary of the conventional division of inputs into three generic categories: land, labor, and capital (Veblen 1921: 27–31). Veblen, like Neurath, found 'capital' especially troublesome, though unlike Neurath, Veblen did not gainsay altogether the possibility of designating other, more appropriate categories as factors of production. The increasing reliance upon mechanization in production led Veblen, not unlike Neurath, to see the rise of a new set of economic structures through which the economy operated; these were typically much larger entities, subject to cartelization.

Putting all this together, Veblen called for 'technical experts' to assume the leading role in managing the economy, appearing to echo, perhaps even more than was the case for Neurath, the St.-Simonian model of social engineering. For his part, it should be noted, Neurath's social engineering always entailed an imaginative leap. In Veblen's case the war years left their mark. He advocated for 'technical experts' or 'production engineers' to form a 'general staff of industry' (Veblen 1921: 53). In this way Veblen took up the notion that the command economy constructed during wartime might serve as a model, at least in part, for a more efficient and beneficial mode of operation in peacetime. One further ironic – and Veblenesque– twist: in 1919 the military model of the 'general staff' was that of the German army, adopted by the United States only in World War II. That army had just been defeated in World War I.

There is at least one other point of agreement between Neurath and Veblen that is quite striking. In a contemporaneous sketch of Veblen contained in a set of intellectual biographies entitled *American Masters of the Social Sciences,* published in 1927, Veblen is described as challenging the "metaphysical" assumptions central to conventional political economy, or what Veblen would refer to as the 'canon' of the classical school. These constituted the following trio: (1) the principle of hedonism, whereby the value of all economic activity was registered as either pleasure or pain; (2) a belief in the universality of natural law, making the rules of behavior and exchange found within and from the perspective of the classical school congruent with nature, that is, with equal applicability everywhere; and (3) a tendency toward the 'melioration' of human affairs, which might be taken as a restatement of the Whig theory of progress or history (Homan 1927: 241–243).

The most significant common ground here is to be found in their expressly 'anti-metaphysical' stance, casting the struggle in the first decades of the twentieth century to attain a 'scientific conception of the world' within a broader context than the salient made by the Vienna Circle. Veblen had attacked the scientific claims of economics, making of it instead a religious or metaphysical canon in his 1898 essay on "Why Economics is not an Evolutionary Science" (Veblen 1898).

As to the trio of principles and beliefs noted above, there is both an overlap between Neurath and Veblen, but also nuances of differences. Neurath, like Veblen, favored a more complex calculus for gauging satisfaction or happiness, but Neurath's social epicureanism led him to adopt a more favorable, if nonetheless somewhat mixed, outlook on utilitarianism, seeking to capture the greatest collective good in comparing the efficiency of different economic arrangements, systems, and orders. Early on Neurath took the position that had animated the first generation of the German Historical School, namely that political economy must embrace as its central task the study of social organization and attend to the different principles and rules that would obtain under different economic orders. Hence, no claim to universality held. Later Neurath saw economic laws as bound by history, contrasting Malthus' treatment of population changes with that of Marx (Neurath [1931] 1973: 384, 396–397). Finally, one might infer from the subtext of *Modern Man in the Making* that to some, perhaps even considerable degree Neurath envisioned a progression to modernity that might correspond to an arc of melioration.

In the case of Charles Houston, his use of social engineering casts it in a light at some remove from any St.-Simonian notion of a perfected social order guided by professional experts, but instead links it to the possibility, even the necessity, of social change. It was Houston who in the 1920s and 1930s transformed Howard University Law School into a center for training African-American lawyers, most notably Thurgood Marshall, who would serve as the legal phalanx over the course of three decades to mount the legal challenges to racial segregation in the United States, culminating in the 1954 U.S. Supreme Court decision in *Brown v. Board of Education*.

Houston described himself as a "Legal Social Engineer for a Just Society" (Andrews 2014: 1). The terminology is Houston's own. It was his belief "that a lawyer was either a social engineer or a parasite on society"; further, "[he] saw his role as a legal educator as part of his social responsibility" (Andrews 2014: 6). One might add that he fulfilled this goal in an extraordinary way, as the lawyers he trained were essential to the civil rights movement in the twentieth century.

What is the pertinence of this in surveying, analyzing, and weighing Otto Neurath's economic thought or actions? Quite a bit. Neurath freely made use of the term social engineer, identifying it with what he understood as the current task facing those who were seeking to improve society; hence, he treated it with approbation. Critics of Neurath opposed to his utopianism and advocacy of economic planning have taken his positive references to social engineering as a clear indication of his descent from the St.-Simonians, the followers of Auguste Comte, and latter-day positivists who thought they could consciously reorder and remake society. On occasion Neurath himself referenced such a descent.

However, Houston, who was roughly a contemporary of Neurath, if on a different continent, also viewed the notion of social engineering positively, and one might claim reasonably that his overarching goal was to engage in a conscious effort, effectively a campaign, to remake society. This would not require classifying Houston as a St.-Simonian or positivist for that reason. Similarly, one might well view Neurath's references to social engineering as his own desire and effort to take conscious steps to improve society. What appears to have happened is a conflation of his support for and involvement in economic planning with his embrace of the idea of social engineering. Neurath's invocation of this term should not be cast as somehow mechanistic; rather, it was meant if anything to be a paean to the possibilities afforded by the imagination. In that sense it is Neurath's utopianism that is at issue.

Modernity: social fact or social trend?

Is modernity a 'social fact' or set of 'social facts', or is it the product of 'social trends'? Neurath appears to state that both are the case. Is that possible? Neurath does suggest one plausible way that might be achieved. In the preface to *Modern Man in the Making* Neurath spoke of the connections made among facts ascertained as having the power to explain on their own accord, rather than be subject to external explanation (Neurath 1939: 7–8). Hence, one assumes, those social facts would reveal, or be seen as displaying, pertinent social trends. This was intended to comport with Neurath's claim, also entered into the preface, that no economic or social theory propelled the narrative of the text.

Several questions follow from this. First of all, did Neurath succeed in the task he set out for himself? There is no doubt that he put together a fascinating universal text, encompassing a global history, long-range social developments, a historically layered economic geography, and a consideration of political and institutional forms, all in a dispassionate tone evoking a declarative rather than ideological presentation. But can it rightly be said that the facts – or the connections that exist or are discerned among them – speak for themselves? The statistics presented may be illuminating, but it was Neurath who selected which ones were presented.

One could make the case that certain indices of well-being ought to be highlighted, but they do represent a conscious choice. Their selection in retrospect might be viewed as the ecological counterpart of the standard macroeconomic measures that gained common currency by the mid-twentieth century. That in itself is telling, as it suggests the emergence of a consensus with regard to one set of measures where alternatives exist; hence in reality it might be understood that any measure so selected constituted the adoption of a convention. From the vantage point of Poincaré, who figured significantly in Neurath's conceptualization of political economy and philosophy, reliance upon such conventions placed limits on the scope of their scientificality.

Second, one may ask more generally if any statement of facts can provide an explanation without the introduction of some theoretical apparatus or other. On this count Neurath appears to be of two minds: on the one hand, the notion of physicalism which he championed builds science solely from observable statements, a subset of which would be statistics like those which fill the pages of *Modern Man in the Making;* on the other, the inexorable intermingling of theory and fact was a mainstay of Neurath's thought and reflected especially the influence of Pierre Duhem. Which one prevails? Do these two possibilities comport with modernist and postmodernist tendencies respectively?

What is inescapable in the text of *Modern Man in the Making* is how conventional the notion of modernity is, as it would have been treated and understood in the first part of the twentieth century. This is a version of modernity rooted in history and philosophy, in which a pathway opened up by the Enlightenment led to the 'modern' world. It is in accord with Philipp Frank's description of the figures, from Kant through Mach to Poincaré, who inspired the First Vienna Circle and the anti-metaphysical impulse within it (Frank 1949: 7–8). Hence it proceeds with the securing of the rational and the secular against traditional practices and mystical beliefs.

It also comports with Neurath's favorable account of the 'enlightened' statism of the Habsburg emperor, Joseph II, and the beginnings of the systematic collection of statistics, putting the state, especially the centralized state, on a more scientific footing.

Modern Man in the Making adds an important economic element to this, by highlighting the economic and social impact of the Industrial Revolution. While Neurath was careful in *Modern Man in the Making* to recognize nuances, overall one comes away with the sense that there is a linear progression to modernity, grounded in increasing urbanization, mechanization, use of technology, and secularism, and manifested in far longer average life-spans, changing family structure, new appurtenances of everyday life, and re-formed patterns of work (Neurath 1939: 56–58). For example, the section on 'Trends Towards Modernity' began with "[u]rbanization [as] a characteristic of modernity" (Neurath 1939: 45). It would be fair to say that all the topics listed above would be subsumed as the social trends that emerge from the social facts. However, might this same transformation be viewed more skeptically as a Hegelian confirmation of 'whatever is, is right'; namely, that modernity is simply a label given to the current state of the world, and no other connotations of modernity need obtain?

Should this be framed a bit differently, as a matter of the bounds of intellectual discourse? Neurath was clearly aware of the largely Eurocentric nature of his text, as he took note of imbalances in the exploitation and use of resources, the differences in the state of development across the globe, and, at least in brief, the contributions of non-Western civilizations. Neurath's implicit definition of modernity – he expressly stated that he did not have a definition of it, yet one might infer such from his text nonetheless – comes within the purview of the early to mid-twentieth century convention about it. In that sense Neurath can and should be seen as a modernist.

Within the text Neurath does advocate for the virtues of planning, seeing it as well as a marker of the modern age, and in that general form it would not be unreasonable to think of the emergence of the liberal social democratic state, with its regulatory safeguards, as the dominant socio-political structure and organization by mid-century. Here a set of mirror images within the discourse of the time is instructive. F.A. Hayek, a nemesis of Neurath (and vice versa), wrote *The Road to Serfdom* in 1944 as a call for sustaining or reinstating nineteenth century liberalism in the face of what he saw as the increasing collectivism of advanced societies. While his target appeared to be, and was, the totalitarianism of Nazi Germany and the Soviet Union, the proximate objective was to head off the rise of the social welfare state in places like Great Britain, where the launching of the National Health Service was emblematic. As Neurath himself saw by the early 1940s, a far cry in certain respects from his outlook two decades earlier, when he was at the center of efforts to attain 'total socialization', there might be a blending of planning and institutional changes in such societies that might not neatly be classified as either capitalist or socialist (Neurath [1943] 2004: 529). Thus the United Kingdom of the National Health Service might fit within this aspect of modernity as conceived by Neurath.

The postmodern wellspring

In assessments of Otto Neurath's philosophical outlook, including his evocation of the unity of science across all disciplines, his championing of positivism, recast as 'logical', has been taken to be the epitome of modernism, a view of the world and a conception of the knowledge of it that seems fully capable of subjecting it all to rational comprehension. In the realm of economic thought and action Neurath's call for greater social engineering was thought to exemplify the modernist perspective on science and economic life, a twentieth-century reworking of nineteenth-century positivism.

Nonetheless, Neurath's continuing references to science as an encyclopedia rather than a system, and the necessarily incomplete nature of knowledge within scientific disciplines and about the world, reflected what has been described as his anti-foundationalism. Neurath's 'boat', which is necessarily assembled at sea rather than in drydock, appears to encapsulate this anti-foundationalism, and the evolution of the 'boat' as a metaphor has been carefully charted by Jordi Cat, who has identified three stages in its development. That incompleteness was inexorable also served as a hallmark of Neurath's case against the constituting of any full-blown scientific system. Neurath consistently set himself apart from, and indeed in opposition to, the 'absolutism of Laplace' (Neurath [1946] 1983: 232), the notion that in potential complete knowledge of subject, field, or universe was possible, even if it was not within reach at present (see also Neurath [1913] 1983). For Neurath it would always be a work in progress.

As an aside it might be worthwhile considering how Laplacean systems might emerge in economics. Perhaps one of the best examples may be found in the work of Gerard Debreu, the French-American theoretical economist and

Nobel Prize winner. His concise text, *The Theory of Value,* lays out an abstract, mathematical model of a general equilibrium in which not only the present, but also the future, position and magnitude of all inputs and outputs could be known (Debreu 1959). Its resolution depends upon the capacity to project rationally into the future.

Without question Neurath's anti-foundationalism runs against the grain of the modernism and positivism identified above. When one encounters Neurath's notion that knowledge and experience form complexes or clots, never fully formed and always subject to change, it appears possible to fashion a claim that Neurath, if anything, was more akin to a postmodernist than a modernist.

There is something worth examining in the oppositional pairing of modernism and postmodernism that affords a better insight into where Neurath stands within it, but also more generally about the notion of modernism and modernity. In Neurath's early piece – first a lecture, then a paper – on systems of hypotheses, he examined the history of optics, and the competing views of light as either a particle, in what was known as the emissions theory, or a wave. As part of his philosophical reflection upon the notion of these two longstanding competing theories Neurath noted the conventional reliance upon dichotomy, effectively an oppositional pairing, that he felt did not square with reality. While his focus was on optics and the physical sciences, he nonetheless made a passing reference to the oppositional pairing of "free trade/tariffs" as an example of a flawed dichotomy in political economy (Neurath [1916] 1983: 15).

Neurath had already pointed to the conventional oppositional pairing of mercantilism and the classical school in his 1910 article on the theory of the social sciences, which he saw as overstating their differences and failing to capture their common ground. Yet that oppositional pairing, especially with regard to the comprehension of the nature of value and wealth, may have had a heuristic role in the construction of the program of the classical school, laying the basis for the emergence of a labor theory of value inhering within productive activity and replacing the mercantilist reliance upon the visible accumulation of bullion. Did David Hume and Adam Smith rely upon the oppositional pairing itself an intermediate construct, perhaps like Wittgenstein's ladder and scaffolding appearing at the end of the *Tractatus,* that could be set aside once the new program took hold and gained coherence?

In the instant case one might consider the possibility that postmodernism, for all that it is purportedly built upon the conscious opposition to and rejection of modernism, may not form a dichotomy with modernism. Instead, such opposition and rejection may serve, at least in part, a similar heuristic role.

A meditation on the fluidity of the modern

This possibility is enhanced by the fluidity of the notion of modernity itself: references to it and the embrace or rejection of it have meant different things at different times. They may even conflict with one another. One can find a general alignment of modernity with the advent and grand sweep of the

Enlightenment in the eighteenth century. Oftentimes this is associated with a new consciousness, as Charles Taylor (1989) would have it, that casts what is regarded as a new set of principles more secular in nature – this, after all, would be characterized as the 'age of reason' – against an older set of settled traditions.

One might shift the focus further back a century, to the intellectual battles described as the rival claims of the 'ancients and the moderns', where the role accorded the 'classics', much of which was recovered or rediscovered during the course of the Renaissance, was a crucial determinant. What relation, if any, did a new discourse of science and literature have and thus owe to the past? 'Modernity' appears as the recognition of the new, hence distinct from what preceded it or the past more generally, or both; it embodies a different consciousness of time, involving a remaking of the relation between past and present, and calling forth a rethinking of the place of the existing canon of thought regarding philosophy, morality, and intellectual inquiry. Paul Hazard dramatized in this way the new intellectual identity associated with the 'modern' and the 'Moderns' as it emerged in the late seventeenth century in western Europe (Hazard 1961: 26).

There is a variation in this whereby the new may depend upon what came before, but constitutes more of a break with the near-present. Here a literal 'radical' change, drawing upon sources and inspiration from an earlier period, has ensued. In Neurath's own estimation, for example, Newton's understanding of motion fell short of that proffered by Descartes, which seemed to accord better with the new physics of the early twentieth century (Neurath [1930] 1983: 42).

More generally, is twentieth-century physics, with its immersion in relativity, quantum mechanics, and cybernetics, to name a few of the most salient fields of exploration, 'modern' or 'postmodern'? Consider the challenge to Newton, idealized as the model for many economic theorists. His embodiment as the consummate figure in the emergence of the 'modern' in scientific inquiry can be set against the fragmentation of reality and seeming breakdown of rational structures in quantum mechanics, or the resurgence, if not the triumph of the counterintuitive, through relativity, or the increased reliance upon probabilistic measures and standards. Accordingly, are these manifestations of the 'modern' or entry ways into the 'postmodern'? See, for example, Michel Bitbol's treatment of the implications of Neurath's notions of physicalism and the unity of science as 'revolutionary' in relation to the new ways of thinking about physics in the twentieth century (Bitbol 2000: 344f).

As a further complication one might note that the stochastic model devised by Norbert Wiener, often referred to as the father of cybernetics, has been cited and applied as the mathematical basis or underpinning for the efficacy of the random-walk, touted by some economists as consistent with the efficient-market hypothesis, and as such a reassertion of a mathematical foundation for laissez-faire economics. Is this a modern or a postmodern development?

Perhaps nowhere is the fluidity of the 'modern' to be found more compelling than in the realm of the arts, which, after all, is often the locus from which historical periodization springs. In the first decades of the twentieth century the notion of the 'modern', and hence modernity, was associated with transformational movements recasting what had come to be regarded as traditional art forms. In music the privileging of certain notes and scales, which informed Western music in the classical and romantic eras, was challenged, sometimes abandoned, to allow for new forms of music: serial, twelve-tone, or dissonant. In Western painting the six-century embrace of increasingly realistic portrayal of object and person between 1300 and 1900, roughly from Giotto to Cezanne, gave way to non-figurative and non-objective art, taken to be the essence of what was new and modern. Nonetheless, from a distance one might not be altogether mistaken in comprehending the breakdown in space and order in the arts as prefiguring the 'postmodern'.

In the realm of the arts, the modernist impulse of the early twentieth century was intended as a challenge to the existing order, in art and elsewhere, exemplified by the outrage evoked by Marcel Duchamp's sculpture at the New York Armory exhibition, or by the program advanced by the Dadaists and the surrealists. In turn, one might take note of the counterattack launched ostensibly in the name of conservative and traditional 'good taste' in the 1937 assault by the Nazi regime in Germany against the 'modern' as 'degenerate'.

There is more than a hint of this seemingly paradoxical association of 'modernity' with the notion of a postmodern disassemblage of reality in Neurath's own evocation of the primacy of images and forms of visual representation in the first decades of the twentieth century, offering up the possibility of transmitting information in new ways – hence the introduction of Isotype as a new visual medium of communication and a new role for museums, like the Social and Economic Museum in Vienna – but also presenting the world through a series of impressions, along the lines of a collage of striking images.

As he stated in a short piece he wrote in the mid-1920s: "Modern man receives a large part of his knowledge and his general education through visual impressions, illustrations, photographs, films. Daily newspapers present more pictures from year to year" (Neurath [1926] 1994: 295).

Might one think of Neurath's resort to new forms of visual communication as not only an effort to unmask and eliminate the ambiguities and obfuscation of written language but also as a response to the cultural and social manifestations of modernity akin to Walter Benjamin's contemporaneous evocation of the transformative element of mechanical reproduction – and a new role for the image in contemporary life – in the modern age?

In matters of philosophy one might see a certain ambiguity of similar regard in the central project of the Vienna Circle. While the primary focus upon the postmodern elements in Neurath's call for the unity of science rests with its incomplete nature, as 'encyclopedia' or the 'orchestration of the sciences' (see, for example, Neurath [1946] 1983), a point emphasized by John O'Neill (1999), one might also attend to the role played by the primacy of language and statement in the construction of logical positivism or logical empiricism. This is more of a halfway measure, in that the focus on language and statement did not lead directly to a concentration on the notion of the text itself, nor the place of encoding and decoding often associated with it, all tropes of a postmodern sensibility.

Modernism and a political frame of reference

The discussion of the division between modernist and postmodernist shadings in Neurath's thought and work, especially as part of the Vienna Circle, has become intertwined with consideration of, first, the impact of the shift in locus for the members of the circle in the face of the rise of fascism and Nazi Germany in the 1930s and the outbreak of world war, and then, the limitations imposed by the advent of the Cold War. In his work, *How the Cold War Transformed Philosophy of Science: Toward the Icy Slopes of Logic,* George Riesch (2005) in particular has devoted great attention to the transformation of the program of the Vienna Circle in light of the political strictures that arose during the Cold War, including, but not limited to, McCarthyite threats to some of the surviving members in the United States, like Philipp Frank.

I have focused more on the transformation of the content of that program when the radical and even revolutionary impetus of the work of the Vienna Circle in Europe in the 1930s was translated into a much more circumscribed world of academic inquiry in the late 1940s and early 1950s. It was in this period that the circle's attention to the implications of a linguistic turn in philosophy and scientific inquiry was translated into the much more narrowly conceived analytic philosophy that attained great prominence in the 1950s (Turk 1975). Also see Pierre Jacob's references to it in *L'empirisme Logique* (Jacob 1980b), as well in the thematic overlay he provides in a series of texts from leading figures in the logical empiricist movement and among analytic philosophers compiled in *De Vienne a Cambridge* (Jacob 1980a). At the least one would note a dampening of an interest in broad changes in intellectual currents that however would resurface in succeeding decades, through works like Paul Feyerabend's *Against Method* or, effectively, the application of Thomas Kuhn's *The Structure of Scientific Revolutions,* that resonate with ideas and themes put forward by Neurath decades before.

Modernism, postmodernism, and economic thought

Finally, what relevance do the categories or oppositional pairing of modernism and postmodernism have for economics and the contours of economic thought in the current era? Presumably one might think along the lines of Schumpeter's century-old volume distinguishing among different 'epochs' in the history of economic thought. This is assuredly the role of history in periodizing prevailing sets of ideas, the patterns they evoke, and the movements they engender and sustain.

In the instant case, though, there are at least two preliminary questions. First, do 'modern' and 'postmodern' constitute such pertinent categories? While 'postmodern' can be delimited rather specifically to the last several decades, 'modern' has gone through several iterations, noted above. These have been posed in different oppositional pairings, and present different features and sensibilities. It is striking that no expression like 'neo-modern' has gained any headway among the appellations applied to different philosophical, scientific, artistic, or political eras. Accordingly, whatever the distinctive qualities of any of the 'modern' moments, all convey a sense of the emergence of something new in the current moment (however broadly or narrowly 'current' might be defined). Hence, it would not be impossible or even out of step to call the 'postmodern' era 'modern'.

Second, beyond these more general concerns about nomenclature and categorization, there is the pressing question as to the applicability of such terms and categories to economic thought. Can one distinguish 'modern' economic thought from a 'postmodern' version, and, if so, what would that entail? Might one classify the formulation of the mid-twentieth century 'neo-classical synthesis' or the separation of the principles of economics into macroeconomics and microeconomics as the birth of the modern? Not all that likely. The notion that the mainstream in economic thought might be conceived as a 'neoclassical synthesis' poses an obvious impediment: is it modern, or is it neoclassical?

Instead, the appearance of concerns about the place of the postmodern in economics is largely a matter of transference, whereby a literary and philosophical debate, initiated mainly as to the nature of signs and language, but extended into matters like the fragmentation and social construction of reality or the place of gender, has been translated to economics. Thus, the tension between 'modern' and 'postmodern' in economics has played out largely through critical inquiries into the discourse of economics.

And as such, this could put Neurath in an interesting position. His focus upon the problematic nature of language in economics can be understood as foreshadowing the more contemporary challenges to the unreflected use of language in forming economic concepts, constructing economic models, and shaping the field's philosophical foundations. Neurath's 1917 essay on the 'conceptual structure of economics' stands out in that regard, as he carefully tied the major concepts for measuring the state of the economy back to a generally unacknowledged reliance upon monetary calculation.

Moreover, Neurath had spoken of 'facts' standing alone as necessarily supplanted by 'relations of order' (Neurath [1910] 2004: 277), a point emphasized by those who have highlighted the postmodern aspects of Neurath's thought (Bitbol 2000: 11–12).

On the other hand, Neurath's vision of knowledge and science as an encyclopedia, necessarily incomplete and always a work in progress, as well as his incorporation of the Duhemian notion that the same set of facts would be amenable to a multiplicity of hypotheses, did not result in his acceptance of an indeterminacy sufficient to fragment reality altogether (Riesch 1997). In matters of terminology rather, for example, it was the lack of precision in their formation of and the ambiguity of language used for economic concepts that troubled Neurath.

Moreover, one would be hard pressed to find in Neurath's writings any awareness of the impact of gender in informing the framework of economic thought. Neurath seems moored in the moment, that is, the first decades of the twentieth century, in his own references to gender roles. This was apparent in his description of the kinds of work and the consumption needs of the population. It also surfaced amidst his appreciation of Emmy Noether and Sonia Kovalevska, both mathematicians, or Marie Curie (Neurath [1930] 1983: 41), in which he discussed the scientific professions in which women were to be found. Yet some feminist thinkers have found a potential source of inspiration in Neurath's anti-foundationalism, historical grounding, and emphasis upon 'external motives' (Okruhlik 2004: 56–61).

In David F. Ruccio and Jack Amariglio's 2003 volume entitled *Postmodern Moments in Modern Economics,* the various strands of postmodernism in economics are highlighted. The conscious assessment of the role of language and the concomitant bounds of economic discourse following from such an assessment stand at the center of the postmodern impulse in economics, evidenced in works like Warren Samuels' volume on *The Discourse of Economics* and Willie Henderson's *Language and Economics.*

However, it extended further in several directions. In part it drew upon the work of French poststructuralists, like Michel Foucault, and French deconstructionists, including Jacques Derrida, as well as American literary critics, like Richard Rorty. Accordingly, a challenge to what was taken to be an objective standard to comprehend economic experience in the age of modernism led to an evocation of its seeming opposite: a complete fragmentation of reality such that competing and conflicting narratives about human experience and activity could not only be sustained, but might in fact be regarded as equally valid. Different linguistic structures might gain preeminence, reflecting underlying power relations, that in turn reinforced the terms of those relations. Through this process of examination new insights were revealed about the hitherto hidden place of gender in economics. Moreover, within the postmodernist impulse was a renewed attack upon the presumed rationality of economic agents as the bedrock upon which economic analysis would be built.

Here one faces a bit of the problem posed by historical amnesia: were there intellectual currents and thinkers a century ago who took up in some measure the concerns and insights of the postmodernist critique of more recent vintage? Beyond the linguistic turn that Neurath himself had set forth, one can find a presaging of sorts in a rather unlikely place, the German Historical School. Among the strands within the postmodernist critique noted above is the notion that economic behavior cannot be deemed rational; that, to the contrary, economic motives are wide-ranging and hence augment the level of subjectivity within economics. However, it is worth noting that among the six elements Schumpeter noted as characteristic of the German Historical School was a rejection of *homo oeconomicus.* Instead, there was a "multiplicity of motives" in economic actions and engagements, whereby "people act according to rules which have not been reasoned out and often appear to them as imperatives which cannot be discussed, or sees people under the influence of obviously illogical impulses" (Schumpeter [1914] 1954: 177). This then served as the basis for what Gustav Schmoller in particular referred to as the "ethical argument" in political economy.

Nor, it should also be noted, did Neurath hitch his construction of a "rational economic theory", the thesis of his 1935 tract, to any such assumed conscious sorting out of self-interest as the basis for and the confines of economic behavior (Neurath 1935). One might in fact contend that Neurath sought to do just the opposite, by conceiving of rationality as grounded in an exacting form of scientific inquiry establishing, in the realm of sociology (but effectively political economy) ways of gauging the 'terrain' of 'life situations' within an existing economic order. Neurath had long regarded the self-interest of individual economic agents as a psychological sketch introduced by the marginalists and adopted for advancing a specific economic model with the profit motive and price theory at its center. At the same time, one might reasonably view Neurath's rejection of the rationality of self-interest within the constraints of the modernist era, as the thesis he counterposed to it was intended to encompass a genuine state of rationality that ought to be accepted broadly.

References

Andrews, Gordon (2014). *Undoing Plessy: Charles Hamilton Houston, race, labor, and the law, 1895–1950*. Newcastle upon Tyne, UK: Cambridge Scholars Publishing.

Balabkins, Nicholas W. (1978). "Der Zukunftsstaat: Carl Ballod's Vision of a Leisure-Oriented Socialism". *History of Political Economy* 10(2): 213–232.

Ballod, Carl [1898] (1927). *Der Zukunftsstaat*. 4th reworked edition. Berlin: E. Laub.

Bitbol, Michel (2000). *Physique et Philosophie de l'esprit*. Paris: Flammarion.

Cartwright, Nancy, Jordi Cat, Bela Fleck, and Thomas Uebel (1996). *Otto Neurath: Philosophy Between Science and Politics*. Cambridge: Cambridge University Press.

Debreu, Gerard (1959). *Theory of Value*. New York: Wiley.

Dekker, Erwin (2014). "The Intellectual Networks of Otto Neurath: Between the Coffeehouse and Academia". *European Studies* 32: 103–121.

Frank, Philipp (1949). *Modern Science and Its Philosophy*. Cambridge: Harvard University Press.

Galison, Peter (1996). "Constructing Modernism: The Cultural Location of Aufbau". In Ronald Giere and Alan Richardson, eds., *The Origins of Logical Empiricism*. Minneapolis: University of Minnesota Press.

Haller, Rudolf (1991). "History and the System of Science in Otto Neurath". In Thomas Uebel, ed., *Rediscovering the Forgotten Vienna Circle*. New York: Springer, pp. 33–40.

Hauser, Arnold (1958). *The Social History of Art*. Trans. in collaboration with the author by Stanley Godman. New York: Vintage Books.

Hazard, Paul (1961). *La conscience europeénne*. Paris: A. Colin.

Hertzka, Theodor (1891). *Freiland: ein sociales Zukunftsbild*. New York: D. Appleton.

Homan, P.T. (1927). "Thorstein Veblen". In Howard W. Odum, ed., *American Masters of the Social Sciences*. New York: H. Holt, pp. 231–270.

Jacob, Pierre, ed. (1980a). *De Vienne a Cambridge: essais de philosophie des sciences*. Paris: Gallimard.

Jacob, Pierre (1980b). *L'empirisme logique*. Paris: Editions Minuit.

McCloskey, Deirdre M. (2001). "The Genealogy of Postmodernism: An Economist's Guide". In Stephen Cullenberg, Jack Amariglio, and David F. Ruccio, eds., *Postmodernism, Economics and Knowledge*. London: Routledge, pp. 102–128.

Neurath, Otto [1910] (2004). "On the theory of the social sciences". In Robert S. Cohen and Thomas E. Uebel, eds., *Otto Neurath: Economic Writings Selections*. [Multiple translators]. Dordrecht: Kluwer Academic Publishing, pp. 265–291.

Neurath, Otto [1913] (1983). "Lost Wanderers of Descartes and the Auxiliary Motive". In Robert S. Cohen and Marie Neurath, eds. and trans., *Philosophical Papers*. Dordrecht/Boston: D. Reidel Publishing Company, pp. 1–12.

Neurath, Otto [1916] (1983). "On the Classification of Systems of Hypotheses". In Robert S. Cohen and Marie Neurath, eds. and trans., *Philosophical Papers 1913–1946*. Dordrecht/Boston: D. Reidel Publishing Company, pp. 13–31.

Neurath, Otto [1917] (2004). "The Economic Order of the Future and the Economic Sciences". In Robert S. Cohen and Thomas E. Uebel, eds., *Otto Neurath: Economic Writings/Selections 1904–1945*. [Multiple translators]. Dordrecht: Kluwer Academic Publishers, pp. 241–261.

Neurath, Otto [1919] (1973). "Utopia as a Social Engineer's Construction". In Marie Neurath and Robert S. Cohen, eds., *Empiricism and Sociology*. Trans. Paul Foulkes and Marie Neurath. Dordrecht: Reidel, pp. 150–155.

Neurath, Otto [1925] (2004). "Economic Plan and Calculation in Kind". In Robert S. Cohen and Thomas E. Uebel, eds., *Otto Neurath: Economic Writings/Selections 1904–1945*. [Multiple translators]. Dordrecht: Kluwer Academic Publishers, pp. 405–465.

Neurath, Otto [1926] (1994). "Statistische Hieroglyphen". In Paul Neurath and Elisabeth Nemeth, eds., *Otto Neurath oder die Einheit der Wissenschaft und Gesellschaft*. Wien: Borlau Verlag, p. 295.

Neurath, Otto [1930] (1983). "Ways of the Scientific World-Conception". In Robert S. Cohen and Marie Neurath, eds., *Philosophical Papers 1913–1946*. Dordrecht/Boston: D. Reidel Publishing Company, pp. 32–47.

Neurath, Otto [1931] (1973). *Empirical Sociology*. In Marie Neurath and Robert S. Cohen, eds., *Empiricism and Sociology*. Trans. Paul Foulkes and Marie Neurath. Dordrecht: Reidel, pp. 319–421.

Neurath, Otto (1935). *Was bedeutet rationale Wirtschaftsbetrachtung?* Wien: Verlag Gerold & Co.

Neurath, Otto (1939). *Modern Man in the Making*. New York & London: A.A. Knopf.

Neurath, Otto [1943] (2004). "Planning or Managerial revolution?" In Robert S. Cohen and Thomas E. Uebel, eds., *Otto Neurath: Economic Writings/Selections, 1904–1945*. [Multiple translators]. Dordrecht: Kluwer Academic Publishers, pp. 527–538.

Neurath, Otto (1944) *Foundations of the Social Sciences*. Chicago: University of Chicago Press.

Neurath, Otto [1946] (1983). "The Orchestration of the Sciences by the Encyclopedism of Logical Empiricism". In Robert S. Cohen and Marie Neurath, eds. and trans., *Philosophical Papers 1913–1946*. Dordrecht/Boston: D. Reidel Publishing Company, pp. 230–242.

Okruhlik, Kathleen (2004). "Logical Empiricism, Feminism, and Neurath's Auxiliary Motive". *Hypatia* 19(1): 48–72.

O'Neill, John (1999). "Socialism, Ecology and Austrian Economics". In Elisabeth Nemeth and Richard Heinrich, eds., *Otto Neurath: Rationalität, Planung, Vielfalt.* Wien: R. Oldenbourg Verlag, pp. 123–145.

Popper-Lynkeus, Josef (1912). *Die allgemeine Nahrpflicht als Lösung der soziale Frage.* Dresden: C. Reissner.

Quine, Willard van Orman (1960). *Word and Object.* Cambridge: Technology Press of the Massachusetts Institute of Technology.

Riesch, George (1997). "How Postmodern Was Neurath's Ideas of Unity of Science?" *Studies in History and Philosophy of Science Part A* 28(3): 439–451.

Riesch, George (2005). *How the Cold War Transformed Philosophy of Science: Toward the Icy Slopes of Logic.* Cambridge: Cambridge University Press.

Rosner, Peter (2006). "Theodor Hertzka and the Utopia of 'Freiland''. *History of Economic Ideas* 14(3): 113–137.

Ruccio, David F. and Amariglio, Jack (2003). *Postmodern Moments in Modern Economics.* Princeton: Princeton University Press.

Scherke, Katharina (2005). "Arnold Hauser and the Social History of Art". In Peter Weibel, ed., *Beyond Art: A Third Culture.* [Numerous translators.] New York: Springer, pp. 478–480.

Schumpeter, Joseph (1914). *Economic Doctrine and Method.* Trans. R. Aris (1954). London: George Allen & Unwin.

Taylor, Charles (1989). *Sources of the Self: the Making of the Modern Identity.* Cambridge: Harvard University Press.

Turk, Michael (1975). *The Vienna Circle in Historical Perspective, 1920–1940.* Unpublished dissertation: Harvard University Archives.

Uebel, Thomas (1992). *The Overcoming of Logical Positivism from Within.* Amsterdam: Rodopi.

Veblen, Thorstein (1921). *The Price System and the Engineers.* New York: B.W. Huebsch, Inc.

Veblen, Thorstein (1898). "Why Economics is not an Evolutionary Science". *The Quarterly Journal of Economics* 12(4): 373–397.

Vossoughian, Nader (2008). *Otto Neurath: Language of the Global Polis.* Rotterdam: NAi Publishers.

Index

Taylor & Francis Group
an informa business

Taylor & Francis eBooks

www.taylorfrancis.com

A single destination for eBooks from Taylor & Francis with increased functionality and an improved user experience to meet the needs of our customers.

90,000+ eBooks of award-winning academic content in Humanities, Social Science, Science, Technology, Engineering, and Medical written by a global network of editors and authors.

TAYLOR & FRANCIS EBOOKS OFFERS:

- A streamlined experience for our library customers
- A single point of discovery for all of our eBook content
- Improved search and discovery of content at both book and chapter level

REQUEST A FREE TRIAL

support@taylorfrancis.com

Routledge
Taylor & Francis Group

CRC Press
Taylor & Francis Group

For Product Safety Concerns and Information please contact our EU representative GPSR@taylorandfrancis.com Taylor & Francis Verlag GmbH, Kaufingerstraße 24, 80331 München, Germany